PASSKEY™ FOR HEALTH INSURANCE LICENSING

6TH EDITION

DEARBORN™
A Kaplan Professional Company

This text is updated periodically to reflect changes in laws and regulations. To verify that you have the most recent update, you may call Dearborn at 1-800-423-4723.

Published by Dearborn Financial Institute, Inc.®

Printed in the United States of America.

Second printing, April, 1999.

Library of Congress Cataloging-in-Publication Data

Passkey for health insurance licensing.—6th ed.
p. cm.
ISBN 0-7931-3537-0 (pbk.); 0-7931-3233-9
1. Insurance, Health—Law and legislation—United States.
KF1183.Z9P37 1998
344.73'022—dc21 98-46492
CIP

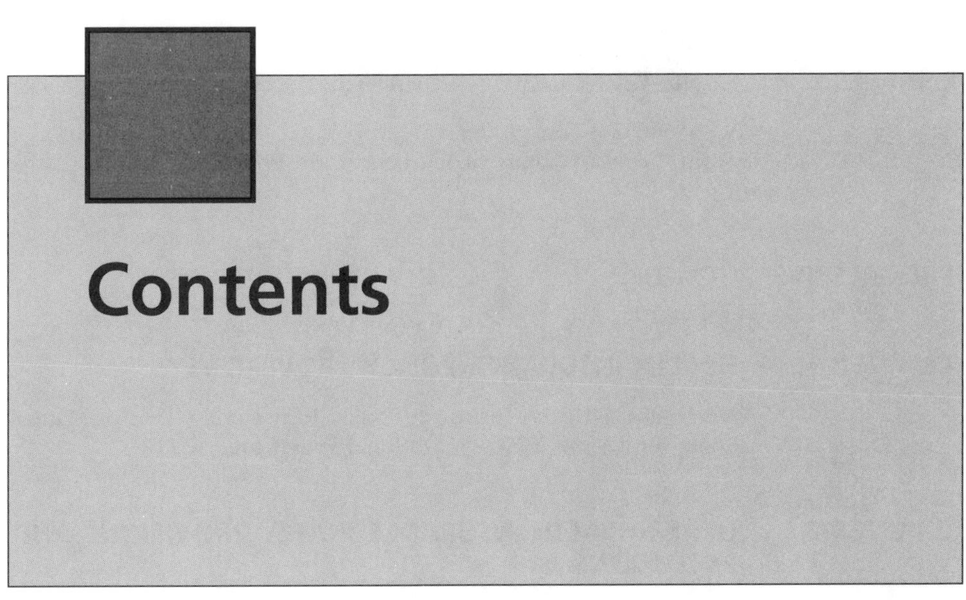

Contents

Introduction to the 6th Edition

Passkey for Health Insurance Licensing has been used successfully for 15 years to prepare candidates for state insurance licensing examinations. In this, the 6th edition, we have revised the book to reflect changes in licensing examinations and to better meet the needs of prospective agents and brokers. We have addressed changes brought about by the Health Insurance Portability and Accountability Act (HIPAA) of 1996, which in many respects are the catalysts behind the development of a new edition. Before writing this 6th edition, we contacted many individuals who had used *Passkey* to study for their licensing exams, and we spoke to instructors who use *Passkey* in their classrooms or who recommend it to students for independent study at home. We asked instructors and students: "What do you like about the book?" and "What do you think would make the book better?" Their responses guided the development of this edition.

While the overwhelming response to *Passkey* was very positive, our research revealed that to better simulate the licensing exams, our test questions needed to be more challenging. Consequently, we rewrote many of the questions to reflect more accurately those on the licensing exams and thus help students better prepare for the type, scope and format of the exam questions. Another request we received was to provide an introduction to health insurance before discussing the types of health insurance policies. In this edition, we begin with an introduction that defines health insurance and the role it plays in society and in our lives.

In most states, one of two testing organizations administers the licensing exam. The remaining states conduct their own exam. In this edition, we have continued to expand the scope of the material so that, instead of focusing on the requirements of one testing organization, we present a comprehensive survey of topics that may appear in any test outline, in any state, by any testing organization.

In our effort to cover the topics in a logical order, we have retained a structure that presents the subject matter in the manner our readers have found the most helpful. The book consists of 15 chapters, designed to flow from topic to topic in a way that helps the reader retain the information logically. We have also expanded on topics affected by HIPAA, particularly long-term care insurance, and have included new information about disability income insurance and health maintenance organizations. We have updated other topics throughout the book. The glossary is indexed with page numbers to allow easy reference and review. Key terms within the text are italicized.

While we have made major changes to the content of *Passkey* to reflect recent federal legislation, we have retained many of the key elements of the previous edition, especially those features customers repeatedly told us they liked and needed. As in the previous edition, the book is written in "red reader" format for programmed instruction, which is a proven way to help students assimilate information quickly and efficiently. The information is presented in a clear and straightforward style, and there are five progressive quizzes and a final exam.

We thank all *Passkey* users who took the time to give us their comments and suggestions. In particular, we extend our appreciation to the following reviewers:

Donna J. Cannon, Special Account Manager, Dearborn Financial Institute, Inc.
Stephen J. Cochilla, J.D.
Jeffrey S. Galper, Director, Dearborn Financial Institute, Inc., Michigan branch
Barbara Gavitt, Instructor, Dearborn Financial Institute, Inc.
Barbara Harrington, Director, Harrington School, Inc.
Timothy Melodick, Instructor, Dearborn Financial Institute, Inc.
Keith E. Worthington, Director, Bankmark School for Business

The input from these reviewers has made this edition a text we believe will guide insurance students to licensure, not only in the waning years of the twentieth century but also into the dawn of the new millennium.

Arthur G. Carvajal, Esq.
Editor

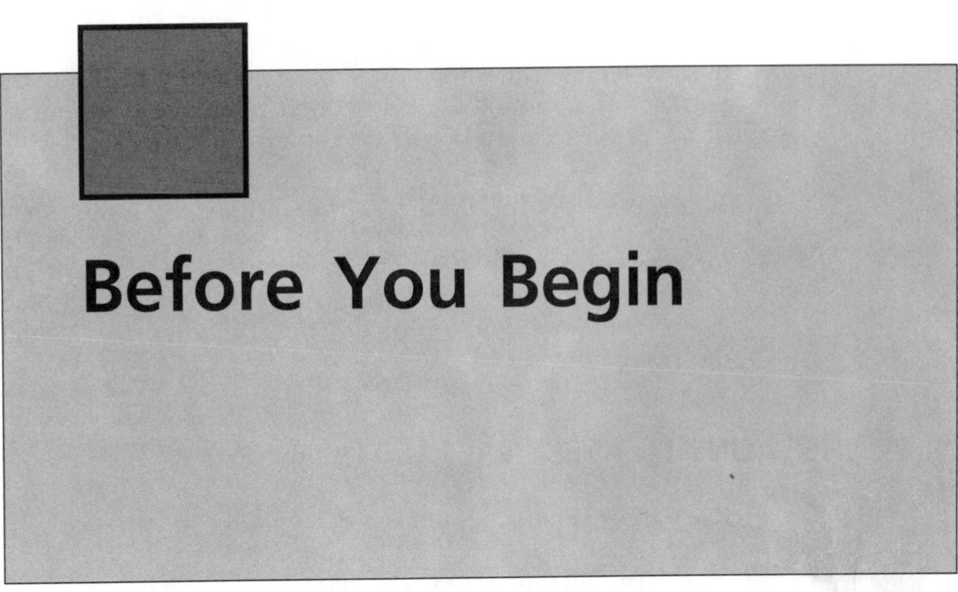

Before You Begin

Passkey for Health Insurance Licensing is a self-study course designed to prepare prospective health insurance agents and brokers for the general health insurance principles portion of the state licensing examination. It also provides an introduction to the business of insurance and a solid foundation of basic insurance information.

Passkey may be used to prepare for the state licensing examination whether licensing exams are conducted and administered by Assessment Systems, Inc. (ASI), Insurance Testing Corporation (ITC) or by your state insurance department. *Please note that your licensing exam will include questions on insurance laws and regulations specific to the state where you are taking the exam. We recommend that you supplement study of* Passkey *with the Dearborn study manual for your state.*

■ ABOUT THE FORMAT

Passkey allows you to learn on your own, at your own pace and when it is convenient for you. This text includes 15 chapters and each chapter contains several sets of review questions that reinforce and help you retain what you have just read. For some questions you will simply select an answer; for others you will need to write your answer in the space provided. Immediately after responding to a review question, check your answer by placing the red plastic strip (found in the small envelope in the front of the book) over the red column. If your response is correct, you should proceed with your reading. If your response is incorrect, reread that part of the text material to ensure you understand the full meaning. Please remember, these review questions are designed to help you understand and retain the information you are studying; your performance on these questions is not necessarily an accurate measure of how you will do on the licensing exam. Later, when you take the *Passkey* Final Examination, you will encounter questions that are very similar to those found on the state licensing exams.

After you have completed a few chapters, you'll come to a multiple-choice "Progressive Quiz" (there are five altogether in the text). These progressive quizzes include questions on subjects covered in the text up to that point. So that you can quickly review, text reference page numbers are located beneath the correct responses to the quiz questions.

When you have completed the final progressive quiz and have reviewed the subjects you needed to review, you should take the Final Exam. Instructions for answering and grading the exam are included. As mentioned earlier, the questions in this exam are more like those you'll find on the state licensing exam. Therefore, you'll probably find them more challenging than those in the rest of the text.

SUGGESTIONS FOR TEST PREPARATION

Here are several suggestions for preparing for the test.

- Thoroughly read each chapter in *Passkey* and answer all of the review questions. Pay attention to key terms and take notes while you read—putting information in writing often helps you commit it to memory.

- After completing and grading your final exam, return to the text and review any topics with which you had difficulty on the exam.

- Read carefully any instructions furnished by your state Department of Insurance.

Licensing exams are administered by either:

1. Assessment Systems, Inc. (ASI);
2. Insurance Testing Corporation (ITC); or
3. your state's Department of Insurance.

In the states where ASI provides the test, handbooks containing information about the licensing examination are available to all candidates. These publications contain vital information—including outlines of specific topics covered in the licensing tests. These handbooks also indicate approximately how many test questions there will be in each subject area and whether your understanding of a topic should be general or comprehensive. These handbooks will be helpful as you prepare for your licensing examination.

In the states where ITC is doing the testing, booklets called *Licensing Information Bulletins* are available to all candidates. These bulletins explain the exam procedures, contain an outline of the topics covered in the exam and include all the forms you need to fill out before and after taking the exam.

The information available to candidates in those states that do their own testing varies from state to state.

YOUR CAREER AS AN AGENT

A successful career in the insurance business is achieved one step at a time. The first step is to become licensed, and it is the purpose of this book to help you prepare for the state licensing examination. It will do so by providing a solid foundation of basic health insurance principles.

However, your professional education does not stop with the licensing exam. An insurance agent's career demands a true sense of professionalism in dealing with the public. For this reason, agents are required not only to be licensed, but, in most states, to fulfill a certain number of continuing education hours each year. Future training and educational activities will be offered to you by insurance industry organizations and associations and by your own company or agency. If you take full advantage of such opportunities to enhance your knowledge and performance, you will soon develop the professionalism necessary for a successful insurance career.

1

Health Insurance Basics

The first step in the study of health insurance is to understand the purpose it serves and the important role it plays for individuals and society. In this chapter, we will explore this purpose and role, by explaining the concept of risk and showing how insurance replaces the uncertainties of risk with guarantees.

THE ROLE OF HEALTH INSURANCE

The health insurance industry serves a vital role in our society. At the end of 1994, approximately 220 million Americans were protected by some form of health care coverage. Health insurers pay out billions of dollars in health insurance claims every year, with commercial insurance companies making approximately half of these payments.

With the dramatic rise in health care costs, health coverage is no longer considered a luxury but a necessity. In fact, health insurance has become a major issue in the business arena. Many businesses, in an effort to control costs, are shifting some of the burden of paying for health insurance to employees. The high cost of medical insurance has stimulated national debate about the merits of several options such as national health insurance, paid for and administered by the government, or mandating that businesses, no matter how small, provide health insurance as an employee benefit. The American public's concern about the cost and availability of health insurance demonstrates that health coverage is a highly valued form of insurance.

THE PURPOSE OF HEALTH INSURANCE

Health insurance, like all forms of insurance, exists as a practical solution to uncertainty and the possibility of economic loss. The uncertainty is whether or when illness or disability will strike; the economic loss is the resulting cost of the illness or disability. Health insurance provides funds for medical expenses due to sickness or injury and to cover loss of income during a disability.

Health insurance offers its solution in the form of a *policy,* which is a device for accumulating funds. The policy is a legally binding contract that sets forth the following:

> Whereby, for a set amount of money (the *premium*), one party (the *insurer*) agrees to pay the other party (the *insured* or his or her *beneficiary*) a certain sum (the *benefit*) upon the occurrence of some event.

In the case of health insurance, the benefit is paid if and when the insured incurs certain illness or injury-related medical expenses or becomes disabled, as defined by the policy.

Health Insurance Is Risk Transference

Health insurance, like all insurance, is a method of *transferring risk* from one party to another, so that the loss is borne by the second party. Though purchasing health insurance does not eliminate the risk of illness or injury, it relieves the insured of the economic loss these risks bring. But how is this possible? How and why can an insurer accept a risk that an individual is not willing to take? The answer lies in two basic principles of insurance —risk pooling and the law of large numbers.

Risk Pooling

To understand the principle of *risk pooling,* consider the following example. Assume that 100 people in the same social club agree that if any member of their group becomes seriously ill, all members will pitch in to provide him or her with $1,000 to cover the costs associated with the illness. Because it is not known if or when any one person in the group will become ill, the decision is made to "pre-fund" the benefit by assessing each member $10, thus creating a $1,000 fund. Without the agreement to provide for each other's potential loss, each member would have to face the economic cost of illness alone. By sharing the burden and spreading the risk of illness over all 100 group members, the most any one member pays is $10.

This is, of course, a very simplified example, but it explains the basic concept of loss sharing. By spreading a risk, or by sharing the possibility of a loss, a large group of people can substitute a small, certain cost ($10) for a large, unknown risk (the economic risk of becoming ill). In other words, the risk is transferred from an individual to a group, all of whom share the losses and have the promises of a future benefit. Insurance companies pool risks among thousands and thousands of insureds, and apply certain mathematical principles to guarantee policyowners that the money will be there to pay a claim when it arises.

Law of Large Numbers

In addition to the spreading of risks, insurance relies on the principle that the larger the number of individual risks (or "exposures") in a group, the more certainty there is as to the amount of loss incurred in any given period. No one can predict when any one person will become ill or disabled. However, it is possible to apply mathematical principles to predict the *likelihood* of disability occurring among a certain group during a certain period. In other words, given a large enough pool of risks, an insurer can predict with reasonable accuracy the number of claims it will face during any given time. This principle, known as the *law of large numbers,* is based on the science of probability and upon mortality (death) and morbidity (sickness) statistics. The larger and more homogeneous the group, the more certain the mortality or morbidity predictions.

ELEMENTS OF INSURABLE RISK

Though insurance is one of the most effective ways to handle risk, not all risks are insurable. To begin with, insurers only insure *pure* risks or those that involve only the chance of loss. *Speculative* risks, or those that involve the chance for both loss and gain, are not insurable. However, not even all pure risks are insurable. Certain conditions must be met before a pure risk can be insured:

1. *The loss must be due to chance.* To be insurable, a risk must involve a chance of loss that is random and outside the insured's control.

2. *The loss must be definite and measurable.* An insurable risk involves a loss that is definite as to cause, time, place and amount.

3. *The loss must be predictable.* An insurable risk is statistically predictable. This enables insurers to estimate the average frequency and severity of future losses and set appropriate premiums.

4. *The loss cannot be catastrophic.* Insurers typically do not insure risks that expose them to catastrophic losses. There must be limits that insurers can be reasonably certain their losses will not exceed.

5. *The loss exposures to be insured must be large.* An insurer must be able to predict losses based on the law of large numbers. Consequently, there must be a sufficiently large pool to be insured and those in the pool (the "exposures") must be grouped into classes with similar risks. Individuals, for example, are grouped according to age, health, gender, occupation, etc.

6. *The loss exposures to be insured must be randomly selected.* The group to be insured must be randomly selected. Insurers must have a fair proportion of good risks and poor risks. A large proportion of poor risks could financially threaten the insurance company, since there would be many losses without sufficient premiums to offset them.

1. The law of large numbers allows insurers to predict which insureds will become ill or disabled.

   (True/False)

False. The law of large numbers allows insurers to predict with reasonable accuracy the number of claims there will be in a certain period. No one can predict who will become ill or disabled.

2. Insurers only insure

   A. pure risks.
   B. speculative risks.
   C. large risks.
   D. catastrophic risks.

A. Only pure risks are insurable.

3. All of the following are elements of insurable risks, EXCEPT:

   A. the loss must be due to chance.
   B. the loss exposures to be insured must be large.
   C. the loss must be statistically unpredictable.
   D. the loss exposures must be randomly selected.

C. In order to be insurable a risk must be statistically predictable.

BASIC FORMS OF HEALTH INSURANCE COVERAGE

The terms "health and accident insurance," "accident and health insurance" and "health insurance" are used interchangeably in the health insurance industry, from state to state and company to company. No matter what it is called in the industry, it all means the same thing to consumers—a critically important type of insurance that provides financial protection from the high costs of illness and injury.

Health insurance (as it will be called in this text) refers to the broad field of insurance plans that provide protection against the financial consequences of illness, accidents, injury or disability.

Within the broad field of health insurance, there are three distinct categories of health coverage: *medical expense insurance, disability income insurance* and *accidental death and dismemberment insurance.* Each of these coverages will be discussed in detail in subsequent chapters, but an introduction is appropriate here.

Medical Expense Insurance

Medical expense insurance provides financial protection against the cost of medical care by reimbursing or indemnifying the insured, fully or in part, for these costs. It includes many kinds of plans that cover hospital care, surgical expenses, physician expenses, medical treatment programs, outpatient care and the like. Medicare supplement insurance and long-term care insurance (discussed in Chapters 5 and 6 respectively) are examples of medical expense insurance plans. Depending on the type of policy (and its specific provisions), coverage can range from limited (coverage for hospital costs only, for example) to very broad (coverage for all aspects of medical services and care). Medical expense insurance is issued on both an individual and a group basis.

Disability Income Insurance

NYS LAW: we can replace up to 60% of the Insured Income.

Disability income insurance is designed to provide a replacement income when wages are lost due to a disability. As such, it does not cover the medical expenses associated with a disability; rather, it provides the disabled insured with a guaranteed flow of periodic income payments, usually on a monthly basis, while he or she is disabled. Like medical expense coverage, disability income insurance is available on both an individual and a group basis.

Accidental Death and Dismemberment Insurance

Accidental death and dismemberment insurance, commonly referred to as AD&D, is the purest form of accident insurance, providing the insured with a lump-sum benefit amount in the event of accidental death *or* loss of one or more body members under accidental circumstances. Typically, AD&D coverage is part of a group insurance plan.

Within each of these three categories are many forms and variations of coverage that have evolved to meet unique insurance needs. Even the type of health insurance provider—of which there are many—can make a difference in the basic makeup of any of these types of coverages. Each of these basic coverages, as well as the many types of health insurance providers, will be discussed in later chapters. They are introduced here to help acquaint you with the health insurance field in general.

■ CHARACTERISTICS OF HEALTH INSURANCE

A brief overview of the distinguishing features of health insurance will set the stage for the more in-depth discussion to follow in later chapters.

Renewability Provisions

Health insurance policies may contain any one of a wide range of *renewability provisions,* which define the rights of the insurer to cancel the policy at different points during the life of the policy. There are five principal renewability classifications: *cancelable, optionally renewable, conditionally renewable, guaranteed renewable* and *noncancelable.* The distinguishing characteristics of each type will be covered in Chapter 8, but generally speaking, the more advantageous the renewability provisions are to the insured, the more expensive the coverage.

Premiums and Premium Factors

Health insurance is funded by the regular payment of *premiums.* Health policies are paid for on a year-by-year basis and, except for the noncancelable type of policy mentioned above, health insurance premium rates are subject to periodic increases. Health premiums can be paid under one of several different payment modes, including annual, semi-annual, quarterly and monthly. Monthly premiums are often paid through some form of preauthorized check method, by which the insurer automatically obtains the premium directly from the policyholder's checking account. In the case of group health insurance, employers may deduct premium contributions directly from employees' paychecks.

Various factors enter into premium calculations for health insurance. These include interest, expenses, types of benefits and *morbidity.* Morbidity is the expected incidence of sickness or disability within a given age group during a given period of time; it is to health insurance what mortality is to life insurance. Still other health insurance premium factors are claims experience and the age, sex and occupation of the insured. All of these factors are discussed in detail in Chapter 10.

Participating vs. Nonparticipating Policies

Health insurance policies may be written on either a *participating* or *nonparticipating* basis. Participating policies allow policyholders to share in company earnings through policy dividends. Nonparticipating policies do not pay dividends. Most individual health insurance is issued on a nonparticipating basis. Group health insurance, on the other hand, is generally participating and provides for *dividends* or *experience rating.* It is important to note, however, that dividends are paid to the policyholder, not the individual insured.

Cost-accounting formulas are complex and vary from insurer to insurer; however, the two major factors that influence whether dividends or experience-rated refunds are payable are the *expenses* and *claims costs* of the insurer. If these factors are less than anticipated, the group policyowner benefits by receiving a dividend or refund credit. If expenses and claims costs are higher than expected, the group policyowner may not qualify for a dividend or refund credit.

Group health plans issued by mutual companies usually provide for dividends, while stock companies frequently issue experience-rated plans. A group policy that is experience-rated may make premium reductions retroactive for 12 months if the claims experience is better than projected. However, if the experience is worse than expected, premium increases for such policies are *not* assessed retroactively. Experience-rated refunds may be contingent upon renewal of the master policy, but the payment of dividends usually is not contingent upon renewal.

Unique Aspects of Health Insurance Contracts

Certain characteristics set health insurance contracts apart from other contracts. A health insurance contract is *conditional* in that the obligation of the insurance company to pay a claim depends on the performance of certain acts by the insured or others, such as the payment of premiums and furnishing proof of loss. A health insurance contract is *unilateral* because it involves the enforceable promises of one party only, the insurer. Though policyowners must pay premiums in order for the contract to perform, they are not contractually obligated to do so. However, if the premiums are paid, the insurer must accept them and meet its full obligations under the contract. *Adhesion* is a legal term relating to the fact that all provisions of a health insurance contract are determined by the insurance company. The applicant has only the opportunity to accept or reject the contract; it is not the result of the negotiations between the two parties. If the contract is accepted, the policyowner has no choice but to adhere to its terms. However, because policyowners must accept the insurance contract as it is written, the courts generally have interpreted any ambiguities in the contract's wording for the benefit of the policyowner.

Reserves

Reserves are set aside by an insurer and designated for the payment of future claims. Part of each premium is designated for the reserves.

Two types of health insurance reserves are *premium reserves* and *loss* (or *claims*) *reserves.* Premium reserves reflect the liability of the insurer for losses that have not occurred but for which premiums have been paid. Reserves earmarked as loss reserves represent the insurer's liability for losses that have occurred, but for which settlement is not yet complete. The details of how reserves are handled and recorded by the company are very technical. State laws dictate the minimum requirements for reserves for both life and health insurance. The annual statements required by state insurance departments break down a company's reserves in considerable detail.

---

1. Which of the following types of health insurance covers the medical expenses associated with a disability?

   A. Medical expense insurance
   B. Disability income insurance
   C. Accidental death and dismemberment insurance

A
Medical expense insurance reimburses the insured for the cost of medical care.

---

2. The expected incidence of sickness or disability in a given group over a certain period of time is referred to as

   A. mortality.
   B. morbidity.

B
Morbidity is to health insurance what mortality is to life insurance.

---

3. Which of the following factors determine whether or not policy dividends will be paid on a participating policy?

   A. Reserves and experience
   B. Expenses and claims costs
   C. Interest and benefits
   D. Premiums and renewability

B
If expenses and claims costs are less than expected, dividends are likely to be paid.

4. Why is a health insurance contract a unilateral contract?

Because it involves the enforceable promises of one party only—the insurer.

HOW HEALTH INSURANCE IS PURCHASED

When it comes to obtaining health insurance coverage, Americans have a variety of providers from which to choose. Those providing health insurance can be divided into three general categories: *private insurers, service providers* and *state* and *federal governments.* In all cases, though, the objective is the same: to provide protection against the costs associated with illness, injury or disability. How each provider approaches this task is unique.

Individual Health Insurance

Individual health insurance is issued by private insurers and service organizations as contracts between the insured and the company. Though all companies have standard policies, most allow an individual to select the various options or benefit levels that most precisely meet his or her needs. Individual health contracts require an application and usually the proposed insured must provide evidence of insurability.

Group Health Insurance

Group health insurance, also issued by private insurers and service organizations, provides coverage under a master contract to members of a specified group. Group health plans are available to employers, trade and professional associations, labor unions, credit unions and other organizations. Insurance is extended to the individuals in the group through the master contract, usually without individual underwriting and usually without requiring group members to provide evidence of insurability. The employer or the association is the policyowner and is responsible for premium payments. The employer may pay the entire premium or may require some contribution from each member. Generally speaking, the provisions and coverages of group health insurance contracts are more liberal than individual health contracts. Group health insurance will be discussed in greater detail in Chapter 11.

Government Programs

Health insurance is also provided through *state* and *federal government* programs. At the state level, workers' compensation provides benefits to employees for work-related injuries, illness or death. Employers are responsible for providing workers' compensation benefits to their employees and do so by purchasing coverage through state programs or private insurers, or by self-insuring. *Medicaid* is also available at the state level. Its purpose is to assist low-income individuals in meeting the costs of medical care. The federal government offers health insurance protection through *Medicare* and *OASDI disability*, components of the Social Security system.

The different types of health insurance providers and the health insurance industry will be discussed in greater detail in later chapters.

2

Medical Expense Insurance

As we mentioned in the first chapter, specific types of health insurance policies include medical expense insurance, disability income insurance and accidental death and dismemberment insurance. In this chapter, we will focus on the various types of medical expense policies. Disability income insurance and accidental death and dismemberment insurance will be the subjects of the next two chapters. For the most part, we will limit our discussion to individual policies rather than group policies.

■ MEDICAL EXPENSE INSURANCE

When people speak of their "health insurance," they are usually referring to insurance that protects against the costs of medical care. Medical expense insurance, which is available in several different forms, reimburses policyowners for part or all of the costs of obtaining medical care. It is a vital form of insurance considered by many to be the one type of insurance they cannot do without.

Purpose of Medical Expense Insurance

Medical expense insurance provides financial protection from the costs of medical care for accidents and sicknesses. Medical expense insurance is available through two different policy plans: *basic medical insurance* or *major medical insurance.* Basic medical insurance limits coverage to certain types of medical care and allocates benefits accordingly. Major medical insurance can be used to supplement a basic medical insurance plan or can serve as a comprehensive, stand-alone plan that provides broader, more complete coverage.

How Benefits Are Paid

Depending on the type of insurer, benefits under a medical expense plan are payable on a *service* basis or a *cash reimbursement* basis.

As we will discuss in greater detail in Chapter 13, service organizations, such as Blue Cross and Blue Shield, provide benefits on a service basis.

Service organizations contract directly with health care providers and pay the providers directly for the medical services given to the insured, instead of reimbursing the insured after the insured pays the provider.

Private insurers have traditionally paid benefits on a reimbursement basis. This means that the insured pays for the medical services out of his or her own pocket and then is reimbursed by the insurance company. This is in contrast to the service approach, used by Blue Cross and Blue Shield.

Policies under which benefits are paid on a reimbursement basis are either "expense-incurred" policies or "flat amount" policies. An "expense-incurred" policy bases benefit payments on the amount of loss or expense the insured actually incurs, up to a stipulated maximum. "Flat amount" policies pay a stated amount for a loss, regardless of the actual expense incurred. Two examples will help clarify these concepts.

Karl owns a medical expense policy that pays benefits on an "expense-incurred" basis, with a lifetime maximum benefit of $200,000. He enters the hospital for ten days and incurs covered medical expenses of $10,000. His policy would base its payment of benefits on $10,000—the expenses Karl actually incurs.

Doris owns a medical expense policy that pays benefits on a "flat amount" basis, providing her with $250 a day for each day of hospitalization (this type of policy is usually called a "hospital indemnity policy" and is discussed in more detail later in this chapter). Doris enters the hospital for ten days and incurs covered medical expenses of $10,000. Doris's policy will pay benefits of $2,500; ten days at $250 per day. If Doris's actual hospital expenses were less than $250 per day (which is not likely, of course), she would still receive $250 a day in benefits from the insurer. Contracts that pay benefits on a "flat amount" basis do not take into consideration expenses or bills; they merely pay the insured a stated amount for a covered loss.

Now we're ready to look at the two types of medical expense policies: *basic* and *major medical.* Within these two categories are many types of plans.

■ BASIC MEDICAL EXPENSE PLANS

Basic medical expense insurance is sometimes called "first-dollar insurance" because, unlike major medical expense insurance, it provides benefits "up front," without requiring the insured to first pay a deductible. For many years it was the leading type of medical expense insurance sold, but today it is overshadowed by major medical insurance. This is largely because basic medical expense policies not only limit the type and duration of medical services covered but also the dollar amounts that will be paid to the insured. Major medical plans are not as limiting.

Basic medical expense policies classify coverages into general categories of medical care: *hospital expense, surgical expense* and *physicians' (nonsurgical) expense.* Additional plans cover *nursing expenses* and *convalescent care.* While all coverages are often contained in one policy, they can be written separately as well.

1. A policy that pays benefits directly to the health care provider is said to pay benefits on a

   A. service basis.
   B. reimbursement basis.

When benefits are paid on a reimbursement basis, the insured pays the health care provider and then is reimbursed by the insurer.

2. What are the two types of medical expense policies?

   1. ______________________
   2. ______________________

1. Basic
2. Major medical
(May be in any order.)

3. With basic medical expense insurance, what does the expression "first dollar" mean?

____

____

____

Covered expenses will be payable from the first dollar of hospital expense incurred by the insured; no deductible is required.

Basic Hospital Expense

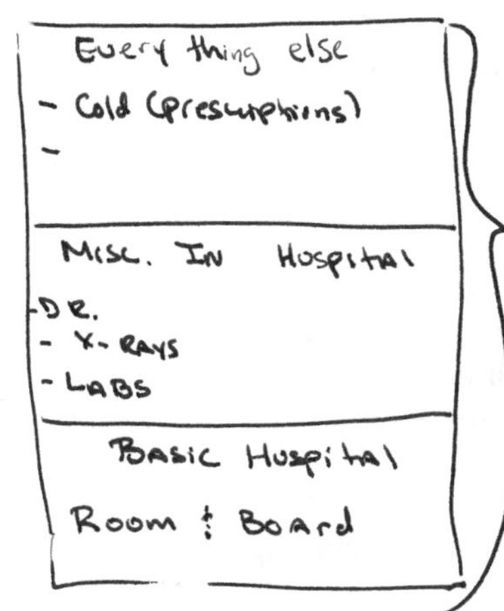

Every thing else
- Cold (prescriptions)
Misc. In Hospital
- Dr.
- X-Rays
- Labs
Basic Hospital
Room & Board

Basic hospital expense insurance reimburses policyowners for the cost of hospitalization. (Many policies also cover outpatient care if it is provided in place of hospitalization.) Basic hospital policies cover (1) daily room and board and (2) other miscellaneous hospital expenses.

Daily Room and Board

Basic hospital expense policies cover the daily cost of room and board. The daily amount payable and length of time covered varies depending on the policy. Some policies pay an in-hospital benefit for as long as 365 days, while others pay benefits for only 90 or 30 days. Of course, the longer the benefit period, the larger the premium. Some policies reimburse the insured for daily room and board up to a specified dollar limit. Others provide a flat amount type of benefit, paying an amount equal to the hospital's daily charge for a semiprivate room.

Miscellaneous Hospital Expenses

In addition to room and board, basic hospital expense policies cover hospital "extras" or miscellaneous charges, up to a specified limit. Covered miscellaneous expenses include drugs, X rays, anesthesia, lab fees, dressings, use of the operating room and supplies. Generally, the maximum miscellaneous expense benefit is expressed as a multiple of the daily room and board benefit (10 times room and board or 20 times room and board, for example) or it may be a stated dollar amount. Some policies may even specify individual maximums for certain expenses within the maximum miscellaneous benefit. For example, the overall maximum for miscellaneous expenses may be $1,000, with maximums of $150 for use of the operating room, $125 for anesthesia, $75 for drugs and so on. But the total miscellaneous benefit would be limited to $1,000.

1. Gerald's basic medical expense policy limits the miscellaneous expense benefit to 20 times the $300 daily room-and-board benefit. During his recent hospital stay, miscellaneous expenses totaled $6,300. How much of the $6,300 will Gerald have to pay?

   A. $210
   B. $300

2. Ken's policy has a 30-day hospital benefit period, while Steve's policy has a 90-day hospital benefit period. Everything else being equal, who pays the higher premium?

   A. Steve
   B. Ken

It is important to note that physicians' services are not covered under a basic hospital expense policy, even in the case of surgery. The cost for a physician is covered under a basic surgical expense or basic physicians' (nonsurgical) expense policy.

Basic Surgical Expense

Basic surgical expense policies cover the cost of a surgeon's services, whether the surgery is performed in the hospital or not. These policies are intended to apply to the total professional fees, so generally included in the coverage are the surgeon's fees as well as the fees of the anesthesiologist and the cost of any post-operative care.

Insurers take three different approaches to providing this type of coverage:

1. the surgical schedule approach,
2. the reasonable and customary approach or
3. the relative value scale approach.

Surgical Schedule

Under the *surgical schedule approach,* the insurer assigns a dollar amount to each surgical procedure. Although the policy itself contains a list of common surgical procedures and the amount payable for each procedure, the insurer keeps a complete listing of all established surgical procedures for use by its claims examiners. When a claim is submitted to the insurer, the claims examiner reviews the policy to determine what amount is payable; if the surgeon's bill is more than the allowed charge set by the insurer, it is up to the insured to pay the surgeon the difference. If the surgeon's bill is less than the allowed charge, the insurer pays only the amount billed; the claim payment will never exceed the amount charged.

Reasonable and Customary

Whereas the surgical schedule approach pays up to a stated dollar amount for a specified surgical procedure, the *reasonable and customary approach* is more open in its determination of benefits payable. Under this approach, the surgical expense is compared to what is considered "reasonable and customary" for the geographical part of the country where the surgery was performed. If the charge is within the "reasonable and customary" parameters, the expense is paid, usually in full. If the charge exceeds the "reasonable and customary" parameters, the insurer pays only the reasonable and customary amount. The remaining charge is the responsibility of the insured.

Relative Value Scale

The *relative value scale approach* is similar to the surgical schedule method, except that instead of a flat dollar amount being assigned to every surgical procedure, a set of *points* is assigned.

The number of points assigned to any one procedure is relative to the number of points assigned to a *maximum procedure.* Typically, something like a triple heart bypass would be considered a maximum procedure and assigned a high number of points (usually 500 or 1,000). Every other procedure is also assigned a set of points relative to that; an appendectomy, which is a major procedure but not as serious as a triple bypass, might be assigned 200 points. Setting a broken finger might rate five points.

How are benefit amounts determined? The policy will carry a stated dollar-per-point amount, known as the *conversion factor,* to determine the benefit. For example, a plan with a $5-per-point conversion factor would pay $1,000 for a 200-point procedure. Generally the larger the conversion factor, the larger the policy's premium.

---

1. The surgical schedule approach to paying benefits includes a schedule of common surgical procedures and the dollar amount the policy will pay for each.

   (True/False)

True. The surgical schedule approach lists amounts payable for specific procedures.

2. Explain a "relative value schedule," as used in some basic surgical expense policies.

Points and not dollar amounts are assigned to listed surgical procedures. Points assigned are relative to the number of points assigned to a maximum procedure. A point multiplied by a conversion factor equals the benefit to be paid.

____

3. Sarah enters the hospital for an appendectomy. The points assigned to this procedure in her basic surgical expense insurance policy are 100. If the conversion factor is $10, what surgical benefit would be paid for Sarah's operation?

$____________

1,000

Basic Physicians' (Nonsurgical) Expense

Basic physicians' expense insurance provides benefits for nonsurgical physicians' services, since insurers recognize that professional medical services are typical, even if no surgery is performed. An example of a covered service is the daily visit made by a physician while a patient is hospitalized. Benefits are usually stated in fixed dollar amounts; for example, a plan might pay a flat fee of $50 per visit (but not to exceed the actual charge, if less). These policies typically carry a number of exclusions, such as X rays, drugs and dental treatment.

Other Basic Plans

Two other basic medical expense plans are worth noting: *nurses' expense benefits* and *convalescent care facility benefits.*

Nurses' expense benefits coverage generally is limited to private duty nursing care arranged in accordance with a doctor's order while the insured is a hospital patient. It may cover both registered professional and licensed practical nurses.

Convalescent care facility benefits coverage provides a maximum daily benefit while the insured is confined in a skilled nursing facility for a specified recovery period following discharge from a hospital. Rest cures and normal custodial care are not covered.

1. Randy was hospitalized for exhaustion. His family doctor paid a visit each of the four days Randy was hospitalized and billed Randy $200 for these in-hospital visits. What kind of basic medical expense policy would cover this cost?

   A. Basic hospital expense
   B. Basic surgical expense
   C. Basic physicians' expense
   D. All of the above

C
Basic physicians' expense policies cover the cost of nonsurgical physician expenses.

---

2. Basic convalescent care facility coverage requires a prior period of hospitalization before benefits are payable.

   (True/False)

True
The insured must be hospitalized before entering the convalescent care facility.

■ MAJOR MEDICAL EXPENSE PLANS

Major medical expense insurance, often called "major medical," has made it possible for many people to achieve substantial protection against the high cost of medical care. It offers broad coverage under one policy, typically paying benefits for hospital room and board, hospital extras, nursing services in-hospital or at home, blood, oxygen, prosthetic devices, surgery, physicians' fees, ambulance services and more. In addition, it provides high benefit limits. It generally is available on both an individual basis and a group basis.

The services and supplies covered under a major medical policy must be performed or prescribed by a licensed physician and necessary for the treatment of an insured's illness or injury. The benefit period may be defined on a calendar-year basis or may be specified as a 2-year to 5-year period. In contrast to basic medical expense insurance, major medical policies provide total maximum lifetime benefits to individual insureds usually from $250,000 to $1,000,000 or more.

Major medical expense insurance usually picks up where basic medical expense insurance leaves off, in one of two ways: as a supplement to a basic plan or as a comprehensive stand-alone plan.

Supplementary Major Medical

A supplementary major medical plan covers expenses not included at all under a basic plan. It also covers expenses that exceed the dollar maximums specified in the basic policy as well as those expenses no longer covered by the basic plan because the benefits have been exhausted.

As a supplemental plan, major medical coverage is coordinated with various basic medical expense coverages, picking up where the basic plan leaves off. For example, a basic plan may provide for hospital room and board benefits for a maximum of 45 days. If that basic plan were supplemented with a major medical plan, the supplementary major medical plan would cover hospital room and board expenses beginning on the 46th day. Or, if a basic plan provides a maximum benefit of $1,500 for a specific surgical procedure and the actual cost of the procedure was $2,000, a major medical supplement would cover the additional $500. In addition, because of the broad coverage associated with most major medical supplements, a supplement will likely cover expenses that are either beyond the scope of the basic plan or excluded from its coverage.

Comprehensive Major Medical

The second type of major medical plan is the comprehensive major medical plan. Comprehensive plans are distinguished by the fact that they cover virtually all medical expenses—hospital expenses, physician and surgeon expenses, nursing care, drugs, physical therapy, diagnostic X rays and laboratory services, medical supplies and equipment, transfusions and more—under a single policy.

Major medical plans, whether supplementary or comprehensive, typically include two important features: deductibles and coinsurance. Both features require the insured to absorb some of the cost of his or her medical expenses, thus allowing the insurer to avoid small claims and keep the cost of premiums down. In contrast, a basic medical plan usually does not include either of these features; instead it imposes limitations in the form of maximum benefit amounts that will be paid.

Deductibles

A *deductible* is a stated initial dollar amount that the individual insured is required to pay before insurance benefits are paid. For example, if a plan has a flat $250 annual deductible, the insured is responsible for the first $250 of medical expenses every year. Covered expenses in excess of $250 are then paid by the major plan (subject to any coinsurance requirements).

Depending on the type of major medical policy, the deductible may be one of three kinds: flat, corridor or integrated.

Flat Deductible

A *flat deductible* is a stated amount that the insured must pay before policy benefits become payable. For example, if an insured has a policy with a $500 deductible and incurs $2,000 of covered medical expenses, he or she must pay $500 toward the total. The insurer will then base its payments on the remaining $1,500. Quite often, policies will include a *family deductible,* usually equal to three times the individual deductible amount. In a family of four, for example, if three members each satisfied the individual deductible in one year, no deductible would be applied to medical expenses incurred by the fourth member.

Corridor Deductible

A *corridor deductible* is typical for a supplementary major medical policy that works in conjunction with a basic medical expense policy. The first covered medical expenses the insured incurs are paid by the basic policy. After the basic policy benefits are exhausted, the insured pays the full deductible, and then the major medical benefits are payable. The deductible the insured pays is considered the "corridor" between the two policies.

For example, Lynda has a supplemental major medical policy that has a corridor deductible of $500. The deductible applies after full payment of up to $2,000 by Lynda's basic medical expense policy and before additional expenses are shared on a coinsurance basis by the insurer and Lynda (see "Coinsurance" below). For example, suppose Lynda incurs a medical bill of $8,500. Responsibility for payment is as follows:

Total expenses:	$8,500
Basic medical expense pays:	−2,000
	$6,500
Corridor deductible paid by Lynda:	− 500
Basis for major medical expense payment and coinsurance:	$6,000

The basic medical expense policy paid for the first $2,000 of Lynda's medical bills. The corridor deductible, which Lynda as the insured is responsible for, is applied next. The medical expenses that remain, in this case $6,000, become the basis for the major medical payment. The amount of this payment is usually determined on a coinsurance or copayment basis whereby the insured pays some percentage of the costs. This is explained under "Coinsurance" below.

Integrated Deductible

An *integrated deductible* is also used with a supplementary major medical plan, but it is "integrated" into the amounts covered by the basic plan. For example, if a supplementary plan carries a $500 deductible and the insured incurs $500 or more of covered expenses under the basic plan, the deductible is satisfied. If the basic policy benefits do not cover the entire deductible amount specified in the major medical policy, the insured must make up the difference.

Each of the preceding deductibles may be figured on one of two bases. If a major medical plan provides for a *calendar year deductible,* the deductible amount is applied only once during each calendar year. Once the deductible has been met in a calendar year, all claims submitted will be treated for the balance of the year without regard to any deductibles.

If a major medical plan has a *per cause deductible,* separate deductibles are required for each separate illness or each separate accident. Per cause deductibles are common in policies that define causes of loss as "each sickness or each injury."

Coinsurance

Coinsurance, or percentage participation, is another characteristic of major medical policies. It is, simply, a sharing of expenses by the insured and the insurer. After the insured satisfies the deductible, the insurance company pays a high percentage of the additional covered expenses—usually 75 or 80 percent—and the insured pays the rest. For example, Joe has an 80 percent/20 percent (often written 80/20) major medical policy, with a $200 flat annual deductible. This year, he incurs $1,200 in medical expenses, all of which are covered by his policy. The responsibility for payment is as follows:

Total expenses:	$1,200
Deductible Joe pays:	− 200
Basis for insurer's payment:	$1,000
Coinsurance percentage:	× .80
Amount insurer pays:	$ 800
Coinsurance amount Joe pays:	$ 200

So, after Joe has paid the deductible, the insurer pays 80 percent of the remaining charges, or $800. Joe must pay the $200 deductible and 20 percent of the remaining expenses, for a total of $400.

Now, let's assume Joe has two separate medical problems this year. The first required hospitalization and surgery and totaled $7,500. Under his major medical policy, Joe submitted his claim and paid his $200 deductible. The insurer paid 80 percent of the charges above the deductible, or $5,840; Joe paid the remaining 20 percent, or $1,460. Three months later, Joe incurs another round of medical expenses amounting to $900. Since his policy has a flat annual deductible, which Joe has already paid, the insurer will pay 80 percent of the full $900; Joe must pay the remaining 20 percent or $180.

Coinsurance provisions are effective throughout the life of a policy.

Stop Loss Feature

Many major medical policies contain a *stop loss feature* that limits the insured's out-of-pocket expenses. This means that once the insured has paid a specified amount toward his or her covered expenses—usually $1,000 or $2,000—the insurer pays 100 percent of covered expenses after that point. This provides valuable protection for the insured.

How a stop-loss cap is defined depends on the policy. One policy may provide that the contract will cover 100 percent of eligible expenses after the insured incurs $1,000 in out-of-pocket costs. Another policy may provide that the coinsurance provision applies only to the first $5,000 of covered expenses after the deductible is paid, with remaining expenses covered in full.

Assume that Bill has a policy like the last one described above. After a $500 deductible, the policy provides for an 80 percent/20 percent coinsurance on the next $5,000 in covered expenses. Amounts above $5,500 are fully absorbed by the policy. If Bill were to incur hospital and surgical bills of $20,000 this year, this is how payment would be assigned:

Total expenses:	$20,000
Deductible Bill pays:	– 500
	$19,500
Coinsurance Bill pays (20 percent of the next $5,000 in expenses):	– 1,000
Amount insurer pays:	$18,500

With a $500 deductible and $1,000 in coinsurance for the next $5,000, Bill's insurance plan provides for a maximum out-of-pocket expenditure by the insured of $1,500.

Preexisting Conditions

Another common feature in major medical policies is the exclusion for *preexisting conditions.* In individual plans, a preexisting condition is an illness or condition that existed before the policy's effective date and that the applicant did not reveal on the application. (A condition that *is* noted on the application may be excluded by rider or waiver.) Consequently, medical costs resulting from a preexisting condition are not covered under plans that contain this exclusion. However, this exclusion only applies for a limited time. After the time limit passes, existing conditions are no longer considered "preexisting" and will be covered in full, subject to any other policy limitations.

The exclusion for preexisting conditions is designed to protect insurers against *adverse selection* by those who know they have a medical ailment and who face certain medical costs. Adverse selection is the tendency of less favorable insurance risks to seek or continue insurance to a greater extent than others.

---

1. Thelma incurs a hospital bill of $8,300. Her basic hospital insurance pays $2,400. Thelma pays a $200 deductible, and her major medical plan takes care of the balance of covered expenses. Thelma's deductible would be classified as a ______ deductible.

---

2. An *integrated* deductible amount is $2,000. If basic hospital benefits do not satisfy the $2,000 deductible before major medical benefits become payable, who makes up the difference?

   ______

---

3. Dale incurs hospital expenses totaling $5,500. His major medical policy has a flat deductible amount of $300 and an 80 percent/20 percent coinsurance feature. Dale will pay the first ______ and his major medical will pay ______ percent of $5,200 or ______. Dale will also pay the balance, which will be ______.

4. Wanda is hospitalized for two weeks. Before her hospital bill can be settled, Wanda must pay the first $500 of covered expenses because of her major medical policy's

   A. exclusion allowance.
   B. deductible provision.

Deductible amounts vary according to the policy.

---

5. From an underwriting standpoint, what is the purpose of the deductible provision in major medical insurance?

   ____
   ____
   ____

To eliminate small claims, thereby helping to control the administrative expenses of the insurer and to keep premium rates as low as possible.

---

6. Explain how a major medical stop loss provision works.

   ____
   ____
   ____

The company pays 100 percent of covered expenses after an insured's out-of-pocket eligible medical expenses reach a specified amount.

■ OTHER TYPES OF MEDICAL EXPENSE COVERAGE

As we've discussed, basic medical expense plans and major medical expense plans are the two major types of health policies that provide coverage for accidents and illness. However, our discussion of medical expense plans would not be complete without mentioning a number of other plans, particularly hospital indemnity policies, limited risk (or dread disease) policies and medical savings accounts. (Medicare supplement policies and long-term care policies are other important kinds of medical expense policies, and we will discuss them at length in later chapters.)

Hospital Indemnity Policies

As mentioned earlier, a *hospital indemnity policy* simply provides a stated daily, weekly or monthly amount based on the number of days the insured is hospitalized. For example, a hospital indemnity plan may provide the insured $100 a day for each day he or she stays in the hospital.

This type of insurance has been available for many years, but has been promoted more heavily in recent years due to skyrocketing health care costs. Many insurers are able to offer high benefit indemnity plans at reasonable premiums because underwriting and administration are relatively simple and claim costs are not affected by increases in medical costs.

Benefits may run as high as $4,500 per month, based on a daily hospital confinement benefit of $150, and some are even higher. Maximum benefit periods range from about six months to several years or even for a lifetime. Benefits are paid directly to the insured and may be used by the insured for any purpose.

Limited Risk Policies

Policies that provide medical expense coverage for specific kinds of illness are called *limited risk* or *dread disease* policies. They are available primarily due to the high cost associated with certain illnesses, such as cancer or heart disease. In order to protect consumers, limited risk policies must state on their front pages that: "THIS IS A LIMITED POLICY." It should be noted, furthermore, that some states prohibit the sale of these policies, since they invite questionable sales and marketing practices that may take advantage of people's fear of these diseases. Limited risk policies that cover specified accidents are also available and are discussed in Chapter 4.

Medical Savings Accounts

Medical savings accounts (MSAs) are a new method for small businesses and the self-employed to provide medical expense coverage. MSAs are trust accounts set up for the express purpose of paying the qualified medical expenses of the MSA account holder. Under federal law, the MSA is being tested and evaluated for a four-year period beginning January 1, 1997. During this period, a maximum of 750,000 MSAs may be established on a first-come, first-served basis by self-employed individuals or companies with 50 or fewer employers.

MSAs are designed to cover routine medical expenses; they are not meant to provide catastrophic coverage. Consequently, participation in a high-deductible catastrophic coverage plan is required in order to establish an MSA. The minimum/maximum deductibles for these plans are $1,500/$2,250 for individual coverage and $3,000/$4,500 for family coverage.

Once an individual has established an MSA, he or she may set aside funds to the MSA on a tax-advantaged basis to help pay health care costs. Contributions to an MSA, up to certain limits, are not taxable to the MSA account holder. The maximum tax-free contribution to an MSA is set with reference to the catastrophic coverage plan deductible discussed above. With individual coverage, the maximum annual MSA contribution is 65 percent of the deductible amount; with family coverage, the maximum annual MSA contribution is 75 percent of the deductible.

Similarly, distributions from the MSA are not taxable to the MSA account holder if they are used to pay "qualified medical expenses" of the account holder. Qualified medical expenses are amounts paid by the account holder for medical care for the account holder, his or her spouse or dependents to the extent that these expenses are not paid for by insurance or other means. If distributions are used for purposes other than the account holder's qualified medical expenses, they are subject to taxation including a possible 15 percent penalty tax.

MSA funds belong to the insured; if they are not spent, they accumulate to prefund future health care expenses.

1. Explain why premiums for hospital indemnity policies are economical.

____

____

____

Premiums for hospital indemnity policies are reasonable because of the simple underwriting and administrative procedures as well as the fact that the benefit amount paid under such policies is not affected by increases in medical costs.

---

2. Which of the following statements is/are true regarding hospital indemnity policies?

   I . Benefits are paid directly to the hospital.
   II. Benefits are paid only for specified illnesses.

   A. I only
   B. II only
   C. Both I and II
   D. Neither I nor II

D

Benefits are paid directly to the insured and are based on whether or not the insured is hospitalized, not what type of illness the insured has.

---

3. Distributions from an MSA are not taxable to the individual

   A. under any conditions.
   B. if they are used to pay qualified medical expenses of the account holder.

B

Distributions from an MSA used to pay unreimbursed medical expenses of the individual, his or her spouse or dependents are not taxable; distributions used for other purposes are taxable.

3

Disability Income Insurance

Disability income insurance is often called "the forgotten need." All too frequently, what is thought to be a well-planned insurance program—a program consisting of life insurance and medical expense coverage—is proven completely inadequate when the one risk not covered materializes. The risk associated with disability is *loss of income*—if an individual can't work due to a disability, he or she won't be able to earn a living. The purpose of this chapter is to describe the important role disability income insurance serves and to explain the features of these policies.

PURPOSE OF DISABILITY INCOME INSURANCE

Disability income insurance is designed to provide an individual with a stated amount of periodic income in the event he or she cannot work due to a disabling illness or accident. Statistics prove that the probability of disability greatly exceeds the probability of death during an individual's working years. The need for protection against the *economic death* of a wage earner cannot be overemphasized, and it is this need that disability income insurance fills.

Disability income policies provide coverage for disabilities resulting from either accidents alone or from both accidents and sickness. Because sickness-related disabilities represent only a small fraction of all disabilities, it is not economically feasible to issue sickness-only disability policies. To obtain sickness income protection, one normally has to purchase accident income coverage as well.

Disability income policies are available as individual plans and group plans. They also serve a very important function for businesses and business owners. In this chapter, we will focus on the basics of individual disability policies; group disability insurance is discussed in Chapter 11 and business uses of disability income insurance are discussed in Chapter 15.

■ DISABILITY INCOME BENEFITS

The benefits paid under a disability income policy are received by the insured in the form of weekly or monthly *income payments.* Unlike life insurance, which insurers will issue for almost any amount the applicant applies for (and qualifies for), disability insurance is characterized by benefit limits. Insurers typically place a ceiling on the amount of disability income protection any one applicant can obtain. This ceiling is usually defined in terms of a maximum percentage of the person's salary or wages. For example, an individual earning $2,000 a month may be limited by Company A to a monthly disability benefit of 60 percent of income, or $1,200. If that individual already has an existing disability policy from Company X that provides for $400 in monthly income, Company A would issue a policy for no more than $800 in monthly benefits. Some companies now provide for income protection as high as $10,000 a month, but never to exceed the applicant's gross earnings.

Some insurers do use a flat amount method, whereby the insured receives a flat income benefit amount if he or she becomes disabled. Normally this amount is payable regardless of any other income benefits the insured may receive.

"Disability" Defined

With only one exception (partial disability), an insured must be *totally disabled* before benefits under a disability income policy are payable. However, what constitutes "total disability" varies from policy to policy and an insured must meet the definition of total disability as it is set forth in his or her contract. Basically, there are two definitions: any occupation and own occupation.

Any Occupation vs. Own Occupation

Some policies stipulate that in order to collect disability benefits, the insured must be disabled to the extent that he or she is unable to work at *any occupation* for which he or she is reasonably suited "by education, training or experience." Other policies use an "own occupation" definition and pay benefits if the insured is unable to work at his or her *own occupation* because of disability resulting from injury or sickness.

A disability income policy with an "own occupation" definition of disability is more advantageous to the policyowner. Consequently, it is more expensive and difficult to qualify for. Often, disability income policies provide benefits based on the "own occupation" definition for a certain period of time (usually the first two years of a disability) and then change the basis to the "any occupation" definition.

1. All other factors being equal, which is likely to be less expensive—a policy that uses an "own occupation" definition of disability or one that uses an "any occupation" definition?

____

2. Which of the following statements is true?

   A. Disability income benefits are not subject to limits.
   B. An individual's disability income benefits cannot exceed his or her regular income by more than 60 percent.
   C. Disability income benefits are typically based on a percentage of an individual's earned income.

3. Insurance Company A limits the amount of disability benefits an applicant can apply for to 60 percent of income. Frank has an income of $4,000 a month and currently has no disability income coverage. Frank may apply for how much monthly coverage from Company A?

____

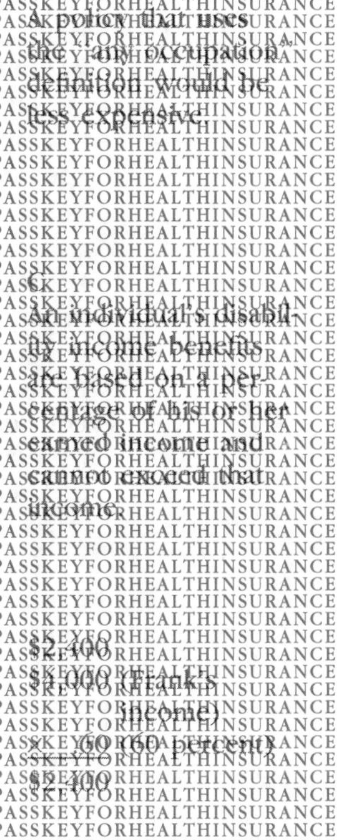

Partial Disability

The exception to the "total disability" requirement are those policies that also pay benefits in the event of a *partial disability.* By most definitions, partial disability is the inability of the insured to perform *one or more important duties of his or her job* or *the inability to work at that job on a full-time basis,* either of which results in a decrease in income.

Normally, partial disability benefits are payable only if the policyowner has first been totally disabled. This benefit is intended to encourage disabled insureds to get back to work, even on a part-time basis, without fear that they will lose all their disability income benefits. The amount of benefit payable when a policy covers partial disabilities depends on whether the policy stipulates a flat amount or a residual amount.

Flat Amount Benefit

A *flat* partial disability benefit is a set amount stated in the policy. Usually this amount is 50 percent or less of the amount that would be paid for a total disability.

Residual Amount Benefit

A *residual* disability benefit is based on the proportion of income the insured has actually lost, taking into account the fact that he or she is able to work and earn some income. (Usually, residual benefits are payable even if the insured was not first totally disabled.) For example, if the insured suffered a 40 percent loss of income due to the partial disability, the residual benefit payable would be 40 percent of the total disability benefit. This percentage is subject to change as the disabled insured's income varies. Generally, residual benefits are provided through a rider to the policy, which specifies that no residual benefits are paid if the loss of income is less than 20 or 25 percent.

Let's look at an example. Quintin, a printer, suffered a disabling back injury following a car accident. He was not able to work at all for seven months, during which his disability policy provided a full benefit. After seven months, he returned to work on a limited part-time basis, earning 60 percent of his predisability salary. If Quintin's policy provided for partial disability benefits on a flat amount basis, he would receive the amount specified in his policy. If Quintin's policy provided for partial disability benefits on a residual basis, he would receive 40 percent of the total disability benefit.

Insurers require proof of an insured's total or partial disability before they will pay benefits. To be eligible for benefits, the disabled insured must be under the care of a physician.

Presumptive Disability

Many policies today contain a *presumption of disability* provision. Basically, these policies provide that certain disabilities, such as permanent loss of sight in one or both eyes, or the loss of both hands or both feet, are so serious that normal monthly income benefits are paid because such injuries are *presumed* to be total and permanent.

Cause of Disability

Another important aspect of disability income policies is the way in which they define the *cause* of disability. Some policies state that benefits are payable when injuries are caused by "external, violent and accidental means." Others provide for payment based on "accidental bodily injury."

Policies that use the *accidental means* provision require the cause of the injury to be unexpected and accidental. Policies that use the *accidental bodily injury* provision require the result of the injury—in other words, the injury itself—be unexpected and accidental. This latter is also known as the "results" provision.

For example, assume Jim, the insured, took an intentional dive off a high, rocky ledge into a lake, struck his head on some rocks and ended up partially paralyzed. If his policy had an accidental means provision, the benefits would probably not be payable since the cause of his injury—the dive—was intentional. However, if his policy had an accidental bodily injury (or results) provision, benefits would be payable since the result of the accident—his injury—was unintentional and accidental.

Today, most disability income policies use the accidental bodily injury or results provision, which is far less restrictive than the accidental means provision. In fact, many states now require all accident-based insurance benefits to be based on the accidental bodily injury provision.

Occupational vs. Nonoccupational Coverage

Disability income policies can be classified as *occupational* or *nonoccupational.* Occupational policies cover work-related ~~and nonwork-related~~ injuries or illnesses. Nonoccupational policies cover only injuries or illnesses that are not work-related.

Insurance companies will not offer occupational coverage to individuals who work in certain hazardous occupations, such as test pilots. In these cases, most companies will sell the individual a nonoccupational policy. All other factors being equal, an occupational policy will cost more than a nonoccupational policy since it provides more extensive benefits.

Group disability income policies are generally issued on a nonoccupational basis since coverage for work-related losses is already provided by workers' compensation coverage.

---

1. Policies that pay benefits based on accidental means require that only the injury be unexpected and accidental.

   (True/False)

False

Policies that use the accidental means provision require that the *cause* of the injury be unexpected and accidental.

---

2. Which definition of the cause of disability is also known as the "results" definition?

   A. Accidental means
   B. Accidental bodily injury

B

The accidental bodily injury definition requires only that the result (i.e., the injury itself) be accidental, so it is also known as the results definition.

---

3. Disability income benefits for partial disability may be payable under which of the following circumstances?

   I. The insured is unable to perform one or more important duties of his or her job.
   II. The insured is unable to work at his or her job full-time.
      A. I only
      B. II only
      C. Both I and II
      D. Neither I nor II

C

By most policy definitions, partial disability is the inability to perform one or more important duties of a job or the inability to work at that job on a full-time basis.

4. Which of the following terms relates to disability income insurance?

   A. Service basis
   B. First-dollar
   C. Residual amount
   D. Coinsurance

C. A residual disability benefit is one way of paying disability benefits.

---

5. Sidney has a monthly total disability benefit of $2,500 under a policy that pays partial disability benefits on a residual basis. If Sidney returns to work but suffers a 40 percent loss of his pre-disability income, how much will his partial disability benefit be?

   A. $2,500
   B. $1,500
   C. $1,000

C. $2,500 (total disability benefit)
× .40 (actual income loss)
$1,000 (partial disability benefit)

DISABILITY INCOME POLICY PROVISIONS

In addition to specifying the amount of benefit payable and the circumstances under which a benefit is payable (plus complying with required policy provision standards), disability income policies contain a number of other important provisions. The most notable of these are as follows.

Probationary Period

The *probationary period* specified in a disability insurance policy is the period of time that must elapse *following the effective date of the policy* before benefits are payable. It is a one-time-only period that begins on the policy's effective date and ends 15 or 30 days after the policy has been in force. The purpose of the probationary period is to exclude preexisting sicknesses from coverage and provide a guidepost in borderline cases when there is a question as to whether an insured became ill before or after the effective date of the policy. Just as important, it helps protect the insurer against adverse selection, since those who know they are ill are more likely to try to obtain insurance coverage.

Note that a disability income probationary period applies to sickness only; it does not apply to accidents. Whereas a person may be able to anticipate a sickness-related disability (after a visit to the doctor, for example), it is not possible to anticipate an accident.

Elimination Period

Similar in concept to a deductible, the *elimination period* is the time immediately *following the start of a disability* when benefits are *not* payable. Elimination periods eliminate claims for short-term disabilities for which the insured can usually manage without financial hardship and save the insurance company the expense of processing and settling small claims. This, in turn, helps keep premiums down. The longer the elimination period, the lower the premium for comparable disability benefits. An elimination period, also known as a "waiting period," can be compared to a deductible since both are cost-sharing devices that can have a direct bearing on the amount of premium required of the policyowner.

Depending on the policy, elimination periods may apply only to disabilities caused by sickness and not to disabilities caused by accident. In either event, elimination periods usually range from one week to one year or longer, but most are at least 30 days.

Benefit Period

The *benefit period* is the maximum length of time that disability income benefits will be paid to the disabled insured. The longer the benefit period, the higher the cost of the policy. For individual policies, there are basically two types of benefit periods and accordingly they serve to classify a disability income policy as either "short term" or "long term." Individual short-term policies provide benefits for six months to two years, after which payments cease. Individual long-term policies are characterized by benefit periods of more than two years, such as 5, 10 or 20. In some cases, a long-term policy will provide for benefits until the insured reaches age 65. The classifications of short term and long term are not necessarily the same for individual and group plans. See Chapter 11 for a discussion of group disability plans.

Delayed Disability Provision

In some cases, total disability does not occur immediately after an accident, but develops some days or weeks later. Most policies allow a certain amount of time during which total disability may result from an accident and the insured will still be eligible for benefits. The amount of time allowed for a *delayed disability* may be 30, 60 or 90 days, for example.

Recurrent Disability Provision

It is not unusual for a person who experienced a total disability to recover and then, weeks or months later, undergo a recurrence of the same disability.

Most policies provide for *recurrent disabilities* by specifying a period of time during which the recurrence of a disability is considered a continuation of the prior disability. If the recurrence takes place after that specified period, it is considered a new disability and will be subject to a new elimination period before benefits are again payable.

For example, Rachael has a short-term disability policy that stipulates that a new benefit-paying period begins if the insured is disabled, recovers and returns to work for six months and then becomes disabled again. Rachael is totally disabled and off work from January 15 to April 15, when she returns to work. She is stricken again the same year and is off work from September 1 to November 10. Rachael's policy would resume paying benefits, classifying her recurrence as a continuation of her prior disability, since her return to work did not last six months. She would not be subject to a new elimination period.

Nondisabling Injury

Frequently, a person covered by a disability income policy will suffer an injury that does not qualify for income benefits. Such injuries are referred to as *nondisabling injuries.* While a nondisabling injury does not result in loss of working time or income, it may require medical care. Many disability income policies include a provision for a medical expense benefit that pays the actual cost of medical treatment for nondisabling injuries that result from an accident.

This benefit is generally limited to a percentage of the weekly or monthly income benefit specified in the policy. It is payable to eligible insureds in lieu of other benefits under the policy.

---

1. All of the following statements pertaining to recurrent disabilities are true, EXCEPT:

   A. A recurrent disability is one that the insured experiences more than once.
   B. Recurrent disability policy provisions have no effect on the payment of benefits.
   C. A new waiting period may or may not be required for a recurrent disability.
   D. A recurrent disability may begin a new benefit period.

2. Benefit periods for individual short-term disability policies typically vary from

   A. 1 to 12 months.
   B. 3 months to 3 years.
   C. 6 months to 2 years.
   D. 1 to 5 years.

3. Sidney is hospitalized with a broken back and, upon checking his 2-year-old disability income policy, learns that he will not be eligible for benefits for at least 30 days. This indicates that his policy probably has a 30-day

   A. elimination period.
   B. probationary period.

4. Karl is totally disabled as a result of an auto accident. He immediately qualifies for benefits under his disability income policy because it has no probationary period for disabilities caused by______.

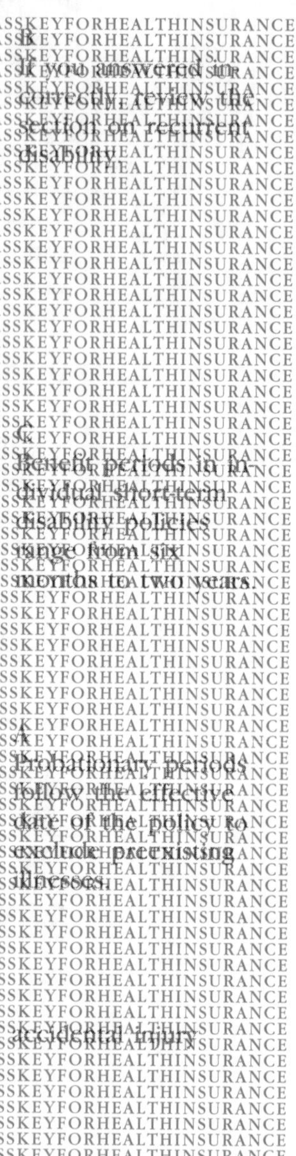

B
If you answered incorrectly, review the section on recurrent disability.
C
Benefit periods in individual short-term disability policies range from six months to two years.
A
Probationary periods follow the effective date of the policy to exclude preexisting illnesses.
accidental injury

5. Define the term "nondisabling injury" as used in disability income policies.

An injury received in an accident that does not qualify the insured for income benefits.

6. What does the "nondisabling injury" benefit provide?

Payment for medical treatment of an injury received in an accident, which is usually limited to a percentage of the weekly or monthly income benefit.

7. All of the following statements pertaining to elimination periods in disability income policies are true, EXCEPT:

   A. Elimination periods may apply to disabilities due to sickness and not accidents.
   B. Benefits are not payable during an elimination period, but are paid retroactively to the beginning of the period if the insured remains disabled throughout the period.
   C. An elimination period follows the start of a disability.
   D. Elimination periods help keep premiums down.

B. Disability income benefits are not payable until after the elimination period.

DISABILITY INCOME POLICY RIDERS

Disability income policies may be purchased with *riders* or *options* that will enhance their value to the insured. Some of the more common riders are discussed below.

Waiver of Premium Rider

A *waiver of premium rider* generally is included with guaranteed renewable and noncancelable individual disability income policies. It is a valuable provision because it exempts the policyowner from paying the policy's premiums during periods of total disability. To qualify for the exemption, the insured must experience total disability for more than a specified period, commonly three or six months. In some cases, the waiver retroactively applies to the original date of disability and any premiums paid for that period are refunded. The trend is to have the waiver apply to the entire period of total disability, rather than to just the benefit period.

The waiver of premium generally does not extend past the insured's age 60 or 65. When the waiver is added, policy premiums are adjusted upward to cover the additional risk. Premiums then are reduced when the waiver is dropped due to the insured reaching the specified age limit.

Social Security Rider

The *Social Security rider,* sometimes called the "social insurance substitute" rider, provides for the payment of additional income when the insured is eligible for social insurance benefits but those benefits have not yet begun, have been denied or have begun in an amount less than the benefit amount of the rider. Usually covered under the definition "social insurance" are disability benefits from Social Security as well as state and local government programs or workers' compensation programs.

When applying for the rider, the applicant states the amount of benefit expected from Social Security and any other programs for which he or she might be eligible. Of course, the level of expected benefits must be realistic in light of the applicant's earnings level. When total disability strikes, the applicant must show that social insurance benefits have been applied for. After the Social Security Administration (or comparable administrative body of a state or local program) determines the benefit payable, the *difference* between the actual benefit and the "expected" benefit listed in the rider is payable as an additional disability income benefit.

Cost of Living Adjustment Rider

The *cost of living adjustment* (COLA) *rider* allows the disability benefit to keep pace with inflation. Specifically, it provides for indexing the monthly or weekly benefit payable to changes in the Consumer Price Index. Typically, the benefit amount is adjusted on each disability anniversary date to reflect changes in the CPI (though often a minimum CPI change, such as 4 percent, is required to trigger a disability income benefit increase.) When the disability ceases, the policyowner can elect to maintain the policy at the new (increased) benefit level by paying additional premiums or can choose to let the benefit return to the originally scheduled amount for the same premium as was paid before the disability commenced.

Guaranteed Insurability Rider

A disability income policy is the only type of health insurance policy to which a *guaranteed insurability rider* may be attached. This option guarantees the insured the right to purchase additional amounts of disability income coverage at pre-determined times in the future *without evidence of insurability.* Of course, the insured may not exceed the insurer's normal benefit limits; the insured may be required to meet an earnings test before each purchase.

Most guaranteed insurability riders require the insured to exercise the option for additional coverage prior to a specific age, such as age 50.

1. Which of the following riders provides for changes in the benefit payable based on changes in the consumer price index (CPI)?

   A. Guaranteed insurability rider
   B. Cost of living adjustment rider
   C. Social Security rider
   D. Waiver of premium rider

B

The cost of living adjustment rider (COLA) provides for benefits to be adjusted when the CPI changes.

---

2. An "earnings test" might be used with a

   A. guaranteed insurability rider.
   B. Social Security rider.
   C. waiver of premium rider.
   D. cost of living adjustment rider.

A

Because a guaranteed insurability rider allows the insured to purchase additional amounts of insurance, insurers protect against overinsurance by subjecting insureds who wish to increase their coverage to an earnings test.

---

3. All of the following statements pertaining to the waiver of premium rider in health insurance policies are correct, EXCEPT:

   A. It exempts an insured from paying premiums during periods of permanent and total disability.
   B. It may apply retroactively.
   C. It generally drops off after the insured reaches age 60 or 65.
   D. It normally applies to both medical expense and disability income policies.

D

The waiver of premium rider may be included in guaranteed renewable and noncancelable individual disability income policies, not medical expense policies.

Progressive Quiz No. 1

(Text page reference numbers are shown under each correct response in the red column.)

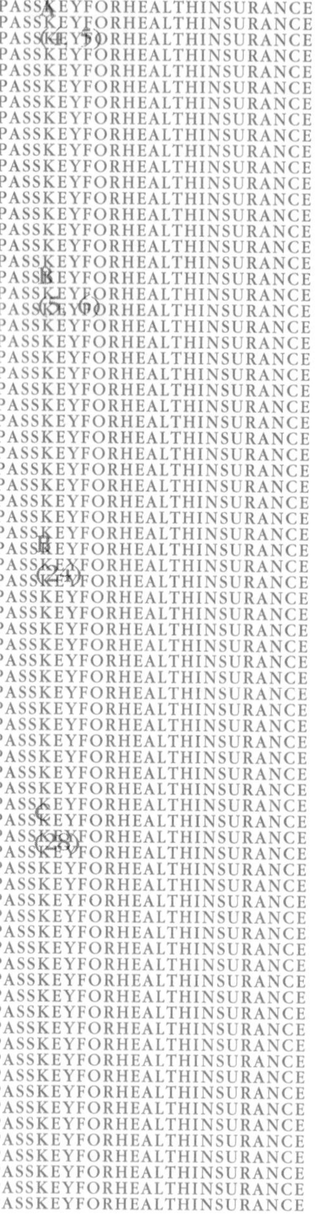

1. Which type of health insurance plan would most likely cover the cost of hospitalization due to a disabling accident?

   A. Medical expense
   B. Disability income
   C. Accidental death and dismemberment

---

2. Like life insurance, health insurance can be purchased on a limited pay basis, allowing the policyowner to have a paid-up policy with protection that extends until his or her death.

   A. True
   B. False

---

3. Which type of policy typically ties its maximum benefit payable to the insured's wages or salary?

   A. Medical expense
   B. Disability income
   C. Accidental death and dismemberment

---

4. Which of the following correctly defines the *elimination period* in a disability income policy?

   A. The period of time immediately following the issue of the policy when benefits are not payable
   B. The period of time between application and policy issue when benefits are conditionally payable, depending on the applicant's insurability
   C. The period of time immediately following the start of a disability when benefits are not payable
   D. The period of time immediately following an accident or illness during which benefits are retroactively payable if the insured later becomes disabled

5. A basic hospital expense policy typically covers

   A. hospital room and board as well as surgeon expenses.
   B. surgeon expenses and anesthesia.
   C. private duty nursing and skilled care facility expenses.
   D. hospital room and board as well as miscellaneous hospital expenses.

D
(11)

---

6. Under what type of basic surgical expense plan are surgical procedures assigned a dollar value to determine benefit amounts payable?

   A. Relative value scale
   B. Surgical schedule
   C. Reasonable and customary approach
   D. Surgical indemnity

B
(12, 13)

---

7. Camille owns a health insurance policy that pays benefits of $125 a day for each day of hospitalization, regardless of the actual expenses she incurs. These amounts are paid directly to her. Camille has a

   A. limited risk policy.
   B. Medicare supplement policy.
   C. disability income policy.
   D. hospital indemnity policy.

D
(20)

---

8. Which of the following statements regarding a disability income policy's probationary period is/are true?

   I. It is the period of time following a disability before benefits are payable.
   II. It is applicable to sicknesses only; it does not apply to accidents.

   A. I only
   B. II only
   C. Both I and II
   D. Neither I nor II

B
(28)

---

9. Under a disability income policy, benefits to cover medical expenses for nondisabling injuries are

   A. prohibited.
   B. limited to a percentage of the weekly or monthly income benefit specified in the policy.
   C. payable with no effect on other benefits under the policy.
   D. limited to nondisabling injuries that result from sickness.

B
(30)

10. The principle of the law of large numbers allows insurers to predict

I. when any one person in a given group during a given period will become ill or disabled.
II. the likelihood of illness or disability that will occur in a given group during a given period.

A. I only
B. II only
C. Both I and II
D. Neither I nor II

---

11. All of the following are elements of an insurable risk, EXCEPT the loss

A. must be measurable.
B. must be within the insured's control.
C. must be predictable.
D. cannot be catastrophic.

---

12. Jean owns a conditionally renewable health insurance policy, and John owns a guaranteed renewable health insurance policy. Based on these facts alone, whose policy is likely to be more expensive?

A. Jean's
B. John's

---

13. "The expected incidence of sickness or disability within a given age group during a given period of time" is the definition of

A. risk pooling.
B. law of large numbers.
C. morbidity.
D. mortality.

---

14. Which authority establishes minimum requirements for health insurance reserves?

A. The insurer
B. The federal government
C. The state government
D. The National Association of Insurance Commissioners (NAIC)

15. Which type of health plan provides coverage under a master contract to members of a specified group?

A. Workers' compensation
B. Medicare
C. Medicaid
D. Group health insurance

---

16. The term "first dollar" is associated with which type of health insurance policy?

A. Major medical
B. Partial disability
C. Basic medical
D. Accidental death and dismemberment

---

17. With a major medical policy, the initial amount the insured must pay before any insurance benefits are payable is the

A. deductible amount.
B. coinsurance amount.
C. stop loss amount.
D. cost-share amount.

---

18. Policies that provide medical expense coverage for specific kinds of illnesses are known as

A. limited risk policies.
B. single risk policies.
C. supplemental risk policies.
D. wraparound policies.

---

19. In February, Wilt incurs his first hospital expenses of the year, which total $12,500. All of these expenses are covered by his major medical policy. The policy contains a $250 annual deductible and a 80/20 coinsurance feature. Of the total expense, how much will Wilt have to pay?

A. $2,500
B. $2,700
C. $2,750
D. $3,000

20. Based on the facts in the above question, assume that six months after Wilt's initial hospitalization, he is involved in an automobile accident and is again hospitalized. This time the bill is for $16,300, all of which his policy covers. How much of this $16,300 will Wilt have to pay?

A. $3,210
B. $12,790
C. $3,260
D. $13,040

---

21. With regard to deductible provisions in medical expense policies, all of the following statements are correct, EXCEPT:

A. They help eliminate small claims.
B. They provide that initial medical expenses up to a specified amount are to be paid by the insured.
C. They are most commonly found in basic medical expense policies.
D. They help hold down premium rates.

---

22. In order to qualify for a medical savings account (MSA), an employer can have no more than how many employees?

A. 1
B. 10
C. 25
D. 50

---

23. A "stop loss" provision is typically associated with

A. basic hospital expense policies.
B. major medical expense policies.
C. disability income insurance policies.
D. All of the above

---

24. Which of the following types of medical expense plans would contain a corridor deductible?

A. Comprehensive major medical
B. Supplementary major medical medical
C. Hospital indemnity
D. Basic hospital expense

25. Andrew has a major medical policy with a $250 deductible and an 80/20 percent coinsurance provision. Due to a serious accident, he incurred the following losses: a $3,000 hospital expense, a $2,000 physician expense and a $1,250 loss of income. Andrew would be eligible for a benefit of

A. $3,800.
B. $4,800.
C. $4,750.
D. $6,250.

A (17)

4

Accidental Death and Dismemberment

So far we've discussed medical expense insurance and disability income insurance. The third major form of health insurance coverage is *accidental death and dismemberment insurance,* commonly referred to as AD&D. Actually, it is something of a hybrid, paying benefits in the event of death or dismemberment. Though the circumstances under which it pays these benefits are somewhat limited, it is a popular form of insurance protection and is widely utilized in group insurance plans. In this chapter we will review the nature and principles of AD&D policies and benefits.

NATURE OF AD&D POLICIES

Accidental death and dismemberment insurance is the primary form of pure *accident coverage.* As such, it serves a rather limited purpose: it provides a stated lump-sum benefit in the event of accidental death *or* in the event of loss of body members due to accidental injury. This latter includes loss of one or both hands or feet or the loss of sight in one or both eyes. ("Loss of body member" is typically defined as actual severance from the body, though it may include loss of use, depending on the policy.) Separate benefits for hospital, surgical and other medical expenses are generally not included in AD&D policies, although a few may pay a medical reimbursement benefit up to a stated amount.

AD&D Benefits

AD&D policies make benefits payable in the form of a *principal sum* and a *capital sum.*

Principal Sum

The principal sum under an AD&D policy is the amount payable as a *death benefit.* It is the face amount of insurance purchased—$10,000, $25,000, $50,000, $100,000 or more. The principal sum represents the maximum amount the policy will pay.

Capital Sum

The capital sum paid under an AD&D policy is the amount payable for the accidental loss of sight or accidental dismemberment. It is a specified amount, usually expressed as a percentage of the principal sum, that varies according to the severity of the injury. For example, the benefit for the loss of one foot or one hand is typically 50 percent of the principal sum. The benefit for the loss of one arm or one leg is usually two-thirds of the principal sum. The most extreme losses, such as both feet or sight in both eyes, generally qualify for payment of the full policy benefit, which is 100 percent of the principal sum.

Let's say, for example, Kevin has an accidental death and dismemberment policy that pays $50,000 for accidental loss of life. Thus, $50,000 is the policy's principal sum. The same policy pays $25,000 for accidental loss of sight of one eye or dismemberment of one limb. Therefore, $25,000 is the policy's capital sum.

Some AD&D policies provide for payment of double, triple or even quadruple the principal sum if the insured dies under specified circumstances. A double payment is referred to as "double indemnity." If three times the principal sum is payable, it is called "triple indemnity."

Accidental Means vs. Accidental Results

As we learned in the last chapter, an insurance policy that provides benefits in the event of an injury due to an accident must define "accident." In all cases, an accident is "external and violent," but accidental death and dismemberment policies (like disability income policies) make a distinction between injuries due to *accidental means* and those due to *accidental results* (or accidental bodily injury).

As you will recall, policies that base their benefit payments on accidental means require that both the cause and the result of an accident must be unintentional. Policies that use the more liberal accidental bodily injury (or results) definition stipulate that only the injury resulting from an accident be unintentional. If Ted, the insured under an AD&D policy, intentionally jumps from the roof of his house after fixing his antennae (instead of climbing down the ladder) and so severely injures his leg that it must be amputated, he would be paid the appropriate percentage of the capital sum only if his policy used the "results" definition. If his policy used the "means" definition, no benefit would be payable because Ted intentionally performed the action (the jump) that resulted in the injury.

As noted in Chapter 3, most states require that policies that provide any form of accident benefit, including AD&D policies, base the definition of "accident" on the results definition, not the means definition.

1. The amount payable as a death benefit in an accidental death and dismemberment policy is known as the

   A. primary amount.
   B. capital sum.
   C. indemnity amount.
   D. principal sum.

2. Theodore received a $15,000 cash benefit from his $50,000 accidental death and dismemberment policy for the accidental loss of one eye. The amount he received is the policy's

   A. principal sum.
   B. secondary sum.
   C. capital sum.
   D. contingent amount.

3. Which of the following examples pertaining to accidental death and dismemberment insurance is correct?

   A. Merrill is the insured under a $50,000 AD&D policy and dies unexpectedly of a heart attack. His beneficiary will receive $50,000 as the death benefit.
   B. Linda has a $40,000 AD&D policy that pays triple indemnity. If she should be killed in a train wreck, her beneficiary would receive $120,000.
   C. Paula has an AD&D policy that pays $15,000 for the loss of one hand or foot or the sight of one eye. That benefit amount is called the principal sum.
   D. Eric has an AD&D policy. He is killed in an auto accident. The $30,000 his beneficiary receives as a death benefit is the policy's capital sum.

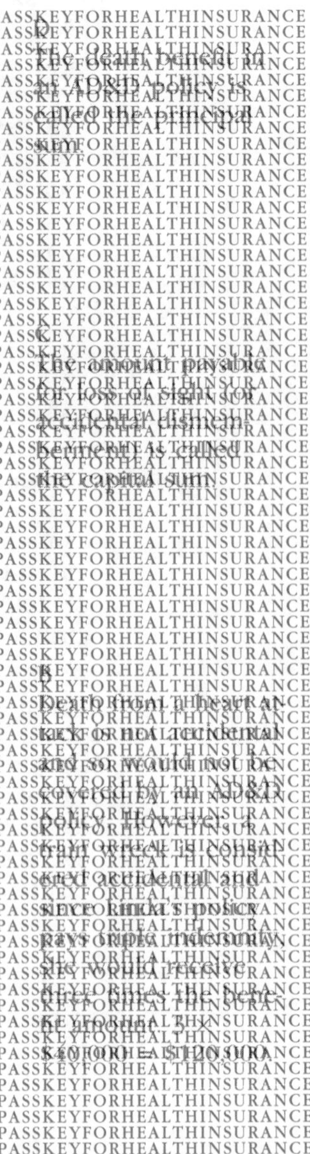

OTHER FORMS OF AD&D

Accidental death and dismemberment coverage is made available in a variety of ways. It can be purchased by individuals as a single policy or it may be a part of an individual disability income policy. Quite typically, however, it is an aspect of a group insurance plan—either group life or group health—or it may constitute a group plan by itself. Usually, AD&D benefits are payable whether the injury occurred on the job or off.

As we have seen, AD&D policies are somewhat narrow by their very nature, providing benefits only in the event of death or dismemberment due to an accident. However, there is another type of AD&D coverage, even more narrow in scope, that provides protection against accidental death or dismemberment only in the event of certain *specified* accidents. These are *limited risk policies* and *special risk policies.*

Limited Risk Policies

As noted in Chapter 2, *limited risk policies* set forth a specific risk and provide benefits to cover death or dismemberment due to that risk. For example, an *aviation policy* provides benefits for accidental death or dismemberment only if death or injury results from an aviation accident during a specified trip. An *automobile policy* provides benefits for accidental death or injury only while riding in a car. *Travel accident* covers most kinds of travel accidents, but only for a specified period of time, such as one year.

Special Risk Policies

Lloyds of London

A distinction should be made between limited risk and *special risk* policies. A special risk policy covers unusual hazards normally not covered under ordinary accident and health insurance. An actress who insures her legs for $1 million or a pilot test-flying an experimental airplane who obtains a policy covering his life while flying that particular plane, are both purchasing special risk policies. But a traveler who purchases an accident policy at the airport to provide coverage while he or she is a passenger on a commercial airlines flight is purchasing a limited risk policy.

---

1. Agnes purchases a round-trip travel accident policy at the airport before leaving on a business trip. Her policy is which type of insurance?

   A. Limited risk
   B. Special risk

2. Clyde, a popular comedian with very unusual facial features, insures his face for $500,000. His policy would be a ______ risk policy.

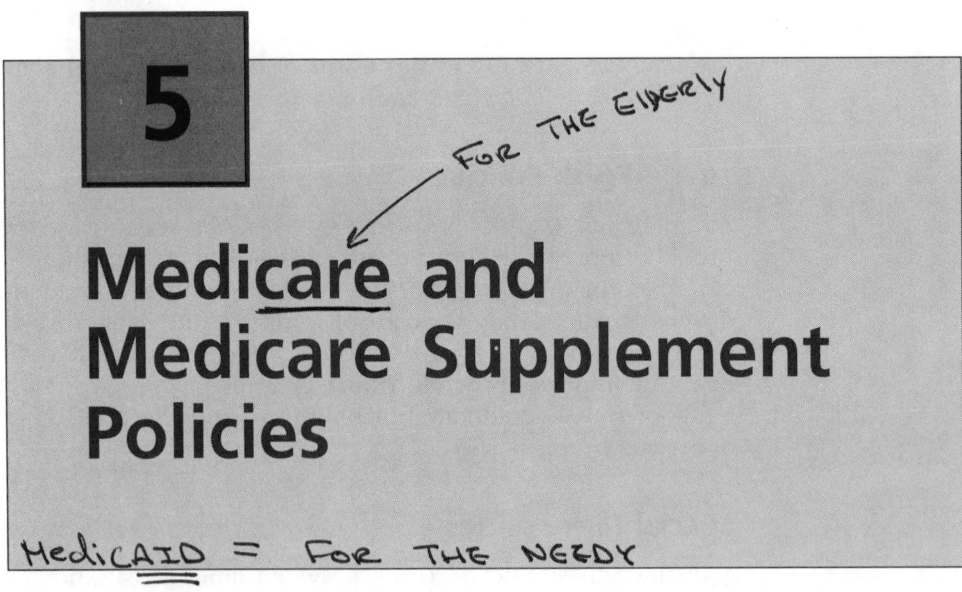

5 Medicare and Medicare Supplement Policies

In this chapter and the next, we will focus on two types of health care policies designed to protect the elderly from the high cost of health care. These two types of coverages, Medicare supplements (the subject of this chapter) and long-term care (the subject of the next chapter), have received a great deal of attention in recent years since, due to medical breakthroughs, individuals now are living longer and, therefore, encountering more medical problems and requiring more care. The cost of treating these problems has spiraled, leading to an ever-growing concern over how these costs will be paid.

In order to understand Medicare supplement policies, it is important to be clear about what these policies seek to supplement. For this reason, we will start this chapter with an overview of the Medicare system.

■ MEDICARE

The federally administered *Medicare* program took effect in 1966 as part of the Social Security program. Its purpose is to provide hospital and medical expense insurance protection to those aged 65 and older, to those of any age who suffer from chronic kidney disease or to those who are receiving Social Security disability benefits.

Medicare consists of two parts: Medicare Part A and Medicare Part B. *Medicare Part A* is compulsory hospitalization insurance (HI) that provides specified in-hospital and related benefits. It is compulsory in that all workers covered by Social Security finance its operation through a portion of their FICA tax and are automatically provided with benefits once they qualify for Social Security benefits.

Medicare Part B is a voluntary program designed to provide supplementary medical insurance (SMI) to cover physician services, medical services and medical supplies not covered under Part A for those who desire the coverage. It is financed by monthly premiums from those who choose to participate and by tax revenues.

Medicare Eligibility

An individual becomes eligible for Medicare:

1. at the beginning of the month in which he or she turns 65 and qualifies for Social Security or Railroad Retirement benefits;

2. after he or she has been receiving Social Security disability benefits for two years; or

3. if he or she has chronic kidney disease requiring dialysis.

An individual automatically applies for Medicare at the same time he or she applies for Social Security retirement benefits. When applying, the individual is given the opportunity to enroll in both Part A and Part B of the program, or Part A only. As noted, Medicare Part B is optional, and those who do enroll in Part B must pay a monthly premium ($43.80 in 1998). There is no premium required for Part A coverage.

Those who elect not to enroll in Part B when first applying for Medicare may do so later (though they may have to pay higher premiums). An "open enrollment period" occurs each year from January through March. When an individual signs on during this open enrollment period, Part B coverage becomes effective the following July 1.

Medicare Part A Coverages

Medicare Part A provides coverage for inpatient hospitalization and post-hospital skilled nursing facility care and home care. For the first 60 days of hospitalization during any one benefit period, Medicare pays for all covered services except for an initial deductible ($764 in 1998). Covered services include semi-private room, nursing services and other inpatient hospital services.

For the 61st through the 90th day of hospitalization. Medicare pays a reduced amount of the covered services. The patient is responsible for a daily copayment ($191 per day in 1998). These daily copayments are also called "coinsurance."

This 90-day hospitalization coverage is renewed with each benefit period. A *benefit period* starts when a patient enters the hospital and ends when the patient has been out of the hospital for 60 consecutive days. Once 60 days have passed, any new hospital admission is considered to be the start of a new benefit period. If a patient reenters a hospital before the end of a benefit period, the deductible is not reapplied but the 90-day hospital coverage period is not renewed. However, if the patient reenters a hospital after a benefit period ends, a new deductible is required and the 90-day hospital coverage period is renewed.

Medicare patients also have a *lifetime reserve* of 60 days of hospital coverage. If a patient is hospitalized longer than 90 days in a benefit period, he or she can tap into this 60-day reserve. The lifetime reserve is a one-time benefit; it does not renew with a new benefit period. For each reserve day a patient uses, he or she will be charged a higher daily copayment or coinsurance ($382 in 1998).

If a patient is hospitalized beyond the 60th lifetime reserve day, thereby exhausting the reserve, he or she is responsible for all hospital charges.

Hospital Benefits

The hospital services Part A covers are fairly comprehensive. They include:

- semiprivate room and board;
- regular nursing services;
- drugs furnished by the hospital;
- lab tests, X rays and medical supplies;
- blood transfusions (except for the first three pints);
- use of wheelchairs and similar appliances;
- use of operating room, recovery room and special-care units; and
- rehabilitation services, such as physical therapy.

---

1. In-patient hospital care is covered by Medicare Part ______.

A
Medicare Part A covers in-patient hospital expenses.

2. Participants must pay premiums for coverage under Medicare Part ______.

B
Medicare Part B requires the payment of a monthly premium; Part A does not require premium payments.

3. Under Medicare Part A, the participant must pay his or her deductible

   A. annually.
   B. once per benefit period.

B
The Medicare Part A deductible must be paid for each new benefit period.

4. Byron is insured under Medicare Part A and enters the hospital for surgery. Medicare will help to pay his hospital bill for up to _____ days, assuming Byron has not yet tapped into his lifetime reserve days.

   A. 60 days
   B. 90 days
   C. 150 days

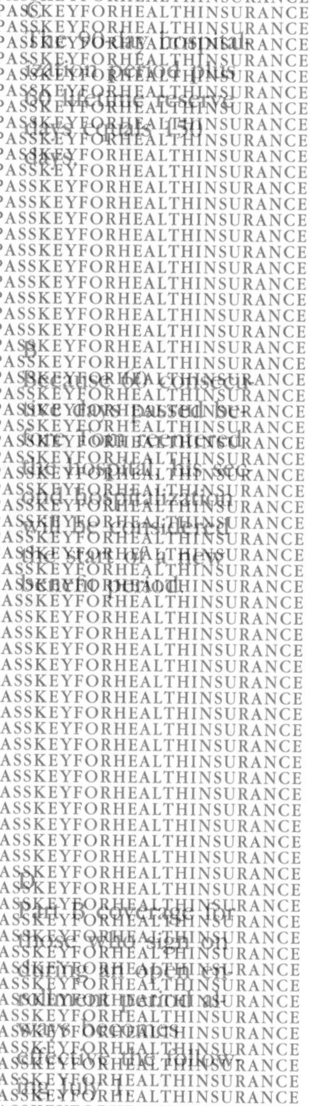

---

5. Tom is covered under Medicare Part A. He spends a week in the hospital and is discharged June 16. It was his first hospital stay in years. He is not admitted to the hospital again until November of that same year. Which of the following statements is true?

   A. Tom will not have to pay the Part A deductible again.
   B. The second admittance will be considered the start of a new benefit period.
   C. Tom will have to pay the Part A deductible again only if the second hospital stay is for a different illness than the first.
   D. Tom need not pay the Part A deductible, but must make a daily copayment.

---

6. Jeff signs up for Medicare Part B on March 21 during the open enrollment period. His coverage will become effective

   A. March 21.
   B. April 1.
   C. June 30.
   D. July 1.

Other Part A Benefits

In addition to benefits for in-patient hospital care, Part A also provides benefits for skilled nursing facility care, hospice care, home health services and, to a limited degree, inpatient psychiatric care. In all cases, Part A covers only those services that are medically necessary and only up to amounts deemed "reasonable" by Medicare.

Skilled Nursing Facility Benefits

Skilled nursing facility benefits are only available following a hospital stay of a least three days and beginning within 30 days of leaving the hospital. Part A pays all covered charges for the first 20 days in a skilled nursing facility. After 20 days, and for the next 80 days, Medicare pays part of the cost and the patient must make a daily copayment ($95.50 in 1998). After 100 days of care, no benefits are available.

Custodial care (care given at retirement and nursing homes for day-to-day living and personal needs) is *not* covered by Medicare.

Home Health Care Benefits

Part A provides benefits for homebound patients, including part-time skilled nursing care, physical and speech therapy, medical social services, rehabilitation services and use of some types of rehabilitation equipment. The home care must be prescribed by a physician. All covered services will be paid for if provided by a home health agency that participates in Medicare.

Hospice Care Benefits

A hospice provides inpatient, outpatient and home care for the terminally ill and their families. Hospice treatments covered by Medicare include counseling, control of disease symptoms and pain relief, as well as physician and nursing services, medical appliances and supplies. Benefits are available for as long as the doctor certifies care is needed, up to 210 days (though this benefit period can be extended, in some cases).

A hospice patient pays 5 percent of the cost of prescription drugs (not to exceed $5), and a copayment of 5 percent for respite care, not to exceed five consecutive days or the current Part A deductible ($764 in 1998).

---

1. For how many days of care in a skilled nursing facility will Medicare Part A pay benefits?

   A. 25
   B. 60
   C. 75
   D. 100

2. Medicare covers custodial care in a skilled nursing facility. (True/False)

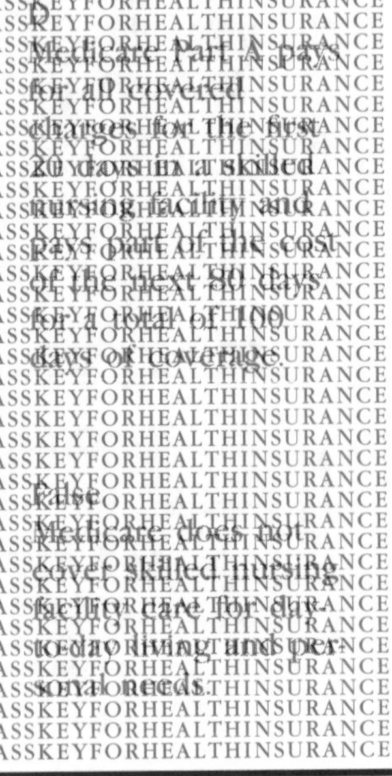

Medicare Part B Coverages

For those who elect it, additional coverage is available under Medicare Part B for physician services, diagnostic tests, physical and occupational therapy, medical supplies and more.

Specifically, Part B covers, among other items, the following types of physician and outpatient hospital charges:

- doctors' fees;
- medical lab fees;
- blood for transfusions, after the first three pints;
- ambulance costs;
- X rays and other diagnostic tests;
- physical and occupational therapy;
- radium therapy;
- the cost for artificial limbs;
- mammography screening;
- surgical dressings, splints, casts and braces; and
- rental (and, in some cases, purchase) of durable medical equipment.

As mentioned earlier, Part B participants are required to pay a monthly premium ($43.80 in 1998) and are responsible for an annual deductible ($100 in 1998). After the deductible, Part B will pay 80 percent of covered expenses, subject to Medicare's standards for reasonable charges.

How Medicare Part B Is Administered

Part B of Medicare coverage is complex, due in part to the wide disparity in doctors' fees and other medical expenses—from one section of the country to another, from one state to another, from city to rural community. Adding to the complexity are the issues of *recognized* (or *allowable) charges* and *participating* vs. *nonparticipating physicians,* key concepts to the Medicare program.

Recognized Charges

The allowable or *recognized* charge is the maximum amount Medicare allows for a medical procedure, treatment or service. This *Medicare-approved amount* is used as the basis for Medicare's 80 percent share of the cost.

Participating Physicians and Assignment

A *participating physician* is one who "accepts assignment," meaning that he or she accepts Medicare's recognized charge as the maximum and will not charge more than that amount. In accepting the Medicare maximum charge for the treatment, a participating physician takes Medicare's 80 percent payment. The patient is then responsible for the copayment, or 20 percent of the charge.

A nonparticipating physician's charges may be higher than those recognized by Medicare but only up to 15 percent higher. The Medicare 80 percent share of a nonparticipating physician's fee is based on the recognized charge. The patient is responsible for any excess charges. For example, if the recognized charge for an operation is $1,000, but a nonparticipating physician charges $1,100, Medicare will only pay $800 (80% × $1,000). The patient will have to pay $300.

Primary Payor and Secondary Payor

Individuals aged 65 or older who are eligible for Medicare and who work for an employer employing 20 or more employees are entitled to the same health insurance benefits offered to younger employees. In such cases, the employer's health plan is the primary plan or *primary payor*. Medicare is the *secondary payor*, paying only those eligible expenses that the employer's plan does not cover. (This rule also applies to an employee's spouse age 65 or older, regardless of the employee's age.)

This arrangement also applies to a disabled Medicare enrollee who is also covered by an employer-provided health care plan as a "current employee" or as a family member of an employee if the employer plan covers 100 or more employees.

Medicare Exclusions

Neither Part A nor Part B of Medicare covers:

- routine physical exams, eye exams, eyeglasses, hearing aids and dental care;
- routine foot care and orthopedic shoes (except for diabetics);
- custodial care;
- cosmetic surgery (except after an accident);
- private hospital rooms (unless medically necessary);
- hospital room "extras," such as telephones and televisions;
- care and services received outside of the USA;
- most prescription drugs taken at home;
- most immunizations; and
- private nurses.

1. A patient covered under Medicare Part B must pay the Part B deductible on a/an

   A. annual basis.
   B. per benefit period basis.

A

Part B has an annual deductible.

---

2. Under Medicare Part B, the participant must pay 80 percent of the covered charges above the deductible.

   (True/False)

False

Medicare Part B pays 80 percent of covered charges above the deductible, leaving 20 percent for the participant to pay.

---

3. A physician who accepts Medicare's recognized charge as the maximum he or she will bill for a procedure is called a ______.

participating physician

---

4. All of the following are excluded from coverage under Medicare, EXCEPT:

   A. X rays.
   B. eyeglasses.
   C. immunizations.
   D. foot care.

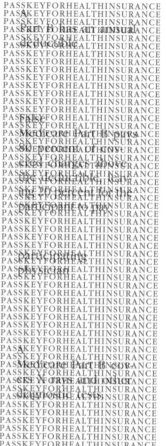

A

Medicare Part B covers X rays and other diagnostic tests.

MEDICAREPLUS CHOICE PROGRAM

The Balanced Budget Act of 1997 created a new Medicare program called the *MedicarePlus Choice Program*. Scheduled for implementation after December 31, 1998, the program will offer Medicare beneficiaries a variety of health coverage alternatives, each of which must include currently covered Medicare services. The health coverage options to be offered under the MedicarePlus Choice Program include:

- health maintenance organization (HMO);
- preferred provider organization (PPO);
- provider-sponsored organization (PSO), an HMO created by doctors and hospitals;
- a combination of private fee-for-service health plans and self-funding;

- private contracts with doctors for particular services; and

- a combination of a tax-free medical savings account (MedicarePlus Choice MSAs) for routine medical bills and a government-funded high-deductible MedicarePlus Choice health plan (MSA plan) for catastrophic expenses. This program is part of a four-year pilot program. It will be available on a first-come, first-served basis to 390,000 eligible seniors.

Under the program, Medicare will pay each plan a certain amount per enrollee. The beneficiary will pay out-of-pocket costs that will vary according to the health coverage plan he or she selects. All beneficiaries will continue to pay the premium for Medicare Part B.

Beneficiaries who return to the traditional Medicare program within 12 months of their first enrollment in a MedicarePlus Choice plan or who move out of the health plan's service area will be able to obtain Medicare supplement policies.

---

1. Under the MedicarePlus Choice program, beneficiaries will be offered a variety of health care coverage options, each of which must

   A. not duplicate Medicare benefits.
   B. be entirely paid for by the beneficiary.
   C. include currently covered Medicare services.
   D. prohibit enrollees from returning to the traditional Medicare program.

2. The MedicarePlus Choice program is scheduled for implementation after ______________

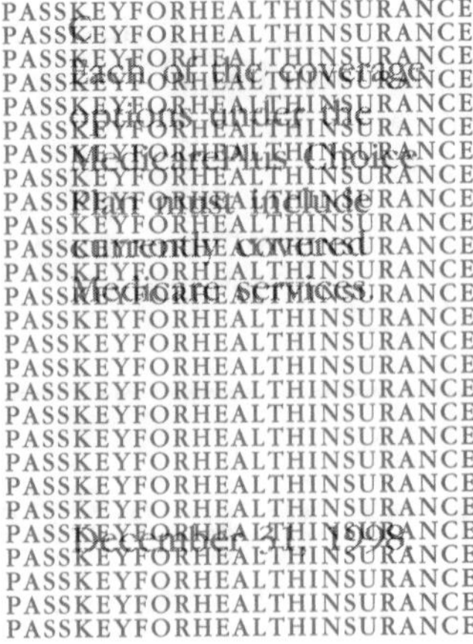

■ MEDICARE SUPPLEMENT POLICIES

As you can see from our previous discussion, Medicare leaves many "gaps" in its coverage. With its structure of limited benefit periods, deductibles, copayments and exclusions, the coverage it provides is limited, at best. To help fill these gaps, private insurance companies market *Medicare supplement* insurance policies to consumers. Medicare supplement policies are designed to pick up coverage where Medicare leaves off.

NAIC Model Policies

The term "Medicare supplement" implies that the policy covers what Medicare does not. Unfortunately, some policies have not lived up to what was expected of them. To combat this, in 1990 Congress passed a far-reaching "Medigap" law that required the National Association of Insurance Commissioners (NAIC) to address the subject of Medicare supplement policies. Specifically, the NAIC's task was to develop a standardized model Medicare supplement policy, which would provide certain "core" benefits, plus as many as nine other supplement policies that would provide increasingly more comprehensive benefits. These ten "model" policies could then be adopted by the states as prototype policies for their insurers.

The purpose of this law was to reduce the number of Medicare supplement policies being offered for sale and to eliminate some of the questionable marketing practices associated with these policies. It was intended that these model policies would help consumers better understand Medicare supplement policies (thereby allowing them to make more informed buying decisions) by:

- standardizing coverages and benefits from one policy to the next;
- simplifying the terms used in these policies;
- facilitating policy comparisons; and
- eliminating policy provisions that may be misleading or confusing.

The result of the NAIC's work are ten standard Medicare supplement policies, ranging from the basic "core" policy, with a minimum of supplemental coverage, to those with more comprehensive coverage. Following is a brief description of Plan A.

Plan A: Core Benefits

Plan A is the "core" plan. It includes coverage for:

- Part A copayment amounts;
- 365 additional (lifetime) days of Medicare-eligible expenses once the Medicare lifetime reserve days are exhausted;
- the 20 percent Part B copayment amounts (for Medicare-approved services); and
- the first three pints of blood each year.

At a minimum, all Medicare supplement policies must contain these "core" benefits. In addition, any company that markets and sells Medicare supplement policies must make available the basic core Plan A as a separate policy.

The following chart summarizes all ten standard plans, each of which includes the core benefits of Plan A.

As you can see, no provision of any of these Medicare supplement plans duplicates benefits provided under Medicare—instead, each plan provides *supplemental* coverage. Of course, the more benefits a supplement plan offers, the more expensive it will be.

THE Higher the letter the more comprehensive.

A	B	C	D	E	F	G	H	I	J
Basic Benefits	Basic Benefits	Basic Benefits	Basic Benefits	Basic Benefits	Basic Benefits	Basic Benefits	Basic Benefits	Basic Benefits	Basic Benefits
		Skilled Nursing Copayment	Skilled Nursing Copayment	Skilled Nursing Copayment	Skilled Nursing Copayment	Skilled Nursing Copayment	Skilled Nursing Copayment	Skilled Nursing Copayment	Skilled Nursing Copayment
	Part A Deductible	Part A Deductible	Part A Deductible	Part A Deductible	Part A Deductible	Part A Deductible	Part A Deductible	Part A Deductible	Part A Deductible
		Part B Deductible			Part B Deductible				Part B Deductible
					Part B Excess (100%)	Part B Excess (80%)		Part B Excess (100%)	Part B Excess (100%)
		Foreign Travel Emergency	Foreign Travel Emergency	Foreign Travel Emergency	Foreign Travel Emergency	Foreign Travel Emergency	Foreign Travel Emergency	Foreign Travel Emergency	Foreign Travel Emergency
			At-Home Recovery			At-Home Recovery		At-Home Recovery	At-Home Recovery
							Basic Drugs ($1,250 Limit)	Basic Drugs ($1,250 Limit)	Extended Drugs ($3,000 Limit)
				Preventive Care					Preventive Care

Source: National Association of Insurance Commissioners.

The NAIC recommends that if a state authorizes the sale of only some of these plans, the letter codes of each plan—A, B, C, D, E, F, G, H, I and J—should be preserved. This uniform "naming" system will enable consumers to compare specific policy plans.

1. All of the following are reasons that the NAIC developed ten model Medicare supplement policies, EXCEPT:

   A. to increase the number of policies for sale.
   B. to standardize coverages.
   C. to simplify terminology.
   D. to facilitate policy comparison.

2. Which is the most comprehensive of the NAIC's ten standard Medicare policies?

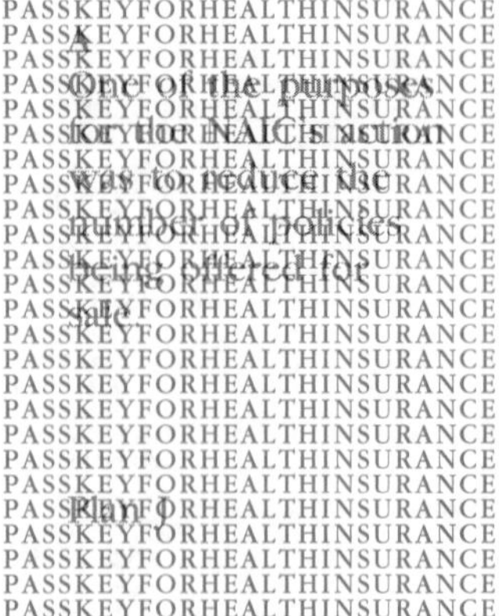

3. Warren is a Medicare participant. He has purchased a Medicare supplement policy based on Plan A, the NAIC model policy that is referred to as the "core" policy. His policy will pay which of the following?

   A. His Part A deductible
   B. His Part A copayment

4. The least expensive Medicare supplement plan that offers coverage of the daily copayment amount for skilled nursing facility care is

   A. Plan B.
   B. Plan C.
   C. Plan D.
   D. Plan E.

6

Long-Term Care Insurance

The cost of the extended day in, day out care some older people need can be staggering: as much as $30,000 or $40,000 a year or more for nursing home care and upwards of $1,000 a month—or more—for aides who come to one's home. A study by the U.S. Department of Health and Human Services indicates that people who turned 65 at the beginning of this decade face a 40 percent risk of entering a nursing home, and of those who enter, about 10 percent will stay there five years or longer.

As beneficial as Medicare and Medicare supplement insurance are to the elderly in protecting them against the costs of medical care, neither of these covers long-term custodial or nursing home care. Medicaid covers some of the cost of long-term care; but, as you will learn, a person is not eligible for Medicaid until he or she is practically destitute. How can these costs be paid? The solution for many is *long-term care insurance*.

WHAT IS LONG-TERM CARE?

Long-term care (LTC) is the broad range of medical, personal and environmental services for individuals who have lost their ability to remain completely independent in the community. LTC refers to care provided for an extended period of time, normally more than 90 days. The need for such ongoing assistance is usually a result of a physical or mental impairment brought on by the aging process. Depending on the severity of the impairment, assistance may be given at home, at an adult day care center or in a nursing home.

WHAT IS LONG-TERM CARE INSURANCE?

Long-term care insurance is another type of insurance product. More and more insurance companies are beginning to offer this coverage as the need for it grows. It is similar to most insurance plans, in that the insured, in exchange for a certain premium, is promised the payment of specified benefits in the event he or she requires long-term care, as defined by the policy. Most long-term care policies pay the insured a fixed dollar amount for each day he or she receives the kind of care the policy covers, regardless of what the care costs.

Insurers offer a wide range of benefit amounts, ranging from, for example, $40 a day to $200 a day for nursing home care. The daily benefit for at-home care is typically half the nursing home benefit. Many policies include an inflation rider or option to purchase additional coverage, enabling the policies to keep pace with increases in long-term care costs.

---

1. Which of the following statements is true regarding long-term care?

   A. It is strictly care given to those with terminal illnesses.
   B. Medicaid covers none of the costs of long-term care.
   C. Long-term care refers solely to care given in a nursing home.
   D. Long-term care refers not only to medical care but to care for personal and environmental needs as well.

2. Long-term care policies usually pay a fixed daily benefit.

   (True/False)

3. The daily amount long-term care policies typically pay for at-home care is

   A. the same as the daily amount paid for nursing home care.
   B. 25 percent of the daily amount paid for nursing home care.
   C. 50 percent of the daily amount paid for nursing home care.
   D. 75 percent of the daily amount paid for nursing home care.

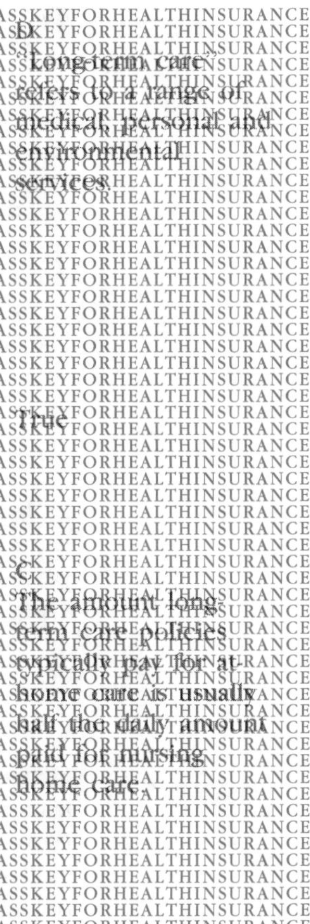
D.
Long-term care refers to a range of medical, personal and environmental services.
True
C.
The amount long-term care policies typically pay for at-home care is usually half the daily amount paid for nursing home care.

LONG-TERM CARE COVERAGES

Currently, there are a variety of long-term care policies on the market, some of which are characterized by innovative coverage concepts. The following is a brief discussion of some typical coverages that may be found in a long-term care policy. Note that the definition of the kind of care provided is a determining factor in where it is administered. It is important to understand the distinctions among the levels of nursing home care as well as the extent and limitations of other kinds of care.

Skilled Nursing Care

This is continuous, around-the-clock care provided by licensed medical professionals under the direct supervision of a physician. Skilled nursing care is typically administered in nursing homes.

Intermediate Nursing Care

Intermediate nursing care is provided by registered nurses, licensed practical nurses and nurses' aides under the supervision of a physician. Intermediate nursing care is typically provided in nursing homes for stable medical conditions that require daily, but not 24-hour, supervision.

Custodial Care

Custodial care is care given to meet daily personal needs, such as bathing, dressing, getting out of bed, toileting and similar activities. Such care does not require specialized medical training, but it must be given under a doctor's order. Custodial care is usually provided by nursing homes, but can also be given by adult day care centers, respite centers or at home.

Home Health Care

Home health care is care provided in the insured's home, usually on a part-time basis. It can include skilled care (such as nursing, rehabilitative or physical therapy care ordered by a doctor) or unskilled care (such as help with cooking or cleaning).

Adult Day Care

Services at an adult day care center are designed for those who require assistance with various activities of daily living, while their primary caregivers (usually family or friends) are absent. These adult day care centers offer skilled medical care in conjunction with social and personal services, but custodial care is usually their primary focus. Some communities have established adult day care centers that specifically serve the special needs of those with Alzheimer's disease.

Respite Care

Respite care is designed to provide a short rest period for a family caregiver. There are two options: either the insured is moved to a full-time care facility or a substitute care provider moves into the insured's home for a temporary period, giving the family member a rest from his or her caregiving activities.

Continuing Care

A fairly new kind of LTC coverage, continuing care coverage is designed to provide a benefit for elderly individuals who live in a continuing care retirement community (CCRC). Continuing care communities are geared to senior citizens' full-time needs, both medical and social, and are often sponsored by religious or nonprofit organizations.

---

1. Which type of long-term care coverage is designed to provide a break for the full-time caregiver?

   ____

2. Which type of long-term care coverage was specifically designed to provide a benefit for those living in a retirement community?

   A. Home health care
   B. Continuing care

3. Skilled nursing care differs from intermediate care in which of the following ways?

   A. Skilled nursing care must be performed by skilled medical professionals while intermediate care does not require medical training.
   B. Skilled care must be available 24 hours a day while intermediate care is daily, but not 24-hour, care.

4. Home health care coverage includes only skilled care.

   (True/False)

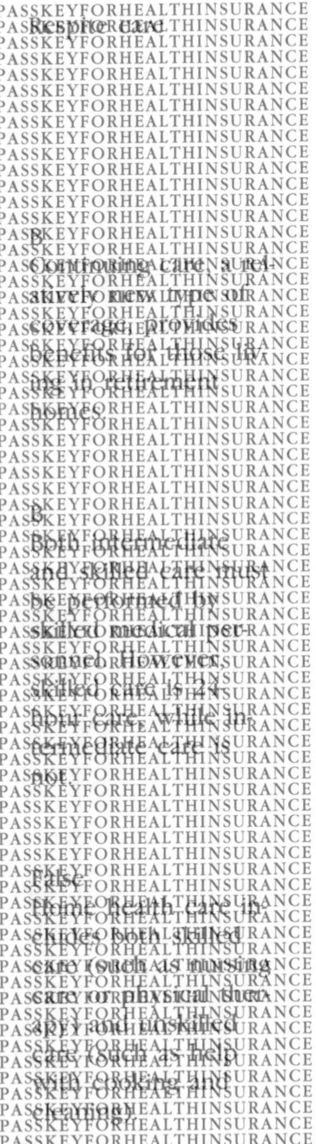

Respite care
B.
Continuing care, a relatively new type of coverage, provides benefits for those living in retirement homes.
B.
Both intermediate and skilled care must be performed by skilled medical personnel. However, skilled care is 24-hour care, while intermediate care is not.
False.
Home health care includes both skilled care (such as nursing care or physical therapy) and unskilled care (such as help with cooking and cleaning).

LONG-TERM CARE POLICY PROVISIONS, LIMITS AND TAXATION

As we have stated, there are a number of LTC policies on the market today, each characterized by some distinguishing feature or benefit that sets it apart from the rest. However, there are enough similarities to allows us to discuss the basic provisions of these policies and their typical limits or exclusions.

The typical provisions found in an LTC policy issued today have been affected by the passage of the Health Insurance Portability and Accountability Act of 1996 (HIPAA) which provided that LTC policies meeting certain standards would receive favorable tax treatment. Among other things, these standards concern how the policy defines LTC services and how the policy triggers benefits. A policy meeting these standards is referred to as a "qualified" LTC policy and benefits received under a qualified LTC policy are exempt from tax.* Since the tax benefits of a qualified LTC policy are significant, insurers are crafting and offering policies that meet these standards.

LTC Services

The definition of qualified LTC services encompasses ". . . necessary diagnostic, preventive, therapeutic, curing, treating, mitigating and rehabilitative services, and maintenance or personal care services" required by a chronically ill individual and provided under a plan of care set forth by a licensed health care practitioner.

Benefit Trigger

When LTC policies were first introduced, insurers frequently required at least three days of prior hospitalization or skilled nursing home care before the LTC policy benefits were "triggered," that is, before benefits became payable. Under HIPAA, a qualified LTC plan cannot use prior hospitalization as a benefit trigger; instead, the diagnosis of an individual as "chronically ill" must be used to trigger benefits. A person can be diagnosed as chronically ill based on either physical or cognitive factors.

Under a qualified LTC policy, a physical diagnosis of chronic illness is based on an individual's inability to perform the *activities of daily living* (ADLs). For these purposes, ADLs are eating, toileting, transferring, bathing, dressing and continence; a qualified LTC policy must take into account at least five of these ADLs. When an individual is certified by a licensed health practitioner as being unable to perform at least two ADLs as defined under the policy, he or she must be diagnosed to be chronically ill.

An individual must also be found chronically ill under a qualified LTC policy when he or she requires substantial supervision to protect his or her own health or safety owing to severe cognitive impairment and such condition has been certified by a licensed health practitioner within the previous 12 months.

---

*LTC policies issued after December 31, 1996, must meet HIPAA's requirements in order to be considered qualified long-term care policies. However, HIPAA also grandfathered certain policies issued before that time. Generally speaking, a policy issued before January 1, 1997, that was approved as long-term care insurance in the state where the policy was issued will be treated as qualified long-term care insurance.

Benefit Limits

Almost all LTC policies set benefit limits, in terms of how long the benefits are paid and/or how much the dollar benefit will be for any one covered care service or a combination of services. Maximum dollar amounts vary considerably from policy to policy. Maximum coverage periods also vary. In fact, it is not unusual for one policy to include separate maximum coverage periods for nursing home care and home health care. Generally speaking, maximum coverage periods extend anywhere from two to six years. Some policies offer unlimited lifetime coverage.

Age Limits

Long-term care policies typically set age limits for issue, the average being about 79. However, some newer policies can be sold to people up through age 89. Many policies also set a minimum purchase age, the average being age 50.

Renewability

Under HIPAA, all qualified LTC policies must be guaranteed renewable, meaning the insurance company cannot cancel the policy and must renew coverage each year, as long as premiums are paid. A guaranteed renewable policy allows the insurer to raise premiums, but only for entire classes of insureds. (''Classes'' of insureds is defined in Chapter 8.)

Probationary Periods

As we've discussed, a probationary period is the period of time from the inception of a policy during which benefits will not be paid. Long-term care probationary periods can range from 0 to 365 days, and many insurers give the insured the option of selecting the period that best serves his or her needs. The longer the deductible or probationary period, the lower the premium.

The primary purpose of a probationary period is to control adverse selection and protect the insurer from individuals who may have a preexisting condition (a condition for which the insured received treatment within a certain time period prior to policy issue). Individuals who have preexisting conditions may find that their policies will not cover any claims arising from that condition for the first six or 12 months after policy issue.

Specified Exclusions

Most long-term care policies exclude coverage for drug or alcohol dependency, acts of war, self-inflicted injuries and non-organic mental conditions. Organic cognitive disorders, such as Alzheimer's disease, senile dementia and Parkinson's disease are almost always included.

Premiums

The cost for a long-term care policy is based on a number of factors: the insured's age and health, the type and level of benefits provided, the inclusion or absence of a deductible or probationary period and the length of that period, and whether or not options or riders are included with the policy (such as the option to purchase additional coverage in the future or the inflation-adjustment rider, which automatically increases the policy's coverage to match inflation levels). Generally, the more beneficial the policy's terms are for the insured, the more expensive it will be.

Taxation of LTC Policies

Benefits under a qualified LTC insurance policy are treated in the same manner as accident and health insurance policies: amounts received as benefits under such a policy are excluded from income because they are treated as amounts received for personal injuries and sickness.

However, there is a limit on the amount of benefits one can receive tax free under a qualified LTC policy to the extent such benefits exceed actual costs. In cases where the benefits exceed actual costs, the limit on tax-free benefits is $175 a day for a per diem policy or $63,875 a year. In other words, if LTC benefits exceed actual LTC costs, the amount of benefits above $175 a day is taxable. Benefits payable under a qualified LTC policy that cover incurred costs are not taxable at all.

The tax treatment of premiums paid for a qualified LTC policy is also important. As you may be aware, an individual may deduct unreimbursed medical expenses exceeding 7.5 percent of his or her adjusted gross income. As a result of HIPAA, premiums paid for qualified LTC insurance can be included as a medical expense for the purposes of the medical expense deduction, up to certain limits that are adjusted annually. The following amounts of qualified LTC premiums are the maximum that can be included with other unreimbursed medical expenses in 1998 (if a couple files a joint return, these amounts are per person):

Age	Amount
40 or younger	$210
41-50	$380
51-60	$770
61-70	$2,050
71 or older	$2,570

One final tax-related note: an employer's contributions to an LTC insurance plan on behalf of an employee are excluded from the employee's income unless the contributions are made as part of a cafeteria plan.

---

1. The shorter a long-term care policy's probationary period, the (lower/higher) the premium.

2. When a long-term care policy is guaranteed renewable, which of the following is true?

   A. The policy premiums cannot be raised.
   B. The policy must be renewed every year as long as premiums are paid.

B

If you answered incorrectly, please review the section titled "Renewability."

3. What is the main purpose of the probationary period in a long-term care policy?

A

A probationary period helps control adverse selection and protect the insurer from individuals who have preexisting conditions.

4. All of the following would be covered by a long-term care policy, EXCEPT:

   A. Alzheimer's disease.
   B. Parkinson's disease.
   C. alcoholism.
   D. arthritis.

C

Alcoholism is often excluded from coverage by long-term care policies.

5. Assume that Walter receives benefits under a per diem qualified LTC policy of $200 per day for 30 days of long-term care. The actual costs incurred for his care during this period were $175 per day. What portion of Walter's LTC benefits is taxable?

$750

Since Walter's LTC benefits exceeded his costs, the portion in excess of $175 per day is taxable: $200 − $175 = $25 per day; $25 × 30 days = $750.

6. Assume the same situation as above except that the actual costs of Walter's care during the period were $250 per day. What portion of Walter's LTC benefits is taxable?

None

Benefits payable under a qualified LTC policy that cover incurred costs are not taxable. Since all the LTC benefits Walter received covered incurred costs, no portion of the amount is taxable.

Progressive Quiz No. 2

(Text page reference numbers are shown under each correct response in the red column.)

1. Which of the following would be covered by Part A of Medicare?

   A. A visit to a doctor for a routine checkup
   B. A physical therapy regimen following surgery
   C. A mammography screening
   D. Custodial care in a nursing home

   B
   (46)

---

2. A typical long-term care policy would likely exclude from coverage

   A. Parkinson's disease
   B. Alzheimer's disease
   C. self-inflicted injuries
   D. All of the above

   C
   (61)

---

3. Which of the following provides coverage for custodial care in a nursing home?

   I. Medicare Part A
   II. Medicare Part B
      A. I only
      B. II only
      C. Both I and II
      D. Neither I nor II

   D
   (48, 50)

4. Which of the following statements is correct?

A. Lynn, the insured under a $150,000 AD&D policy, dies suddenly of a heart attack. Her beneficiary will receive the policy's principal sum of $150,000.
B. Andy, the insured under a $50,000 AD&D policy, dies unexpectedly in a car accident. His beneficiary will receive $50,000 as the policy's capital sum.
C. Carl, the insured under a $250,000 AD&D double indemnity policy, severs his foot while mowing the lawn. He will receive $500,000 as the policy's capital sum.
D. Jim, the insured under a $100,000 AD&D double indemnity policy, loses his right hand in a farming accident. He will receive the policy's capital sum of $50,000.

D
(40, 41)

---

5. What type of coverage would be most appropriate for extended custodial care provided in one's home?

A. Medicare
B. Medicaid
C. Long-term care
D. Comprehensive major medical

C
(50, 58)

---

6. All of the following are contracts that pay a fixed, predetermined amount, EXCEPT:

A. long-term care policy.
B. accidental death and dismemberment policy.
C. hospital indemnity policy.
D. basic medical expense policy.

D
(10, 11, 20, 40, 57)

---

7. Curt suffered a disabling back injury when he intentionally dove into a shallow lake. Fortunately, his disability policy covered him. From this, we can assume Curt's policy defines disability based on

A. accidental means.
B. accidental results.

B
(26, 41)

---

8. Which of the following would tend to reduce the cost of a long-term care policy?

I. The absence of a probationary period
II. The inclusion of a deductible
  A. I only
  B. II only
  C. Both I and II
  D. Neither I nor II

D
(61)

9. Which of the following individuals is eligible for Medicare coverage?

I. Jules, age 67, who just applied for his Social Security retirement benefits
II. Mary, age 44, who has been receiving Social Security disability benefits for a year

A. I only
B. II only
C. Both I and II
D. Neither I nor II

---

10. With regard to Medicare coverage, a *benefit period* begins when an individual

A. officially enrolls in the Medicare program and ends at his or her death.
B. is admitted to the hospital and ends when he or she is released from the hospital.
C. is admitted to the hospital and ends after 60 days of hospitalization.
D. is admitted to the hospital and ends after he or she has been out of the hospital for 60 days.

---

11. Medicare supplement insurance is available through

A. Social Security.
B. the NAIC.
C. state guaranty associations.
D. private insurers.

---

12. All other factors being equal, the premiums for a medical expense policy that has a 70/30 coinsurance provision would be less than those for a policy that has a 80/20 coinsurance provision.

A. True
B. False

---

13. Which of the following would qualify for a group health plan?

I. a credit union
II. A professional association

A. I only
B. II only
C. Both I and II
D. Neither I nor II

14. Which of the following statements is correct regarding distributions from a medical savings account (MSA) that are used for a purpose other than the qualified medical expenses of the individual, his or her spouse or dependents?

  A. The MSA is immediately terminated.
  B. The individual using distributions in this manner is guilty of a criminal misdemeanor.
  C. The distributions are subject to taxation, including a possible 15 percent penalty tax.
  D. The distributions must be returned to the MSA within 60 days to avoid termination of the MSA.

---

15. Under which of the following health plans would the actual cost of medical treatment have no bearing on the amount of benefits the insured receives?

  A. Major medical
  B. Basic hospital
  C. Hospital indemnity
  D. Medicare

---

16. Which of the following disability income insurance riders would increase the benefit amount payable on the disability anniversary dates?

  A. Guaranteed insurability rider
  B. Social Security rider
  C. Cost of living adjustment rider
  D. Waiver of premium rider

---

17. Which of the following provides a lump-sum benefit if the insured dies accidentally?

  A. Hospital indemnity policy
  B. Supplemental major medical policy
  C. Accidental death and dismemberment policy
  D. Comprehensive major medical policy

---

18. Another term for risk pooling is

  A. loss sharing.
  B. morbidity.
  C. law of large numbers.
  D. loss exposures.

19. Which of the following statements is/are true?

    I. Premium reserves reflect an insurer's liability for losses that have not occurred but for which premiums have been paid.
    II. Loss (or claims) reserves reflect an insurer's liability for losses that have occurred, but for which claims payment has not been completed.

    A. I only
    B. II only
    C. Both I and II
    D. Neither I nor II

---

20. Jean owns a basic hospital expense policy. Which of the following would not be covered by her plan?

    A. The cost of the operating room
    B. The surgeon's fee
    C. X rays
    D. The cost of a semiprivate hospital room

---

21. With regard to Medicare supplement policies, which statement is true?

    A. Their purpose is to duplicate the coverage provided by Medicare to ensure that all expenses are fully paid.
    B. All Medicare supplement policies that follow the NAIC models must cover preventive screening and preventive medical care.
    C. All Medicare supplement policies that follow the NAIC models must cover long-term care administered in a nursing home.
    D. They are designed to provide additional medical expense benefits beyond what Medicare covers.

---

22. Qualified LTC policies must trigger benefits when an individual is found to be

    A. morbid.
    B. impaired.
    C. hospitalized.
    D. chronically ill.

23. An individual who buys an AD&D policy that covers him on a commercial airline flight from Chicago to San Francisco has purchased a

A. commercial accidental death and dismemberment policy.
B. special risk policy.
C. limited risk policy.
D. dread accident policy.

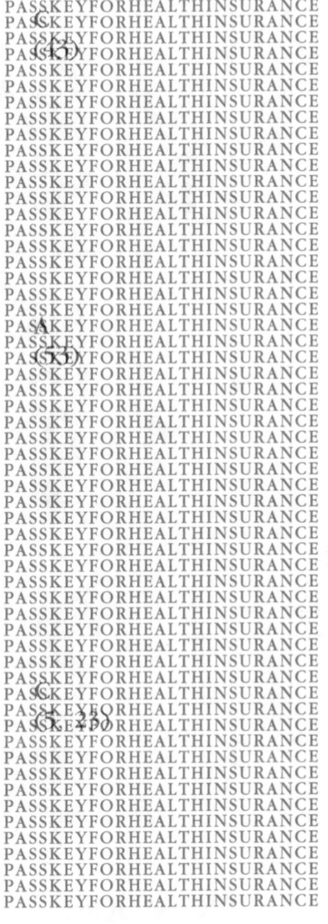

---

24. All Medicare supplement plans that follow the NAIC models must cover

A. the Medicare Part A daily copayment amounts.
B. the cost of a semiprivate hospital room for the first 60 days of hospitalization.
C. all drugs administered in a hospital while the patient is hospitalized.
D. the cost of a hospital recovery room following surgery.

---

25. Which of the following policies would provide a monthly income if the insured could not work due to an accident?

A. Medicare
B. Accidental death and disability
C. Disability income
D. Major medical

7

Health Insurance Policy Provisions

To understand health insurance, it is essential to have a firm knowledge of the contract provisions that distinguish a health insurance policy from other insurance policies. Health insurance, more so than life insurance, is characterized by a number of mandatory provisions that must be included in the contract. The twelve mandatory provisions and eleven optional provisions covered in this chapter add a degree of uniformity to health insurance policies, providing the insured with a high level of regulatory protection.

NAIC MODEL HEALTH INSURANCE POLICY PROVISIONS

Years ago, the National Association of Insurance Commissioners (NAIC) developed a model *"Uniform Individual Accident and Sickness Policy Provisions Law."* Almost all states have adopted this model law or similar legislation or regulations.

The purpose of the NAIC model law was to establish uniform terms, provisions and wording standards for individual health insurance contracts. The result was twelve mandatory policy provisions and eleven optional policy provisions. Because these provisions are to be followed "in substance," insurers may employ different wording from that specifically contained in the law. However, the insurance protection provided can be no less favorable to the insured than the law stipulates.

TWELVE MANDATORY POLICY PROVISIONS

In accordance with the NAIC model law, there are twelve mandatory provisions that must be included in all health insurance contracts.

#1: Entire Contract

The *entire contract* provision in a health insurance policy protects the policyowner in two ways. First, it states that nothing outside the contract—which includes the signed application and any attached policy riders—can be considered part of the contract; that is, nothing can be "incorporated by reference." Second, it assures the policyowner that no changes will be made to the contract after it has been issued. If the insurer changes the policy, such changes are applicable only to future policy sales.

#2: Time Limit on Certain Defenses

Under the *time limit on certain defenses* provision, the policy is incontestable after it has been in force a certain period of time, ~~usually~~ two years. This is similar to the "incontestable clause" in a life insurance policy. However, unlike life policies, a fraudulent statement on a health insurance application is grounds for contest at *any* time, unless the policy is guaranteed renewable, in which case it cannot be contested for any reason after the contestable period expires.

Another part of this provision concerns any preexisting conditions an insured may have. Under the provision, the insurance company cannot deny a claim on the basis of a preexisting condition after expiration of the stated contestable period—unless such preexisting condition has been excluded specifically from the policy by name or description.

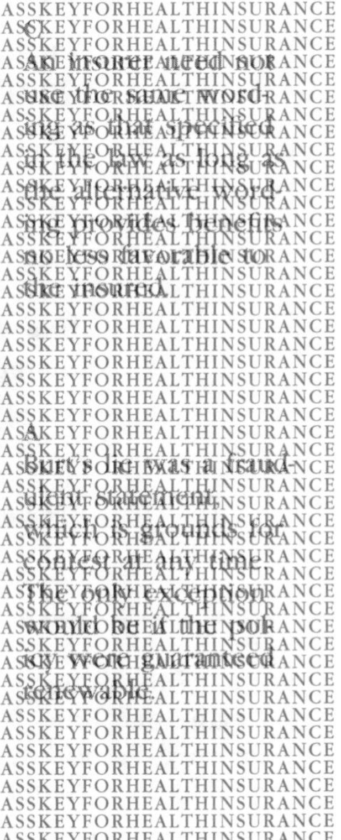

1. An insurer may word a uniform policy provision differently from that used in the law only if

   A. the modified provision is not less favorable to the insurer.
   B. the applicant directs that it be changed.
   C. the modified provision is not less favorable to the insured.
   D. the applicant gives his or her approval of the change.

---

2. Burt lied about his occupation as a demolition expert when he applied for an accident policy. Four years later, the insurer discovered the truth when Burt was seriously injured on a wrecking job and submitted a claim. Which of the following is a correct statement?

   A. The insurer could deny the claim and void the policy on the basis of Burt's fraudulent statement about his occupation.
   B. The insurer could do nothing but honor Burt's claim because the policy's two-year time limitation to contest the policy had expired.

3. The entire contract provision incorporates which of the following into the insurance contract?

   A. The application
   B. Any riders
   C. Both A and B

C
The entire contract provision states that the contract includes the signed application and any attached riders.

#3: Grace Period

The *grace period* provision specifies a number of days after the premium due date during which the premium payment may be delayed without penalty and the policy remains in force.

Depending on the state, the minimum grace periods are typically seven days for policies with weekly premium payments, ten days for policies with monthly premium payments and 31 days for other policies. (Some states, however, require a standard grace period of 31 days, regardless of the frequency of premium payment or policy term.) If the premium is not paid by the end of the grace period, coverage is terminated.

#4: Reinstatement

Under certain conditions, a policy that has lapsed may be reinstated. *Reinstatement* is automatic if:

1. the delinquent premium is accepted by the company or its authorized agent and

2. the company does not require an application for reinstatement.

If a company does require such an application, it may or may not approve the application. If it takes no action on the application for 45 days, the policy is reinstated automatically. To protect the company against *adverse selection,* losses resulting from sickness are covered only if the sickness occurs at least ten days after the reinstatement date. Losses resulting from accidental injury are covered immediately after reinstatement.

---

1. Willard's policy has a grace period of 31 days. A premium came due June 15 while he was on vacation. Willard returned home July 7 and mailed his premium the next day. Which is a correct statement?

   A. Willard's policy would have lapsed.
   B. Willard's policy would have remained in force.

B
The policy remains in force during the grace period.

2. Depending on the premium payment mode, what are the three minimum grace periods specified in the "Grace Period Provision"?

   A. ______ days
   B. ______ days
   C. ______ days

A. 7
B. 10
C. 31

3. Gerald's hospital expense policy was reinstated on September 30 and he became ill and entered the hospital on October 5. Under the policy's reinstatement terms, which are typical, would the hospital be paid? Why?

   ____
   ____
   ____
   ____

No, because losses resulting from sickness are covered only if sickness occurs at least ten days after reinstatement.

#5: Notice of Claims

The *notice of claims* provision describes the policyowner's obligation to provide notification of loss to the insurer within a reasonable period of time. Typically, this period is 20 days after the occurrence or commencement of the loss, or as soon thereafter as is reasonably possible. If the loss involves disability income payments that are payable for two or more years, the disabled claimant must submit proof of loss every six months. Such proof may be submitted to either the company or an authorized agent of the company.

#6: Claims Forms

It is the company's responsibility to supply a *claims form* to an insured within 15 days after receiving notice of claim. If it fails to do so within the time limit, the claimant may submit proof of loss in any form, explaining the occurrence, the character and the extent of the loss for which the claim is submitted.

#7: Proof of Loss

After a loss occurs, or after the company becomes liable for periodic payments (e.g., disability income benefits), the claimant has 90 days in which to submit *proof of loss*. The claim will not be affected in any way, however, if it is not reasonably possible for the claimant to comply with the 90-day provision.

There is a time limit for submitting proof of loss—whether or not it is "reasonably possible" to do so—and that is one year after the company becomes liable for the loss. The only exception to the one-year limit is if the claimant does not have the "legal capacity" to comply.

1. Ella is injured while skiing on January 5. Later she wishes to file a policy claim for medical expenses incurred in connection with the injury. Generally, Ella would be required to submit a notice of claim to the insurance company by what date?

   A. January 20 following the accident
   B. January 25 following the accident

B
Notice of claim is to be filed within 20 days after loss occurs or as soon as is reasonably possible.

---

2. Richard has been totally disabled and receiving benefits for 25 months. The notice of claim provision in his disability income policy requires that he submit proof of loss

   A. every six months.
   B. once a year.

A
Insureds who receive disability income benefits for two or more years must submit proof of loss every six months.

---

3. Furnishing claims forms is the responsibility of the (insured/ insurance company).

insurance company

---

4. Dianna submits notice of claim to her insurance company after she becomes totally disabled.

   A. The company is to supply Dianna with claim forms within ______ days.
   B. What can Dianna do if she does not receive claim forms from the company within this time limit?

   ____
   ____
   ____

15
She may submit proof of loss in any form, explaining the character and extent of loss.

---

5. Velma is badly injured in an auto accident and is hospitalized for more than three months after undergoing emergency brain surgery. She fails to comply with the 90-day provision in her disability income policy for filing proof of loss, but submits the necessary proof six months after the accident. Will the delay affect her claim in any way? Why or why not?

   ____
   ____

No, because it was not reasonably possible for her to comply with the 90-day provision.

---

6. An insured's time limit for filing proof of loss is ______ after the insurance company becomes liable for the loss, unless the claimant does not have ______.

one year
legal capacity

#8: Time of Payment of Claims

The *time of payment of claims* provision provides for immediate payment of the claim after the insurer receives notification and proof of loss. If the claim involves disability income payments, they must be paid at least monthly, if not at more frequent intervals as specified in the policy. In some states, the time of payment of claims is 60 days; in other states, it is 30 days.

#9: Payment of Claims

The *payment of claims* provision in a health insurance contract specifies how and to whom claim payments are to be made. Payments for loss of life are to be made to the designated beneficiary. If no beneficiary has been named, death proceeds are to be paid to the deceased insured's estate. Claims other than death benefits are to be paid to the insured.

In accordance with this required provision are two optional provisions that insurers may add. One gives the insurer the right to expedite payment of urgently needed claim funds and pay up to $1,000 in benefits to a relative or individual who is considered to be equitably entitled to payment. The other optional provision allows the insured to have medical benefits *assigned*—or paid directly—to the hospital or physician rendering the covered services.

---

1. The time of payment of claims provision must provide that disability income payments be paid at least

   A. weekly.
   B. monthly.

2. The only named beneficiary in an accident policy died before the insured was killed in a car accident. To whom would the death benefit be paid, according to the payment of claims provision?

   ____

3. Ernest dies and there is some doubt as to who is legally qualified to receive his $50,000 accidental death benefit. The family is financially hard-pressed to pay some of the insured's final expenses. Depending on how the payment of claims provision is worded, what may the insurer be able to do to help solve the family's financial problem?

   ____

   ____

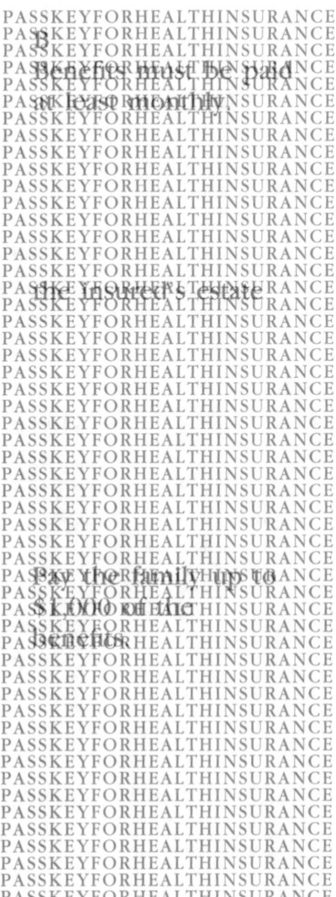

4. A section of the payment of claims provision may give the insured the right to ______ medical expense benefits to a hospital or physician in payment for services.

#10: Physical Exam and Autopsy

The *physical exam and autopsy* provision entitles a company, at its own expense, to make physical examinations of the insured at reasonable intervals during the period of a claim. In the case of death, the insurer has the right to conduct an autopsy on the body of the insured, provided it is not forbidden by state law.

#11: Legal Actions

The insured cannot take *legal action* against the company in a claim dispute until after 60 days from the time the insured submits proof of loss. The same rule applies to beneficiaries. Also, if legal action is to be taken against the company, it must be done within a certain time after proof of loss is submitted (usually two or three years).

#12: Change of Beneficiary

Before we explain the *change of beneficiary* provision, let's first discuss health insurance beneficiaries.

Health insurance policies that provide a death benefit require the designation of a *beneficiary* by the insured. Other health insurance benefits are generally payable to the insured, or to the hospital, physicians or dentists for services rendered.

A *primary beneficiary* is one who is "first in line" to receive a policy's death benefit. If a married applicant buys an accident policy, his or her spouse usually will be named primary beneficiary. An applicant who is single may name a parent or other blood relative as primary beneficiary.

There are also *contingent beneficiaries,* those who are second or third in line to receive benefits. A policyowner can name one or more primary beneficiaries and/or more than one contingent beneficiaries. Beneficiaries who are second in line are called *secondary beneficiaries*. But suppose both the primary and secondary beneficiaries are deceased? In this case, benefits may be paid to a *tertiary beneficiary*—that is, the third in line—if one has been named. If there is no living beneficiary, death benefits will be paid to the estate of the insured.

When death benefits are paid to an insured's estate, however, there usually are delays, settlement costs and probably state death taxes. It's usually not desirable to have proceeds paid to the insured's estate, unless there are special reasons for doing so.

The *change of beneficiary* provision states that the insured, as policyowner, may change the beneficiary designation at any time, unless a beneficiary has been named irrevocably. An *irrevocable beneficiary* is one that cannot be changed by the insured without consent from the beneficiary. So long as the insured reserves the right to change beneficiaries without the beneficiary's consent (a *revocable designation*), the insured may also surrender or assign the policy without obtaining the consent of the beneficiary.

---

1. Beneficiary Theresa submits an accidental death claim September 1 on her husband's policy following his death. The insurer denies the claim on the basis that death was due to natural causes. She decides to talk to her attorney. What is the earliest Theresa could bring legal action against the company?

   A. November 1
   B. December 1

---

2. When a death claim is submitted, the insurer must have the beneficiary's permission before a physical examination and autopsy can be performed on the body of the insured.

   (True/False)

---

3. A policyowner's right to change the policy beneficiary will be eliminated if the policyowner names a(n) _____ beneficiary.

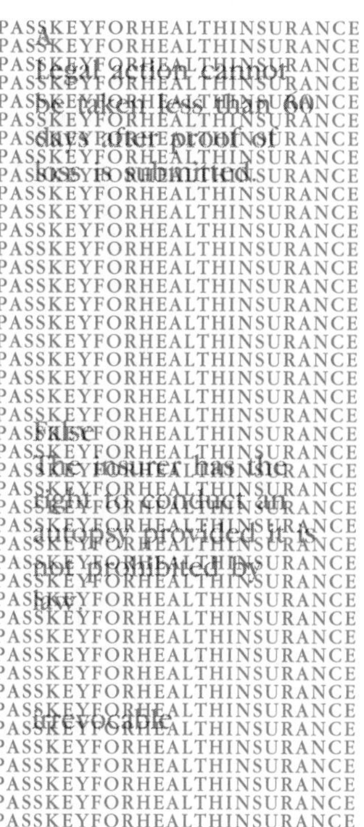

■ ELEVEN OPTIONAL PROVISIONS

In accordance with the NAIC model law, there are eleven optional health policy provisions, and companies may ignore them or use only those that are needed in their policy forms. The provisions pertaining to "other insurance in this insurer," "insurance with other insurers" and "relation of earnings to insurance" seldom are used. They were intended to deal with the problem of overinsurance, but generally proved to be ineffective.

#1: Change of Occupation

The *change of occupation* provision sets forth the changes that may be made to premium rates or benefits payable if the insured changes occupations. An individual's occupation has a direct bearing on his or her risk profile and one's risk profile has a direct bearing on premium charges. Consequently, this provision allows the insurer to reduce the maximum benefit payable under the policy if the insured switches to a *more* hazardous occupation or to reduce the premium rate charged if the insured changes to a *less* hazardous occupation. These changes take effect at the time the insured changes occupations; if a change in jobs is discovered after a disability begins, the changes are made retroactively.

#2: Misstatement of Age

The *misstatement of age* provision allows the insurer to adjust the benefit payable if the age of the insured was misstated when application for the policy was made. Benefits payable in such cases will be what the premiums paid would have purchased at the correct age. The older the applicant, the higher the premium; therefore, if the insured were older at the time of application than is shown in the policy, benefits would be reduced accordingly. The reverse would be true if the insured were younger than listed in the application.

#3: Other Insurance in This Insurer

The *other insurance in this insurer* provision limits the company's risk with any individual insured. This provision restricts the total coverage the company will underwrite for one person to a specified maximum amount, regardless of the number of policies issued. Premiums paid for excess coverage must be returned to the insured or to the insured's estate.

#4: Insurance with Other Insurer

In attempting to deal with the potential problem of overinsurance, the *insurance with other insurer* provision states that benefits payable for "expenses incurred" will be prorated in cases where the company accepted the risk without being notified of other existing coverage for the same risk. When premiums are paid that exceed the amount needed to cover what the company determines it will pay, the excess premiums must be refunded to the policyowner.

#5: Insurance with Other Insurers

Similar to the above, the *insurance with other insurers* provision calls for the prorating of benefits that are payable on any basis other than "expenses incurred." It also provides for a return of premiums that exceed the amount needed to pay for the company's portion of prorated benefits.

---

1. Clarence changes to a more hazardous job than the one he had when he applied for his accident policy. What will happen when he files a claim and the insurer learns of his new job?

   A. There is nothing the insurer can do, if all premiums have been paid.

   B. Clarence's benefit would be reduced to the amount his premiums would have purchased had his occupation classification been changed to reflect his more hazardous job.

2. Kathleen changes to a less hazardous occupation after paying a high premium for her accident policy because of her original occupation classification. The insurer does not learn of her job change until she files a claim a few years later. What action must the insurer take, provided the insured meets the necessary requirements?

   ____

   ____

Pay the full benefit and refund the excess premiums paid based on the less hazardous occupation.

3. The insurer discovers that Mark was really younger than the age shown in his application when he applied for his health policy. In this case, policy benefits would be (increased/reduced).

increased

4. The insurer learns that Vera was actually older than stated in her application when she applied for her health policy. In this case, policy benefits would be (increased/reduced).

reduced

5. Lowell has two medical expense policies issued by different insurers. If each company is unaware of the insured's other coverage, this could result in overinsurance. What might happen to the benefits and premiums if this overinsurance were revealed and one or both of Lowell's policies contained the insurance with other insurers provision?

   1. ______________________________

   ____

   2. ______________________________

   ____

1. Benefits would be prorated

2. Premiums paid for any excess coverage would be refunded

(May be in any order.)

6. The insurance with other insurers provision is almost identical to the insurance with other insurer provision except that it concerns policies with benefits payable on any basis other than ______ (e.g., disability income benefits).

expenses incurred

#6: Relation of Earnings to Insurance

The *relation of earnings* provision states that if benefits from all disability income policies exceed the insured's monthly earnings at the time of disability, the insurer is liable only for that *proportionate* amount of benefits as the insured's earnings bear to the total benefits. In other words, if the insured's earnings only equal 85 percent of the total benefits, the insurer need only pay 85 percent of the total benefits. Any premiums paid by the insured for the excess coverage are refunded. This provision ensures that an insured never collect more than his or her earned income in disability income benefits.

Total benefits payable to the insured may not be reduced below $200 or the sum total benefits under all applicable coverage, whichever is less.

#7: Unpaid Premiums

If there is an *unpaid premium* at the time a health claim becomes payable, the amount of the premium is deducted from the sum payable to the insured or beneficiary. Similarly, if the premium is covered by a note when a claim is submitted, the note payment will be subtracted from the amount payable for the claim.

#8: Cancellation

Though prohibited in a number of states, the provision for *cancellation* gives the company the right to cancel the policy at any time with five days' written notice to the insured. It also provides that the insured may cancel the policy anytime after the policy's original term has expired. Any unearned premium is to be refunded to the insured. If a claim is pending at the time of cancellation, the claim cannot be affected by the cancellation. (See also "Renewability Provisions," Chapter 8.)

#9: Conformity with State Statutes

Any policy provision that is in conflict with *state statutes* in the state where the insured lives at the time the policy is issued is considered automatically amended to conform with the minimum statutory requirements.

#10: Illegal Occupation

The *illegal occupation* provision specifies that the insurer is not liable for losses attributed to the insured's commission of, or being connected with, a felony or participation in any illegal occupation.

#11: Intoxicants and Narcotics

The insurer is not liable for any loss attributed to the insured while *intoxicated* or under the influence of *narcotics,* unless such drugs were administered under the direction of a physician.

---

1. Norman has an accident policy that pays a $50,000 death benefit. He dies of accidental injuries owing a $150 premium. In accordance with the unpaid premium provision, Norman's beneficiary could expect to receive a death benefit check in what amount?

   ____

$49,850

$50,000 (death benefit)
− 150 (unpaid premium)

$49,850

2. Edith has an accident policy that contains the model NAIC cancellation provision. She should know, therefore, that the policy can be canceled at any time by the insurer giving

   A. ten days' written notice.
   B. five days' written notice.

B. Edith also may cancel her policy anytime after the original policy term expires.

---

3. Alvin has submitted a claim to his insurer and soon receives a written notice that his policy is being canceled. The cancellation (will/will not) affect Alvin's claim.

will not

---

4. Explain the conformity with state statutes provision.

If a policy provision conflicts with state statutes in the state where the insured lives when the policy is issued, the provision is automatically amended to conform with minimum statutory requirements.

---

5. Max is injured in an auto accident. He is arrested at the hospital and later convicted of transporting stolen cars across state lines. In this case, the insurer may have a right to deny Max's hospital expense claim on what basis?

   A. Illegal occupation provision
   B. Cancellation provision

A. The illegal occupation provision states that the insurer is not liable for losses due to the insured's commission of a felony.

---

6. Donovan is driving home from a party and is injured when his car strikes a bus. He is arrested for drunken driving and taken to a hospital for treatment. The insurer may be able to deny Donovan's claim for medical expense benefits based on what policy provision?

Intoxicants and narcotics

8

Other Health Insurance Policy Provisions and Exclusions

The twelve mandatory provisions and eleven optional provisions described in the previous chapter comprise the substantive elements of individual health insurance policies. However, there are a number of other very important provisions—some standard, some optional, some restrictive—that are also common to health insurance plans. These provisions are significant in that they give the health insurance contract its form and flexibility.

■ ADDITIONAL POLICY PROVISIONS

In addition to the required and optional provisions, individual health insurance policies contain a number of provisions that define the benefits payable, any exclusions applicable and the rights of the insured to renew the coverage. In addition, there are other provisions that explain and define the insurer's liability.

Insuring Clause

The *insuring clause* is a broad statement on the first page of the health policy, specifying conditions under which benefits are to be paid. While this critical provision varies considerably in health insurance contracts, it basically represents a company's "promise to pay" benefits for specific kinds of losses resulting from sickness or accidents. It legally identifies the insurer and the insured and usually states that benefits are subject to all provisions and exclusions specified in the policy.

Consideration Clause

The *consideration clause* states the amount and frequency of premium payments. If the first premium has not been paid—even though the application has been completed and signed by the applicant—the necessary consideration for a binding legal contract is partially lacking. The legal consideration for a health policy consists of the application *and* payment of the initial premium. A copy of the application is attached to the policy.

Frequently, the consideration clause also lists the effective date of the contract and defines the initial term of the policy. In addition, it may specify the insured's right to renew the policy.

It should be noted that a health insurance policy, though binding on the insurer, is not binding on the policyowner; the policyowner is not obligated to pay the premiums. At any time, an individual has the right to cancel the policy simply by not paying the premium.

Free Look Provision

Most states mandate that their health insurance policies contain a *free look* provision, printed on the first page of the policy, permitting policyowners either 10 or 20 days in which to examine their new policies at no obligation. If they decide not to keep their policies, they may return them within the prescribed time limit and receive full refunds of premiums paid.

Coverage of Dependents

A single health insurance policy may insure more than one person if the applicant is an adult family member and the others to be covered are members of his or her family. Generally, children are eligible for coverage under a family policy until they reach a specified age, usually age 19 or, if they remain in school full-time, age 21 or even age 25. Adopted children, stepchildren and foster children are eligible for coverage. As long as a policy is in force, a child's coverage continues until the child marries or reaches the limiting age. However, a number of states require insurers to continue to insure under the parent's individual health policy any child who reaches the limiting age, but who is dependent on the insured and incapable of self-support because of mental or physical impairment.

Reaching a minimum age, such as 14 days, may be required for coverage; however, some states mandate that health policies insuring family members provide coverage for newborn children from the moment of birth. Typically, such legislation permits the insurer to require that it be notified of the birth of the child and an application be submitted within a specified period after the birth.

Conversion Privilege for Dependents

Under specified conditions, the *conversion privilege* allows dependents to continue their insurance coverage by obtaining their own policy. If the insurance on a covered individual is terminated because he or she no longer fits the policy definition of "family member," that person has a right to take out a conversion policy without evidence of insurability. For example, if Faye divorces Stanley and thus no longer can be covered under his family policy, she has a right to obtain a conversion policy. When their children reach the limiting age for children's coverage, they also will be eligible for conversion policies.

1. Fred reads on the first page of his accident policy that "the company will pay a death benefit of $50,000 providing his death is caused by accidental bodily injury, subject to all provisions, terms and exclusions of the policy." Fred undoubtedly is reading the _____ of his policy.

   insuring clause

2. Who does the insuring clause identify?

   The insurer and the insured

3. Describe the legal consideration for a health insurance policy.

   It consists of payment of the initial premium and the signed application.

4. Give a brief explanation of the free look provision.

   It provides that new policyowners may return their policies within the state's prescribed time limit, e.g., 10 or 20 days, and receive a full refund of premiums paid.

5. A policy with a 20-day free look provision is delivered to Timothy, the insured, on June 5. He decides not to keep the policy and returns it to you on June 22. Which of the following statements applies?

   A. Timothy is entitled to a full refund of premium.
   B. Unfortunately, Timothy waited too long to return the policy so he is not entitled to a refund of premium.

   A. He did return the policy within 20 days so he does qualify for a refund.

6. Children of the insured who are not full-time students remain eligible for health insurance coverage until age

   A. 19.
   B. 21.
   C. 23.
   D. 25.

RENEWABILITY PROVISIONS

One of the distinguishing features of health insurance policies is that they contain a provision that allows the insurer to continue or discontinue coverage; this is known as the *renewability* provision. Every health insurance policy must explain its renewability. Since this is one of the most important aspects of a health policy, we will discuss it in detail here.

The renewability provision varies from policy to policy. Generally speaking, the more favorable the renewability provision is to the insured, the higher the premium.

Cancelable Policies

The renewability provision in a *cancelable* policy allows the insurer to cancel or terminate the policy at any time, simply by providing written notification to the insured and refunding any advance premium that has been paid. Cancelable policies also allow the insurer to increase premiums.

Optionally Renewable Policies

The renewability provision in an *optionally renewable* policy gives the insurer the option to terminate the policy on a date specified in the contract. Furthermore, this provision allows the insurer to increase the premium for any *class* of optionally renewable insureds.* The premium, however, cannot be increased for an individual insured. Usually termination or premium increases take place on policy anniversary dates or premium due dates.

Conditionally Renewable Policies

A *conditionally renewable* policy allows an insurer to terminate the coverage, but only in the event of one or more conditions stated in the contract. These conditions cannot apply to the insured's health; most frequently, they are related to the insured reaching a certain age or losing gainful employment. Usually, the premium for conditionally renewable policies may be increased, but as with optionally renewable policies, the increase must apply to an entire class of insureds.

*A "class" of insureds includes all insureds of policies of a particular kind or all insureds of a specific group. For example, a class of insureds may be those of a particular age or in a specific geographic region.

Guaranteed Renewable Policies

The renewal provision in a *guaranteed renewable* policy specifies that the policy must be renewed, as long as premiums are paid, until the insured reaches a specified age, such as 60 or 65. Premium increases may be applied, but only for the entire class of insureds; again, they cannot be assessed to individual insureds.

Noncancelable Policies

A *noncancelable* or "noncan" policy cannot be canceled nor can its premium rates be increased under any circumstances; these rates are specified in the policy. The term of most noncancelable policies is to the insured's age 65. Noncan provisions are most commonly found in disability income policies; they are rarely used in medical expense policies.

---

1. Kevin's policy gives him the right to renew coverage up to age 65, but the company reserves the right to change the premium rate on a class basis. Which type of policy does Kevin have?

   A. Guaranteed renewable
   B. Noncancelable

2. Merrill has a policy in which the company reserves the right to terminate the coverage at any policy anniversary date or premium due date. What kind of policy does Merrill have?

   ____

3. Eric's policy has a provision that allows him to renew the coverage up to age 65—with one exception. The policy states that it may be terminated earlier if Eric loses his job. As to renewability, what type of policy does Eric have?

   ____

4. Noncancelable policies generally provide what kind of insurance protection?

   ____

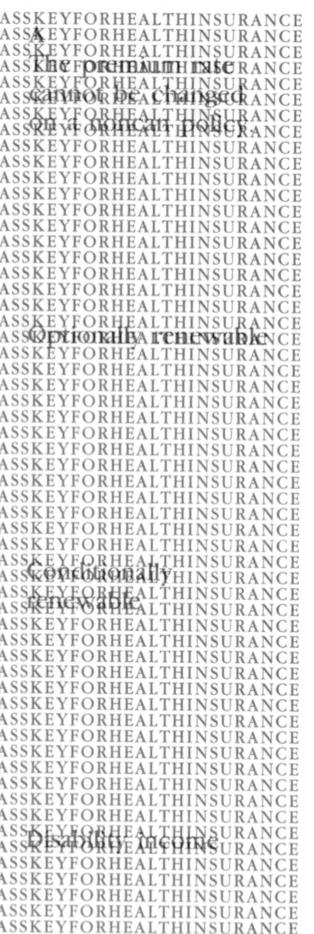

HEALTH INSURANCE POLICY OPTIONS

There are a number of options that health insurance policyowners can elect to tailor their policy to their needs. These options are discussed below.

Modes of Premium Payment

Insureds have a choice of how to pay their health insurance premiums. Premiums may be paid annually (once a year), semiannually (every six months), quarterly (every three months), or monthly—if the payment is not less than the minimum amount permitted by the insurer for that particular payment plan.

All premiums are payable in advance. The first premium is generally paid to the agent at the time of application. If not paid then, the first premium must be paid when the policy is delivered.

There is a small additional charge added to premiums paid more frequently than annually. This is partially because of the insurer's additional administrative expenses for collecting premiums two, four, or 12 times each year instead of only once. In addition, there is the loss of interest; in calculating premiums, the company assumes that a full year's interest will be earned on each annual premium paid in advance.

Elective Indemnity

Another option offered in some health insurance policies is called the *elective indemnity* provision. This gives an eligible insured the opportunity of taking a specified lump sum in lieu of periodic disability benefits or in lieu of all other benefits payable for certain minor or partial disabilities.

The specified amounts usually are listed in a schedule as multiples of the benefit for total disability. For example, the lump-sum benefit may be payable for certain fractures, dislocations and amputations.

To illustrate, Harvey breaks his leg while on a skiing holiday. The doctor estimates that Harvey will be disabled for more than ten weeks. Instead of collecting a weekly benefit for ten weeks or so, Harvey decides to take advantage of the elective indemnity provision in his policy and collects a lump sum. Such lump-sum amounts are usually less than the insured would collect otherwise.

In contrast to the elective indemnity provision, some accident policies contain an "optional provision" that permits the insured to collect a weekly or monthly benefit in lieu of a lump-sum payment.

Assignment

As we've mentioned, medical expense insurance policies commonly include an *assignment* provision that offers insureds the option of having benefits paid directly to a hospital or physician for services rendered.

An assignment form must be signed by the insured before benefits will be paid to a hospital or physician.

For example, an assignment form may be signed by the insured—usually at the request of the hospital at the time of admission—specifying that benefits are to be paid directly to the hospital rather than to the insured. In that case, the insurance company will pay the allowable amount of benefits to the hospital after receiving a statement of charges from the institution.

A statement in such forms generally stipulates that the insured will be responsible for any charges not covered by the insurance. Dental claim forms also usually include space for an assignment authorization.

Disability income benefits also can be assigned. For example, disability income benefits may be assigned on a collateral basis to assure repayment of a loan in the event the debtor (insured) becomes disabled.

---

1. Clint has just paid an annual premium for his major medical policy. Therefore, he has paid the amount due for the 12 months just

   A. completed.
   B. beginning.

2. Joan and Juanita, both age 32, purchase identical major medical policies from Threshold Insurance Company. Joan pays her premiums annually while Juanita prefers to pay her premiums monthly. Which policy will cost less?

   A. Joan's
   B. Juanita's

3. Archie suffers a temporary disability and decides to collect a lump sum in lieu of weekly disability benefits as his policy permits. Thus, Archie has elected to take advantage of which policy provision?

   A. Assignment
   B. Elective indemnity

4. Lump-sum settlements under an elective indemnity provision generally are (more/less) than the total of periodic benefit payments payable to an insured would be.

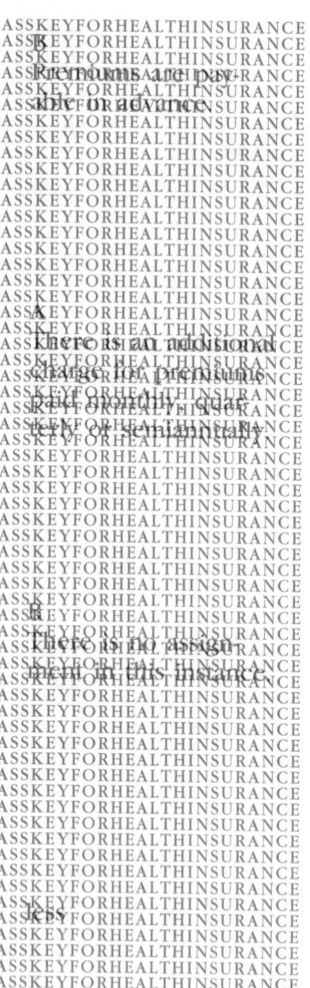

COMMON POLICY EXCLUSIONS OR RESTRICTIONS

Health insurance policies frequently cite a number of *exclusions* or conditions that are not covered. The common ones are injuries due to war or an act of war, self-inflicted injuries and those incurred while the insured is serving as a pilot or crew member of an aircraft.

Other exclusions are losses resulting from suicide, hernia (as an accidental injury), riots or the use of drugs or narcotics. Losses due to injuries sustained while committing a felony, or attempting to do so, also may be excluded. Foreign travel may not be excluded in every instance, but extended stays overseas or foreign residence may cause a loss of benefits.

Maternity Benefits

Maternity benefits generally are handled differently in individual health policies than in group health policies. When available for individual policies, a maternity provision may provide a fixed amount for childbirth or a benefit based upon a specified multiple of the daily hospital room benefit. Frequently, the maternity benefit is available only as an added benefit for an additional premium.

Maternity coverage in group health plans is discussed in Chapter 11.

Preexisting Conditions

As we have learned, medical expense and disability income policies usually exclude paying benefits for losses due to preexisting conditions pertaining to illness, disease or other physical impairments. For purposes of issuing individual health policies, insurers consider a preexisting condition to be one that the insured contracted (or one that manifested) prior to the policy's effective date. Consequently, in the event the insured did not specifically cite the condition on the application and the insurer did not expressly exclude the condition from coverage, the preexisting condition provision would serve to exclude the condition nonetheless. Remember, however, such exclusions are subject to the mandatory "time limit on certain defenses" provision.

Any preexisting condition that the insured has disclosed clearly in the application usually is not excluded or, if it is, the condition is named specifically in an excluding waiver or rider, as we will discuss next.

The treatment of preexisting conditions under group health plans is a little different and is discussed in Chapter 11.

Waivers for Impairments

The majority of health policies are standard and are issued as applied for. However, a few people have an existing impairment that increases the risk and so are required to pay an extra premium. A few people are uninsurable and must be declined. Others, however, fall in between and would not be able to obtain health insurance if *waivers* were not in use. Waivers simply exclude coverage for some specific impairment. They usually are stated in simple language. For example: "This policy does not cover or extend to any disability resulting directly or indirectly from. . . ." A waiver is dated and bears the signature of an officer of the company and, in many cases, the applicant. This is usually called an "impairment rider."

If the insured's condition improves, the company may be willing to remove the waiver. Meanwhile, the person at least has health protection from other hazards, which he or she otherwise could not obtain.

---

1. Which section of a health insurance policy specifies the conditions, times and circumstances under which the insured is NOT covered by the policy?

   A. Coinsurance provision
   B. Coverages
   C. Insuring clause
   D. Exclusions

D.
Exclusions are conditions not covered.

---

2. Common exclusions in a health insurance policy include all of the following, EXCEPT:

   A. loss resulting from suicide.
   B. loss due to war.
   C. loss incurred while committing a felony.
   D. loss sustained while a passenger on a commercial airline.

D.
However, a common exclusion is loss incurred while serving as a pilot or crew member of an aircraft.

---

3. When the insured has an existing impairment that increases the risk, the premium is (higher/lower) than if he or she did not have an impairment.

higher
Increased risks require a higher premium.

---

4. Why might a waiver be valuable to the applicant?

   ____

   ____

The applicant can obtain insurance protection otherwise not available.

9

Completing the Application and Delivering the Policy

Before accepting a health insurance risk, before agreeing to insure an individual or group, an insurer must review and classify the risk. This process is called *underwriting* the risk. The underwriting process can be broken down into two phases: the collection of information by the agent, and the collection and evaluation of information by the insurance company's home office underwriters.

In this chapter, we will discuss the agent's role in the underwriting process. This includes ensuring that the application is completed accurately and fully, submitting the application to the insurer and once the policy is issued, delivering and explaining the policy to the insured. We will also look at the sources of information an insurer uses to evaluate a risk.

THE HEALTH INSURANCE APPLICATION

When an insurer's home office underwriters evaluate a health insurance risk, they use a variety of sources that provide useful information about the risk. Regardless of what other sources the underwriter may draw from, the *application*—the first source to be reviewed—will be evaluated thoroughly.

There are three basic parts to a typical health insurance application:

1. Part 1—General,
2. Part 2—Medical and
3. the Agent's Report.

Part 1—General

Part 1 of the application is where the agent enters general nonmedical information about the applicant, such as the applicant's name, home and business addresses (past and present), occupation, sex, date of birth, name and relationship of beneficiary (if applicable), amount and kind of insurance being requested, existing health insurance, driving record, etc. Generally, there are also questions about the applicant's avocation, aviation activities and plans for foreign travel.

Applicant's Name

The agent should always verify an applicant's name to be sure it is spelled correctly. What sounds like "Smith" might actually be "Smyth," "Smythe" or even "Schmidt."

Age

Some people are vain about their age. If a prospect says, "I'm 39," the agent should put it down as 39. Another question in the application will ask for the date of birth. Applicants will generally give their correct date of birth, which the agent can easily check against the stated age.

Age is obviously important because it affects how much the premium will be (this is discussed in detail in the next chapter). Some companies figure an applicant's age according to the *nearest birthday*. Others base premiums on an applicant's *last birthday*.

For example, Tom was born June 1, 1959. If you were to meet with Tom on April 1, 1999, his age per the "nearest birthday" definition would be 40. If his insurance age were based on his last birthday, however, Tom would be 39. Agents should follow their company's specific rule on determining age.

Sex

Is the applicant male or female? Agents should always be sure it is clearly marked on the application—an applicant's name does not necessarily indicate his or her sex.

Occupation

When listing an applicant's occupation, agents should be certain to record his or her exact duties in addition to the job title. An applicant's income figure shown in an application for disability income insurance is of special significance because, as we've learned, maximum amounts of coverage are generally based on a percentage of income up to a maximum limit.

Part 2—Medical

Part 2 of many applications provides the basics for a medical history. Health questions relate to a list of specific diseases and medical and surgical procedures. Unless a medical examination is required (in which case a physician completes the part of the application that describes the applicant's health), the agent asks the applicant a series of questions about his or her present state of health and any illnesses, injuries or surgical operations experienced in the last five or ten years. The names and addresses of physicians consulted in the last five years or so and the kind of treatment provided also are required. The company may request further information from the attending physicians. Finally, questions must be answered about the applicant's parents and children, living or deceased.

Agents should be especially careful to obtain accurate information concerning an applicant's present health and health history. Make sure the full names and current addresses of any attending physicians are listed. An applicant's existing insurance policies should be recorded in the space provided and all questions pertaining to any possible replacement of one or more of the existing policies must be answered fully.

At this point, it's appropriate to mention that according to the law of most states, all statements made by an applicant for health insurance—whether in an application or to a medical examiner—are considered to be *representations* and not *warranties*.

A representation is a statement made by the applicant that the applicant believes to be true. A warranty is a statement made by the applicant that the applicant guarantees to be true. The practical distinction is this: if a warranty is untrue, the insurer has the right to cancel the contract; but, if a representation is untrue, the insurer has the right to cancel the contract only if the representation was material to the creation of the contract.

Also, the insurer may have grounds for voiding the policy if the applicant is guilty of *concealment*. Concealment occurs when the applicant conceals known material facts from the insurer for the purpose of defrauding the insurer (that is, to get the insurer to issue a policy that might not otherwise be issued). To void a policy on this grounds, the insurer would have to prove concealment and materiality.

Signatures Needed

Several signatures are required to complete an application, so the agent should be aware of their importance. Overlooking a needed signature will delay having a policy issued and cause embarrassment and unnecessary inconvenience for the agent. Each application requires the signatures of the proposed insured, the policyowner, if different than the insured, and the agent who solicits the application. If the policyowner is to be a partnership or corporation, one or more partners or officers other than the proposed insured generally must sign the application.

Agent's Report

The agent's report usually appears on the back of the application and generally is not seen by the applicant. This report provides important underwriting insight into each case, based on the agent's confidential statements about the applicant. Through this report, the agent can furnish valuable additional information to home office underwriters.

Typically, the underwriters want to know how long the agent has known the applicant. They want the agent's opinion as to the applicant's financial standing, character, life-style and environment. Other questions may relate to replacement, e.g., will the policy being requested replace an existing policy? Does the agent believe the applicant to be a good risk? The agent's report is to be completed and signed only by the agent.

Additional Forms

Additional questionnaires regarding an applicant's aviation or avocation activities may be needed for underwriting purposes, and these require the signature of both the applicant and the agent. For example, if an applicant's hobby is scuba diving or skydiving, the insurance company needs detailed information as to the extent of the applicant's participation in order to determine whether the risk is acceptable or whether the hobby should be listed as an exclusion.

In addition, a form authorizing the insurance company to obtain investigative consumer reports or medical information, such as blood testing, from investigative agencies, physicians, hospitals, the Medical Information Bureau or other sources must be signed by the proposed insured and the agent as witness. A Fair Credit Reporting Act notice of disclosure, which is explained later, also is to be completed with the proper signatures.

---

1. All of the following is information that is typically needed in a health insurance application, EXCEPT:

   A. the applicant's age.
   B. the beneficiary's age.
   C. the applicant's birth date.
   D. the applicant's occupation.

2. An agent interviewed Eleanor on November 1, 1992, in order to complete a health insurance application. Her date of birth is January 10, 1962. The premium is based on her nearest birthday for insurance purposes, so the agent should list her age as

   A. 31.
   B. 30.

3. The agent's opinion of the applicant would be found in which section of the application?

   ____

4. Who signs the agent's report?

   A. Agent and applicant
   B. Agent only

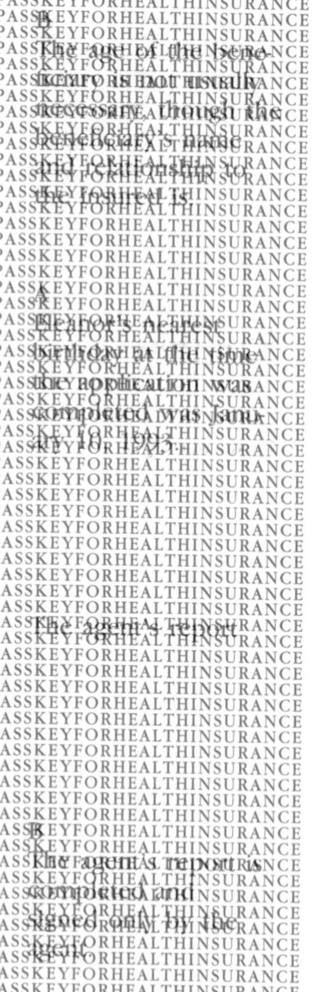

B. The age of the beneficiary is not usually necessary, though the beneficiary's name and relationship to the insured is.

A. Eleanor's nearest birthday at the time the application was completed was January 10, 1993.

The agent's report

B. The agent's report is completed and signed only by the agent.

5. Rebecca inadvertently gave the date of her parents' deaths as 1996 instead of 1997 on her health insurance application. She later called her agent about it and was told that her policy could not be voided because statements made in her application are

   A. warranties and not representations.
   B. representations and not warranties.

B. Her agent is correct since the law in most states provides that statements made in the application are deemed representations, which cannot serve as the basis for voiding the contract unless the representation is material to the contract. In this case, misstating her parents' year of death by a single year was not material to the contract.

---

6. A representation is a statement made by the applicant that the applicant __________ to be true.

   A. believes
   B. guarantees

A. This is in contrast to a warranty, which is a statement made by the applicant that the applicant guarantees to be true.

---

7. How does the legal interpretation that statements made by applicants are generally representations instead of warranties protect policyowners?

____

____

____

It prevents the possible cancellation of their policies on the basis of technicalities.

OTHER SOURCES OF INSURABILITY INFORMATION

As you can see, the completed application provides an extensive amount of information about an insurance applicant. Usually the application itself offers enough information for the home office underwriter to evaluate the risk and make the decision whether or not to issue a policy. However, the older the applicant or the larger the risk to the company, the more diligent the home office underwriters will be. In some cases, they will research all sources of insurability information before judging and classifying the risk. Let's take a look at some of these other sources.

Medical Reports

An insurance company may require certain applicants to undergo a medical examination by a medical examiner. A *medical report* is based on the results of that examination.

Medical examinations and reports must be completed by a qualified person, but that person does not necessarily have to be a physician. Many companies accept reports completed by a paramedic or a registered nurse. Usually the applicant can select the physician or paramedic facility to perform the exam; insurers are also prepared to recommend paramedic facilities where the exam can be given. In almost all cases, the exam is paid for by the insurance company.

When completed, the medical report is forwarded to the insurance company, where it is reviewed by the company's medical director or a designated associate.

Medical Information Bureau (MIB)

Another source of insurability information is the *Medical Information Bureau*, a nonprofit, central information agency that was established by a number of insurance companies. Its purpose is to serve as an aid in the underwriting of life and health insurance. More specifically, the MIB was formed to help disclose pertinent underwriting information in those cases where an applicant either forgets or conceals such information or submits fraudulent information when applying for insurance.

As a central clearinghouse for information, the MIB really helps to hold down the cost of life and health insurance for all policyowners through the prevention of misrepresentation or fraud.

If a member company finds that an applicant has an impairment that is included in a list of specified health conditions, the company pledges to report the information to the MIB in the form of a code number. If the same applicant later applies to another member company for insurance, the home office underwriter can request information from the MIB and readily learn about the preexisting health problem. The information is available only to companies that belong to the MIB and may be used only for underwriting and claims purposes.

Each member company and its medical director sign a pledge that the rules and principles of the MIB will be followed. The rules require that applicants must be notified in writing that the insurance company may make a brief report on their health to the MIB. However, information as to whether or not a policy is issued is not sent to the MIB. Applicants must be advised that, if they should apply to another MIB company for coverage or if a claim is submitted to such a company, the MIB will supply any information in its files to that company, if requested.

If an applicant requests it, the MIB will arrange the disclosure of any information it may have about that individual. Medical information, however, will be given only to the individual's physician who can then best interpret the facts for the patient.

Inspection Reports

Inspection reports may be obtained by insurance companies on applicants who apply for significant amounts of health insurance (particularly noncancelable disability policies) or who represent questionable risks. These reports contain information about the prospective insureds that home office underwriters use to help determine the applicants' insurability. They include information that the agent generally is not in a position to obtain without assistance.

Companies order their inspection reports from investigative agencies, usually called "inspection services." Investigators or inspectors may interview employers, neighbors and associates of an applicant to gather information about the individual's habits, character, financial condition, occupation, health, home life, business life, etc.

These investigations must be carried on within the framework of the Fair Credit Reporting Act, as explained later in this chapter.

Credit Reports

Applicants who are poor credit risks may cause the insurance company to lose money if policies are issued to them. Insureds with poor credit ratings are likely to allow their policies to lapse within a short time—possibly even before a second premium is paid. An insurance company loses money on a policy that is quickly lapsed, because the money the insurer spent in acquiring the business cannot be recovered in a short time.

Thus, in many cases, *credit reports* obtained from a retail merchants' association or other source are a valuable underwriting tool. Home office underwriters usually refuse to insure applicants who have records of nonpayment of bills or who appear to be applying for more insurance than they can reasonably afford.

---

1. Moses, a 45-year-old business executive, applies for the maximum allowable amount of disability income insurance. The home office underwriters decide they need more information regarding Moses's business dealings, his character and financial condition. How can the underwriters obtain such information?

They can order an inspection report.

2. Why are applicants who are poor credit risks usually rejected by insurance companies?

If insured, such applicants generally would be quick to let their policies lapse, which could cause the insurers to lose money.

3. Medical examinations of health insurance applicants must be conducted by a licensed physician approved by the company.

   (True/False)

   False. Examinations must be done by a qualified person, whom the applicant may select.

---

4. What is the purpose of the Medical Information Bureau (MIB)?

   The MIB serves as an aid to underwriting life and health insurance for member companies.

---

5. Can MIB member companies report to the MIB on an applicant's health without first advising applicants that they may do so? Why or why not?

   No, because MIB rules require that applicants be notified in writing that such reports may be filed.

---

6. Kyle is turned down for disability income insurance by an MIB member company and wants to know what information the MIB has on file about his physical condition.

   Will the MIB honor Kyle's request to disclose that information?

   A. (Yes/No)

   Will the MIB release the information directly to Kyle?

   B. (Yes/No)

   To whom would the MIB disclose the requested information concerning Kyle and why?

   C.

   A. Yes

   B. No

   C. The information would be sent to Kyle's physician who can then interpret the medical data for him.

The Fair Credit Reporting Act

To protect the rights of consumers for whom an inspection report or credit report has been requested, Congress in 1970 enacted the *Fair Credit Re-*

porting Act. This law requires that an insurance applicant be notified in writing that:

1. a credit (or consumer) report has been requested and

2. the applicant may request to be advised of the nature and scope of the investigation.

As mentioned earlier, it is the agent's responsibility to obtain the applicant's signature on an appropriate disclosure form and explain to the applicant that an inspection report may be needed for underwriting purposes. In addition, the Fair Credit Act includes the following important requirements:

- The consumer must be provided with the names of all people contacted during the preceding six months for purposes of the report. People contacted who are associated with the consumer's place of employment must be identified as far back as two years.

- If, based on an inspection or consumer report, the insurer rejects an application, the company must provide the applicant with the name and address of the consumer reporting agency that supplied the report.

- If requested by the consumer, the consumer reporting agency—not the insurance company—must disclose the nature and substance of all information (except medical) contained in the consumer's file. Note that the file may be more extensive than the actual report provided to the insurer. The Fair Credit Act does *not* give consumers the right to see the actual report, although most reporting agencies do routinely provide copies of the report, if requested.

- If the applicant/consumer disagrees with the information in his or her file, he or she can file a statement giving his or her opinion on the issue.

■ PREMIUM RECEIPTS

Most applications for insurance will be accompanied by payment of the initial premium. For example, assume you have just closed a sale for a major medical policy. You have completed the application, obtained the necessary signatures and arranged—at least tentatively—for a time for the applicant's medical examination, if necessary. The applicant—let's call her Roselyn—hands you a check for the initial premium and you, in turn, execute a *receipt* for her. You then should explain what the receipt means.

A *conditional receipt* normally is given when the applicant pays the initial premium at the time the application for a health insurance policy is signed. This means the applicant and the company have formed what might be called a "conditional contract," one contingent upon conditions that existed at the time of application or when a later medical examination is completed.

You might explain the receipt to Roselyn in the following manner: "Provided the insurance company finds that as of now (or at the time of the medical exam, if one is needed) you qualify for the policy as it's applied for, your insurance protection begins right now—even though the policy has not been issued or delivered yet."

In issuing a conditional receipt, the company realizes that the applicant is taking a risk if coverage is delayed until the company acts on the application and the policy is issued and delivered. So when a qualified applicant pays the first premium with the application, the risk is taken from the person's shoulders and assumed by the company. The company's only requirement is that all the facts submitted and all investigative results are such that the company normally would have issued the policy at standard rates on the basis of the application as submitted.

Suppose that Roselyn, your applicant, is injured in an auto accident and admitted to the hospital a few days after you submitted her application with premium for the major medical policy to the company (no medical examination required). Later you receive her policy. Should you deliver the policy? Does Roselyn have coverage under the policy? The answer to both questions is "Yes." Roselyn qualified for the coverage as of the date of her application in accordance with the terms of the conditional receipt.

---

1. Complying with the Fair Credit Reporting Act involves disclosure being made to the

   A. reporting agency in writing.
   B. applicant in writing.

2. If requested to do so, the consumer reporting agency must provide the actual consumer report to the applicant.

   (True/False)

3. Bruce signs an application for a disability income policy and pays the initial premium later when the policy is delivered by the agent. Bruce becomes insured when

   A. he signs the application.
   B. he pays the initial premium.

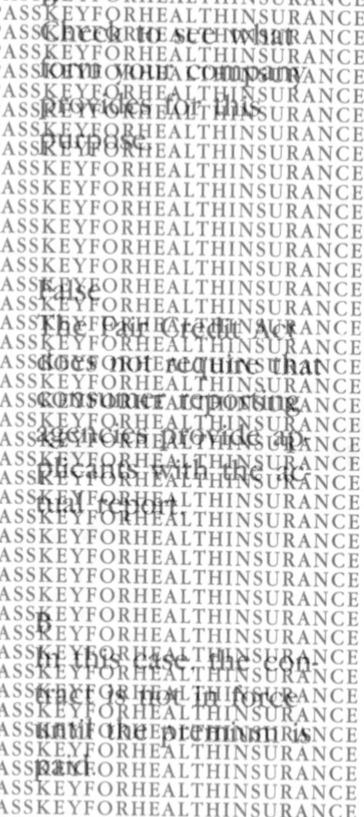

4. Sheila pays the initial premium and is given a conditional receipt at the time she signs an application for a major medical policy. A week later she undergoes a medical examination, as requested by the insurance company. The policy is issued as applied for and delivered by the agent. Therefore, Sheila had coverage from

   A. the date of the medical examination.
   B. the time she signed the application and paid the initial premium.

A. Issuance of the policy was contingent upon the results of the medical examination.

SUBMITTING THE APPLICATION

It is the agent's responsibility to submit signed applications for insurance, together with initial premium checks, if any, for home office underwriting without undue delay. Prior to submitting an application the agent should make sure all questions are answered and that the necessary signatures are in place on all forms.

If the proposed policy contains a death benefit, is the beneficiary listed correctly? Are the names of the insured and the policyowner, if other than the insured, spelled correctly? Does the agent's report include all available information that might affect the risk? Is the proper address shown where premium notices are to be sent? If any existing policy of the applicant's is to be replaced, have the required forms been completed? Is the new policy being applied for properly identified on the application? Has the premium amount been calculated correctly?

These and other details of the application should be given a final check to ascertain that all parts of the form have been properly completed. At that time, essential information regarding the application also should be recorded in the applicant file of the agent.

ASSURING DELIVERY OF POLICY TO CLIENT

From a legal standpoint, policy delivery may be accomplished without physically delivering the policy into the policyowner's possession. Practical considerations, however, dictate that agents should personally deliver policies to their clients.

"Constructive delivery," which satisfies the legal interpretation, is accomplished if the insurance company intentionally relinquishes all control over the policy and turns it over to someone acting for the policyowner, including the company's own agent. Mailing the policy to the agent for unconditional delivery to the policyowner also constitutes constructive delivery—even if the agent never actually delivers the policy. However, if the company instructs the agent not to deliver the policy unless the applicant is in good health, there is no constructive delivery.

Also, it should be noted that a client's possession of a policy does not establish delivery if all conditions have not been met. For example, a policy may be left with an applicant for inspection and an inspection receipt may be obtained to indicate that the policy is not in force during the inspection period or until the initial premium has been paid.

While constructive delivery is legal, personal delivery of policies by the agent is strongly recommended. Personal delivery contributes to the mutual benefit of both agent and policyowner. It affords the agent an opportunity to solidify the sale, build a solid relationship with the client and serve the client on a continuing basis.

---

1. By checking all applications carefully before submitting them to the home office, what might an agent avoid?

Possible delay in having a policy issued, going back to an applicant for additional information, possible rejection of an application, etc.

---

2. Which of the following cases indicates constructive delivery of a health insurance policy?

   A. Agent Tony receives a policy (issued as requested with premium paid) from his company for delivery to the insured, but has not yet delivered the policy.

   B. Agent Pete receives a policy (issued as requested with premium paid) from his company for delivery to the insured. Pete has instructions not to deliver the policy unless he determines that the insured is in good health.

A

In B, the company has made delivery conditional, so there is no constructive delivery.

---

3. Can you think of an additional agent advantage (other than those mentioned in the text) in delivering policies personally?

Laying the groundwork for future sales, obtaining referred leads, etc. (Your answer is acceptable.)

Explaining the Policy

Before delivering a policy, the agent should review it carefully to see that it has been issued as requested. If not, how is it different than the policy applied for? If there is a death benefit, is the beneficiary listed correctly? Is the premium the same as expected? Are there riders attached? Reviewing the policy in advance helps to catch possible errors and makes the delivery interview go more smoothly. Of course, the agent should call in advance for an appointment to deliver the policy.

By personally delivering a policy, the agent can explain the contract, its provisions, exclusions and riders. It is an ideal time for the agent to answer any questions that arise in the mind of the policyowner. This is part of the service due the policyowner and it helps to avert misunderstandings, policy returns and potential lapses. The agent also should reaffirm the insured's buying decision by stressing how the policy meets the specific objectives or needs of the client, i.e., how the policy protects the insured against today's high health care costs.

In cases of rated policies (those with higher premiums for substandard risks), the agent generally can emphasize reasons why the applicant has an even greater need for insurance protection because of the physical impairment or condition. It helps, too, if the applicant can be cautioned in advance that a policy may be rated, when that appears to be a probability.

Obtaining a Signed Statement of Insured's Good Health

In some instances, the initial premium will not be paid until the agent delivers the policy. Common company practice requires in such cases that the agent collect the premium and obtain a signed statement from the insured attesting to his or her continued good health before leaving the policy. The agent then is to submit the premium along with the signed statement of good health to the insurance company.

---

1. What is the advantage of reviewing a policy prior to delivering it to the policyowner?

____

____

____

____

2. An agent mails a policy to a policyowner who decides not to keep it. What might happen?

   A. The policyowner will call the agent to ask if the agent still thinks the policy is a good buy.

   B. The policy probably will be returned for a full refund.

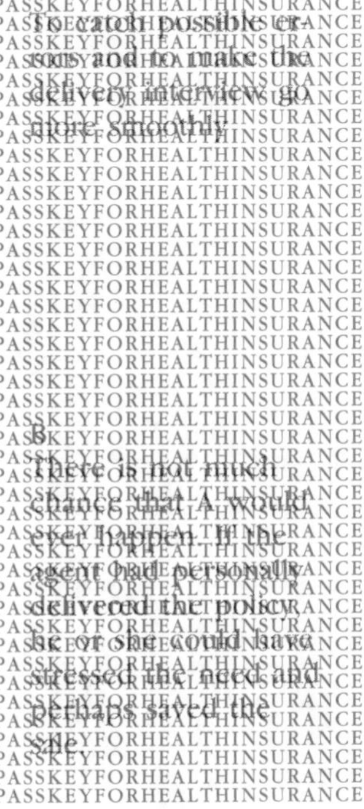

3. Barry is the insured in a newly issued major medical policy for which the premium has NOT been paid. When the agent calls at Barry's home to deliver the policy, he learns that Barry is in the hospital with injuries following an auto accident. In that case, the agent should

A. leave the policy even though he cannot collect the premium.
B. return the policy to the company with an explanation.

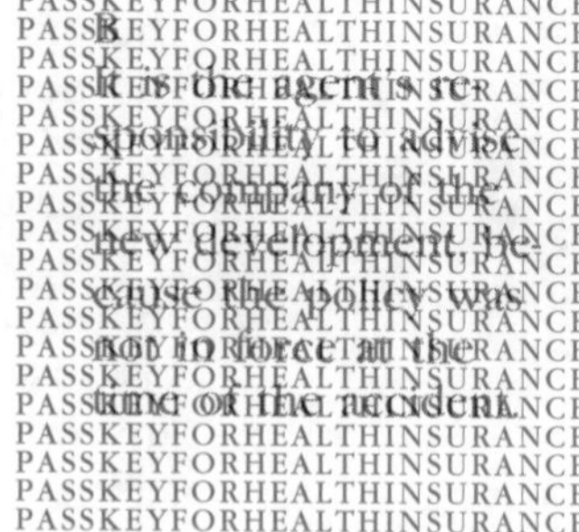

Progressive Quiz No. 3

(Text reference numbers are shown under each correct response in the red column.)

1. Bert obtained a health insurance policy from A-1 Health Insurance Company in June. In October, A-1 made changes in the wording of its health policy provisions. Which of the following provisions guarantees Bert that his policy cannot be changed?

   A. Legal actions
   B. Entire contract
   C. Time limit on certain defenses
   D. Conformity with state statutes

---

2. All of the following provisions must be included in a health insurance policy, EXCEPT:

   A. change of beneficiary.
   B. physical exam and autopsy.
   C. time payment of claims.
   D. misstatement of age.

---

3. Zack's health insurance policy has a 31-day grace period. While Zack is on vacation, he misses a premium payment. He returns home and mails it to the company two weeks late. Which of the following is true?

   A. His policy lapsed when his premium wasn't received on time, but if the company accepts his delinquent premium, his policy will be reinstated.
   B. His policy is still in force, but Zack may have to pay a penalty fee.
   C. The policy will remain in force, and Zack will not be penalized.
   D. None of the above

4. Which of the following types of risks are insurable?

   A. Pure risks
   B. Catastrophic risks
   C. Speculative risks
   D. All of the above

A (83)

---

5. After a policy is reinstated, losses resulting from sickness are covered only if the sickness occurs at least how many days after the reinstatement date?

   A. 7
   B. 10
   C. 14
   D. 12

B (72)

---

6. Under the time payment of claims provision, disability income payments are to be paid to eligible insureds not less frequently than

   A. quarterly.
   B. monthly.
   C. annually.
   D. weekly.

B (75)

---

7. Beulah is killed in an auto accident while she still owes an $80 premium on her $30,000 accident policy. Under the unpaid premiums provision, Beulah's beneficiary would receive a check for

   A. $29,840.
   B. $29,700.
   C. $30,000.
   D. $29,920.

D (80)

---

8. Which section of a health insurance policy specifies the conditions, times and circumstances under which the insured is NOT covered by the policy?

   A. Coinsurance provision
   B. Consideration clause
   C. Exclusions
   D. Insuring clause

C (80)

9. Diana, the beneficiary under her husband's AD&D policy, submits an accidental death claim on September 1, 1993, following his death; however, the company denies the claim on the basis that death was due to natural causes. She decides to talk to her attorney. When is the earliest she could bring legal action against the insurer?

   A. September 2, 1993
   B. October 1, 1993
   C. November 1, 1993
   D. September 1, 1994

---

10. Hubert, the insured, changes to a more hazardous job than the one he had when he applied for his disability income policy. According to the policy's change of occupation provision, what will happen when the insurer learns of his job change?

   A. A specified percentage penalty will be charged against the benefits.
   B. There is nothing the insurer can do as long as Hubert pays the premiums for the policy.
   C. Policy benefits will be reduced to an amount the premiums would have purchased originally based on the more hazardous occupation.
   D. The insurer has the right to cancel the policy unless Hubert pays an additional premium to cover the higher risk.

---

11. Which of the following types of health insurance policies prevents the company from changing the premium rate or modifying the coverage in any way?

   A. Optionally renewable
   B. Noncancelable
   C. Guaranteed renewable
   D. Cancelable

---

12. The wording of a uniform policy provision may be changed by a company in its policies only if

   A. the company's board of directors approves the change.
   B. the modified provision is not less favorable to the company.
   C. the Insurance Commissioner directs that it be changed.
   D. the provision, as changed, is not less favorable to the insured or beneficiaries.

13. Under the misstatement of age provision, what can a company do if it discovers that an insured gave a wrong age at the time of application?

    A. Cancel the policy
    B. Increase the premium
    C. Adjust the benefits
    D. Assess a penalty

---

14. Which of the following terms is associated with basic surgical expense policies?

    A. Relative value scale
    B. Corridor deductible
    C. Residual disability
    D. Accidental means

---

15. With disability income insurance, a policy that provides for a residual disability benefit ties benefit payments directly to the

    A. number of disability days.
    B. proportion of actual earnings lost.
    C. insured's average past earnings.
    D. insured's other disability insurance.

---

16. According to the notice of claim provision, a claimant normally must notify the insurance company of loss within how many days after the loss occurs?

    A. 10 days
    B. 20 days
    C. 35 days
    D. 40 days

---

17. The time limit on certain defenses provision typically provides that the policy cannot be contested after two years except for

    A. nonpayment of premiums.
    B. mental incompetence of the insured.
    C. fraudulent statements in the application.
    D. incomplete policy records.

18. Insured losses are covered immediately after a policy is reinstated when

A. the losses result from accidental injuries.
B. all back premiums have been paid.
C. hospitalization is required.
D. claim forms are submitted with proof of loss.

---

19. Under the claims forms provision, a company MUST furnish the insured with such forms within how many days after receiving a notice of claim?

A. 30
B. 21
C. 15
D. 10

---

20. The consideration clause pertains directly to which of the following?

A. Medical examination and agent's report
B. Exclusions and endorsements
C. Premium payment and application
D. Underwriting recommendations

---

21. Bernard has total hospital expenses of $9,200. His major medical policy includes a $200 deductible and an 80/20 coinsurance provision. Of the total expenses, how much will Bernard have to pay?

A. $7,400
B. $4,500
C. $2,040
D. $2,000

---

22. An application includes all of the following, EXCEPT:

A. Part 1—General.
B. Part 2—Medical.
C. Part 3—Credit History.
D. agent's report.

23. A signed statement of good health is required when D (103)

  A. the applicant submits the application and first premium.
  B. the insured is released from the hospital after a covered illness.
  C. the insured applies for partial disability benefits.
  D. the initial premium is paid at the time the policy is delivered.

---

24. The program that will offer Medicare beneficiaries a variety of health coverage alternatives, each of which must include currently-covered Medicare services, is known as the C (51)

  A. Medicare Savings Account program.
  B. Medical Savings Account program.
  C. MedicarePlus Choice program.
  D. Medicare Part B program.

---

25. Irving has been totally disabled and receiving disability income benefits for 36 months. In accordance with the notice of claim provision in his policy, Irving normally would have to submit proof of loss A (15)

  A. every six months.
  B. one time only.
  C. once a year.
  D. every three months.

---

26. The following terms relate directly to beneficiaries, EXCEPT: D (16)

  A. tertiary.
  B. contingent.
  C. primary.
  D. executor.

---

27. All of the following statements concerning the Fair Credit Reporting Act are correct, EXCEPT: C (88, 89)

  A. It relates to investigative reports on applicants, which are frequently needed for underwriting purposes.
  B. The agent is required to obtain the applicant's signature on an appropriate disclosure form.
  C. It is a state law enforced by all state insurance departments.
  D. The law gives applicants the right to challenge the validity of information about themselves that is included in a consumer report.

28. If a beneficiary were third in line to receive the death benefits from an accident policy, he or she could rightfully be described as a

A. final beneficiary.
B. triad beneficiary.
C. secondary beneficiary.
D. tertiary beneficiary.

---

29. Clara pays the initial premium and is given a conditional receipt when she signs an application for a major medical policy. A week later the policy is issued as applied for and delivered by the agent. Therefore, Clara had coverage from the date

A. the policy was issued.
B. she signed the application and paid the initial premium.
C. the policy was delivered to her by the agent.
D. the policy was submitted to the insurer.

---

30. You interviewed applicant Lois on January 5, 1998, and her date of birth is April 25, 1964. If premiums were based on her nearest birthday for insurance purposes, what would Lois's age be listed as on the application?

A. 32
B. 33
C. 34
D. 35

---

31. A medical report MUST be completed by

A. the agent.
B. a qualified medical person.
C. the applicant's physician.
D. the insurer's medical director.

---

32. Which kind of policy assures renewability up to a specific age of the insured, although the company reserves the right to change the premium rate on a class basis?

A. Noncancelable
B. Conditionally renewable
C. Guaranteed renewable
D. Optionally renewable

33. The agent's report is part of which document?

A. Inspection report
B. Authorization form
C. Fair credit disclosure
D. Application

---

34. Which of the following terms relates to the elective indemnity provision?

A. Policy conversion
B. Reimbursement for expenses
C. Lump-sum benefit payment
D. Long-term disability

---

35. Capital sum is a term that applies to which kind of health insurance?

A. Disability income
B. Major medical
C. Accidental death and dismemberment
D. Business overhead expense

---

36. All of the following are coverages that may be provided under a long-term care policy, EXCEPT:

A. intensive care.
B. custodial care.
C. residential care.
D. skilled nursing care.

10

Health Insurance Underwriting and Premiums

Health insurers increasingly find themselves in a tough position. The high cost of medical care requires them to charge premiums that cover the correspondingly high level of health insurance claims, and yet public sentiment and even competition from within the industry pressure companies to keep rates as low as possible. Health insurers are reacting to these conflicting forces by tightening their underwriting requirements—becoming more selective in the risks they will accept—and controlling claim costs through innovative measures.

In the previous chapter we covered the first step in the underwriting process: the completion and submission of the application. In this chapter we continue to look at the important topic of health insurance underwriting by examining the second stage in the process—how the home office underwriters evaluate a risk. We will also look at the emerging issues of cost control and case management.

THE PURPOSE OF UNDERWRITING

Underwriting is the process of reviewing the many characteristics that make up the risk profile of an applicant to determine if the applicant is insurable and at what rate. Underwriting is also known as *risk selection*.

Each insurer sets its own standards as to what constitutes an insurable risk versus an uninsurable risk, just as each insurer determines the premium rates it will charge its policyowners. Every applicant for a health insurance policy—whether it's an individual or a group—is carefully reviewed by a company underwriter to determine if the applicant meets the standards established by the insurer to qualify for the coverage being sought.

For every applicant, the underwriter must address these questions:

1. "Is there insurable interest?"
2. "Is the applicant insurable?"
3. "If so, at what premium rate?"

■ INSURABLE INTEREST

One of the first areas an insurance company reviews is the question of who has a legal *insurable interest* in the individual to be insured. In health insurance, an insurable interest exists if the applicant is in a position to suffer a loss should the insured incur medical expenses or be unable to work. In all cases, individuals are presumed to have an insurable interest in themselves. Questions arise when the applicant and the insured are not the same person.

One person has a legal insurable interest in the good health of another if they are related by marriage. However, aunt or uncle, niece, nephew, or cousin does not qualify by reason of the relationship alone. An insurable interest may also exist if two people have a business relationship of such nature that the person to be benefited by the insurance contract may reasonably expect to benefit from the continuance of the good health of the insured, or to suffer a loss upon its premature termination.

Policies obtained by a person not having an insurable interest in the life or good health of the insured are not enforceable because they are considered contrary to public policy.

Once the issue of insurable interest has been established, the underwriter must determine whether the applicant is insurable and at what premium. The answers to these questions lie in the risk profile the applicant represents to the insurer.

■ RISK FACTORS IN HEALTH INSURANCE

The factors that determine an individual's risk profile are evaluated carefully by a health insurance underwriter. Unlike life insurance, where there will be but one claim per each insured, health insurance by its very nature may involve multiple claims per insured. Thus, the classification of health insurance risks is critically important. Data accumulated over the years by insurance companies in underwriting health insurance serves as the primary basis for classifying risks.

Classifying risks for health insurance is more complex than simply deciding whether a risk is acceptable or not acceptable. The *degree of risk* is highly important when considering the probable future health of an individual applicant and the amount of premium to be charged. So home office underwriters are charged with the responsibility of scrutinizing health insurance applications with special care.

Many factors are reviewed in underwriting health insurance policies. Three of the most important factors are:

1. physical condition,
2. moral hazards and
3. occupation.

Physical Condition

An applicant's present physical condition is of primary importance when evaluating health risks. For example, the underwriter must know whether the individual has been treated for any chronic conditions. Any physical impairments of the applicant are checked out carefully. Hernias or ulcers, for example, may require surgical correction or treatment in the future and, thereby, represent an additional risk. Persons with an unusual body build, including extreme obesity or height, also represent higher risks to the insurer.

Moral Hazards

The habits or life-styles of applicants also can flash warning signals that there may be additional risk for the insurer. Personalities and attitudes may draw attention in the underwriting process. Excessive drinking and the use of drugs represent serious moral hazards. Applicants who are seen as accident-prone or potential malingerers (feigning a continuing disability in order to collect benefits) likewise might be heavy risks, particularly those applying for disability income insurance. Other signals of high moral hazard can be a poor credit rating or dishonest business practices.

Occupation

A third significant factor involved with health insurance risks is the applicant's occupation. This is because occupation has a direct bearing on both the *probability of disability* and the *average severity of disability*.

Experience shows that disability benefit costs for insurers can vary considerably from occupation to occupation. There is little physical risk associated with professional persons, office managers or office workers, but occupations involving heavy machinery, strong chemicals or high electrical voltage, for example, represent a high degree of risk for the insurer.

Jobs requiring manual labor can also influence the length of recuperation periods for disabled workers and how soon they can return to work. Further, the sporadic nature of employment in certain occupations can have a bearing on claim costs because the number and size of such claims tend to rise when insureds are unemployed.

Some occupations involve irregular hours, uncertain earnings and, in some cases, not even a definite place of business—all of which contribute to higher risks for insurers. Examples are entertainers and authors, who generally do not have regular business hours. In addition, disability benefit costs to insurers also can be influenced by the social and economic character of persons in some occupational classifications.

For underwriting purposes, many insurers divide occupations into five classes: AAA, AA, A, B and C. The five classes range from the top classification (AAA), which includes professional and office workers, to more hazardous occupations in the lower (B and C) classes. Persons in a few occupations, such as steeplejacks, airplane test pilots or stunt flyers usually are uninsurable.

The applicant's occupation and the renewability factor of a policy also are connected from an underwriting standpoint. According to the change of occupation provision, if the insured changes to a less hazardous job, the insurer will return any excess unearned premium; however, if the change is to a more hazardous occupation, the benefits are reduced proportionately and the premium remains the same. The change of occupation clause generally is not included in guaranteed renewable policies, especially long-term disability policies. Noncancelable policies are sold only to individuals in the higher occupational classes in which change of occupation is seldom a factor. Limited and industrial health policies usually are available at standard rates for all occupations, except those excluded by specific policy provisions.

---

1. All of the following are primary risk factors in underwriting individual health insurance policies, EXCEPT:

   A. geographical location.
   B. moral hazard.
   C. occupation.
   D. physical condition.

Geographical location is not a primary risk factor.

---

2. Winston has been treated periodically for ulcers. Why would this pose an extra risk if Winston applies for health insurance?

   ____

Because his ulcer problem might require surgery in the future or contribute to recurring disability.

---

3. Indicate which type of hazard the following individuals would represent to a home office underwriter:

   Cora has changed jobs five times in the last two years.
   A. (physical/moral)
   Burl is 60 pounds overweight, loves to eat fattening foods, but appears to have no other bad habits.
   B. (physical/moral)
   Hugh has been arrested twice for drunken driving in the last year and has a reputation for being a heavy drinker.
   C. (physical/moral)

A. moral
B. physical
C. moral (perhaps also physical, but definitely a moral hazard)

---

4. Who would represent a lower disability risk to an insurance company?

   A. Jack, an office manager
   B. John, a foreman in a farm equipment factory

A
John would be the higher risk because he works around heavy equipment.

5. If both Lola and Ruby experience identical injuries, who would probably be off work the longest based on their occupational duties?

   A. Lola, whose job requires manual labor in a manufacturing plant
   B. Ruby, whose duties as an office supervisor do not require manual labor

A
Jobs involving manual labor usually require longer periods of recuperation.

---

6. Based on occupations, which of the following would be classified as uninsurable?

   A. Kirk, a test pilot for Lockfield Aircraft
   B. Julian, superintendent of a small motor manufacturing plant

A
Test pilots generally are uninsurable.

---

7. How does the change of occupation provision, when used, protect both the insured and the company?

   ____

   ____

   ____

   ____

   ____

If the insured changes to a less hazardous job, any excess unearned premium is returned; if the change is to a more hazardous job, the benefits are reduced proportionately and the premium remains the same.

---

8. John's first cousin, Jim, can have a legal insurable interest in the good health and life of John solely based on the fact that they are related.

   (True/False)

False
Jim must be in a position to suffer a loss should John become ill or disabled.

Other Risk Factors

Additional health insurance risk factors include the applicant's age, sex, medical and family history and avocations.

Age

Generally, the older the applicant, the higher the risk he or she represents. Most individual health insurance policies limit the coverage to a specified age such as 60 or 65 (although some lifetime coverages are available).

Sex

An applicant's sex is also an underwriting consideration. Men show a lower rate of disability than women, except at the upper ages.

History

An applicant's medical history may point to the possibility of a recurrence of a certain health condition. Likewise, an applicant's family history may reflect a tendency he or she has toward certain medical conditions or health impairments.

Avocations

Certain hobbies an applicant may have—such as skydiving or mountain climbing—may increase his or her risk to the insurer. An applicant's avocations are carefully evaluated and waivers may be needed.

■ CLASSIFICATION OF APPLICANTS

Once an underwriter has reviewed the various risk factors associated with an individual applicant and has measured them against the company's underwriting standards, there are four ways to classify the applicant and his or her request for health coverage:

- a standard risk,
- a preferred risk,
- an uninsurable risk or
- a substandard risk.

Standard, Preferred and Uninsurable Risks

Standard risk applicants are usually issued a policy at standard terms and rates. *Preferred risk* premium rates are generally lower than standard risk rates, reflecting the fact that people in this class have a better-than-standard risk profile.

Uninsurable applicants are usually rejected and denied coverage. But, with years of experience to guide them, insurers today reject a smaller percentage of applicants for health insurance than in the past.

Substandard Risks

Substandard risk applicants—those who pose a higher-than-average risk for one or more reasons—are treated differently. Substandard applicants may represent a very low risk on moral and occupational considerations and still pose a high risk because of their physical condition. Other substandard applicants may be in top physical condition, but work at a hazardous occupation. Besides outright rejection, there are three techniques commonly used by insurers in issuing health insurance policies to substandard risks:

1. attaching an exclusion (or impairment) rider or waiver to a policy,
2. charging an extra premium or
3. limiting the type of policy.

Exclusion or impairment riders rule out coverage for losses resulting from chronic conditions or physical impairments. With the questionable risks excluded, policies then are issued at standard rates. When some occupational hazard exists, applicants may be charged an extra premium to compensate for the additional risk. The same may be true when applicants are overweight or show signs of high blood pressure, etc. Extra premiums may be charged only for a few years or on a permanent basis.

Another method of handling substandard risks is to modify the type of policy requested in some manner. For example, a policy may exclude all sickness or a specific kind of sickness, but cover all losses due to accidental injuries. In other cases, a policy may provide protection for a lower amount than requested or provide a shorter benefit period. Or a provision may be inserted calling for a longer waiting period than indicated in the application.

Overall, only a small percentage of applicants are classified as substandard risks.

---

1. At younger ages, which group shows a lower disability rate?

   A. Females
   B. Males

2. Which of the following are health insurance risk factors?

   Sex

   A. (Yes/No)

   Number of brothers and sisters

   B. (Yes/No)

   Age

   C. (Yes/No)

   Type of residence

   D. (Yes/No)

   Family history

   E. (Yes/No)

3. Jack qualifies for a disability income policy at standard rates, except he drives race cars on weekends as a hobby. What is the insurer likely to do?

   A. Reject the application because of Jack's car racing hobby.
   B. Issue the policy, but attach a waiver to exclude any loss resulting from injuries Jack might receive in connection with car racing.

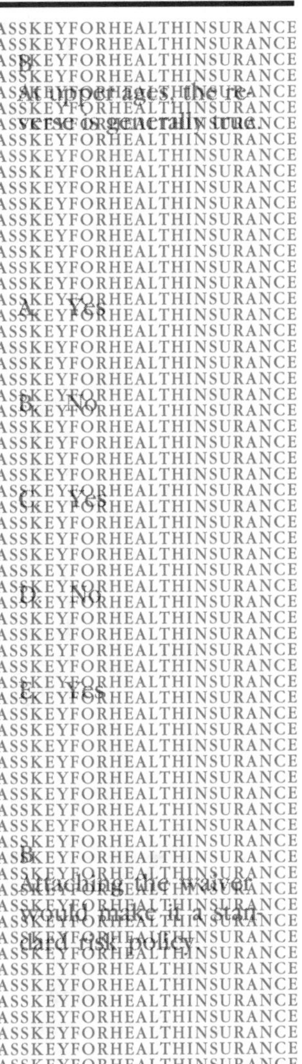

B
At upper ages, the reverse is generally true.
A. Yes
B. No
C. Yes
D. No
E. Yes
B
Attaching the waiver would make it a standard risk policy.

HEALTH INSURANCE PREMIUM FACTORS

Rate-making for health insurance policies is complex, primarily because it involves more than one type of benefit. The average frequency of covered health insurance losses further complicates premium computations. There are a number of variables—primary and secondary—all insurers take into account when determining the premium rate for a particular health insurance product.

Primary Premium Factors

At the base level, there are three primary factors that affect health insurance premiums: *morbidity, interest* and *expenses.* Note how closely these correspond to basic life insurance premium factors, except that morbidity is substituted for mortality.

Morbidity

You will recall from Chapter 1 that *morbidity* is the expected incidence of sickness or disability within a given age group during a given period of time. Morbidity statistics also reveal the average duration of disability, so insurers can approximate not only how many in a large group will become disabled, but how long the disabilities can be expected to last.

Morbidity statistics, which are available to companies offering health insurance, have been collected over many, many years and reflect the disabilities of hundreds of thousands of people. They are compiled into morbidity tables.

Interest

Interest is a major element in establishing health insurance premiums. A large portion of every premium received is invested to earn interest. The interest earnings reduce the premium amount that otherwise would be required from policyowners.

Expenses

Every business has *expenses* that must be paid and the insurance business is no different. Each health insurance policy an insurer issues must carry its proportionate share of the costs for employees' salaries, agents' commissions, utilities, rent or mortgage payments, maintenance costs, supplies and other administrative expenses.

---

1. Agent commissions can be considered a part of which premium factor?

   A. Interest factor
   B. Expense factor

B

Commissions are a part of the company's expenses taken into account in computing premiums.

2. How does interest help to reduce premium rates?

A portion of each premium is invested, so interest earnings help to reduce premium rates, making it possible for policyowners to pay lower premiums than would otherwise be necessary.

3. Why is establishing premium rates complicated for health insurance?

Because it involves various kinds of benefits and frequent claims per policy.

4. Which of the following is a major premium factor for health insurance?

A. Morbidity statistics
B. Mortality statistics

A Insurers rely on morbidity statistics to gauge the average number and duration of disabilities at various age levels each year.

Secondary Premium Factors

In addition to these three primary factors, the actual rate assigned to a specific health policy by the underwriter depends on several other factors, including the benefits provided under the policy, past claims experience, the age and sex of the insured and the insured's occupation and hobbies.

Benefits

A health insurance policy may offer a specific type of benefit or a variety of *benefits*. For example, a hospital expense-only policy offers benefits to cover just hospitalization expenses, while a comprehensive major medical policy covers a much broader range of medical expenses. The number and kinds of benefits provided by a policy affect the premium rate.

Even if two policies provide identical types of benefits, the amount of protection or benefits in one policy may be higher than in another. So, the greater the benefits, the higher the premium, or, to state it another way, the greater the risk to the company, the higher the premium.

Claims Experience

Before realistic premium rates can be established for health insurance, the insurer must know what can be expected as to the dollar amount of the future claims. The most practical way to estimate the cost of future claims is to rely on claims tables based on past *claims experience.*

For example, experience tables have been constructed for hospital expenses based on the amounts paid out in the past for the same types of expenses. Such tables, along with an added factor to account for rising hospital costs, enable companies to estimate the average amounts of future hospital expenses. Similarly, experience tables have been developed for surgical benefits, covering various kinds of surgery based on past experience. The same procedure is followed to estimate average claims expected in the future for other medical expenses. Such tables must be adjusted periodically, of course, to reflect more recent experience.

Age and Sex of the Insured

As discussed earlier, experience has shown that health insurance claims costs tend to increase as the *age* of the insured increases. For any given coverage, the older the insured, the higher the applicable premium rate.

Also, disabilities among women under age 55, on the average, have a greater frequency and longer duration than among men, so female premium rates for certain coverages are higher than the premium rates for males. At the older ages, however, that is generally not true.

Occupation and Hobbies

Because some types of work are more hazardous than others, health insurance premium rates may be affected by the insured's *occupation.* If an insured's occupation indicates a higher than normal risk to the company, the policy may carry an extra premium charge. (Insurers establish their own occupational classifications, which represent another element in the premium structure.) The same concept holds true for any dangerous *hobbies* in which the insured may participate.

Policy Fees

In quoting premiums to prospects, agents quickly learn that a *policy fee,* or a charge by some similar name, is to be included in all premium quotations.

The policy fee, which is payable annually, is a "per policy charge" to cover a portion of the expense to the company in issuing a policy. For example, the basic premium for a health insurance policy might be figured as $430, If the policy fee to be added were $20, the annual premium to be paid by the policyowner would be $450.

1. On what do insurers base their cost estimates of future health insurance claims?

Claims tables of past claims experience

2. Claims experience tables are adjusted periodically to reflect more recent experience.

(True/False)

True. Updating gives the underwriter the most credible data.

3. Milton, age 30, and William, age 38, both qualify for the same amount of disability income insurance with the same company. Other things being equal, who will pay the higher premium?

A. Milton
B. William

B. The older the insured, the higher the premium rate.

4. In question No. 3, Milton and William are an example demonstrating that _____ is a definite premium factor.

age

5. Why are health insurance premiums for women under age 55 generally higher than for men of comparable ages?

Because disabilities among such women, on the average, occur with greater frequency and last longer than for their male counterparts.

6. Which of the following factors would affect a health policy's premium rate?

I. Age of the insured
II. Occupation of the insured
III. Type of benefit provided
IV. The company's expense factor

A. I and II only
B. III only
C. IV only
D. I, II, III and IV

D. I through IV would all affect a health policy's premiums.

7. Is "policy fee" another term for policy premium? Explain.

No, the policy fee is part of the premium. Some companies charge a policy fee on a per policy basis, payable annually, to cover part of the company's expense in issuing the policy.

COST CONTAINMENT

Insurers face a complex dilemma: how to reduce health claims experience so that health insurance, especially medical expense insurance, remains affordable. While there is little direct influence insurers can exert over the medical profession to contain the cost of medical care, there are important actions insurers themselves can take toward the important goal of *cost containment.*

Managed Care

The term *managed care*, as used in this text, refers to a *system* of delivering health care and health care services. It is characterized by:

- selective contracting with efficient and effective health care professionals and organizations;
- financial incentives for members to use providers and procedures approved by the plan;
- controlled hospital admissions and lengths of stay;
- use of utilization management tools such as utilization review (described below) to achieve better outcomes and better case management; and
- emphasis on disease prevention and health promotion programs.

These characteristics have led to lower health care costs for *managed care organizations* (MCOs) than for traditional indemnity plans. We will discuss MCOs such as *health maintenance organizations* (HMOs) and *preferred provider organizations* (PPOs) in Chapter 13.

Policy Design

The design or structure of a policy and its provisions can have an impact on an insurer's cost containment efforts. A higher deductible will help limit claims, for example, and in fact the "average" deductible has increased in recent years. Whereas the typical deductible was $100 for an individual and $300 for a family just a few years ago, it is more common now to find deductibles in the $300 to $500 range for an individual and $900 or higher for a family. As we have seen in previous chapters, coinsurance is another important means of sharing the cost of medical care between the insured and the insurer. Shortened benefit periods can also prove beneficial from a cost containment standpoint, in that they can reduce the tendency some people have to seek medical attention for a condition that has long since been resolved.

Medical Cost Management

Medical cost management is being widely recognized and applauded as the most promising means of controlling claims expenses. Basically, it is the process of controlling how policyowners utilize their policies. There are four general approaches insurers use for cost management:

1. mandatory second opinions,
2. precertification review,
3. ambulatory surgery and
4. case management/utilization review.

Mandatory Second Opinions

In an effort to reduce unnecessary surgical operations, many health policies today contain a provision requiring the insured to obtain a *second opinion* before receiving non-life-threatening surgery. Benefits are often reduced if a second opinion is not obtained.

Precertification Review

To control the number and size of hospital claims, many policies now require policyowners to obtain approval from the insurer before entering a hospital on a nonemergency basis. Even if the admission was on an emergency basis, most policies with this type of provision require the insured to notify the insurer within a short period of time (usually 24 hours) after being admitted. The insurer will then determine how much of the hospital stay it will cover, depending on the reason for the admission. If the insured wants to stay longer, the additional expense will be the responsibility of the insured, not the insurer.

Ambulatory Surgery

The advances in medicine now permit many surgical procedures to be performed on an "outpatient" basis (also known as *ambulatory surgery*) where once an overnight hospital stay was required. To encourage insureds to utilize less expensive outpatient care, many policies offer some sort of inducement. For example, a policy may waive the deductible or coinsurance if the policyowner elects to be treated on an outpatient basis rather than as an admitted patient.

Case Management/Utilization Review

Case management or *utilization review,* as referred to here, involves a specialist within the insurance company, such as a registered nurse, who reviews a potentially large claim as it develops to discuss treatment alternatives with the insured. For example, the insured's policy might state that treatment for a kidney ailment can only be performed in a hospital or registered hemodialysis center. However, if it makes economic sense to the insurer—and practical sense to the insured—to have treatments conducted at the insured's home, the case manager might negotiate with the insured to allow treatment to be performed at home as long as certain conditions are met.

The purpose of these procedures is to let the insurer take an active role in the management of what could potentially become a very expensive claim.

---

1. The purpose of medical cost management is to

   A. influence hospital charges and doctors' fees.
   B. discourage individuals from utilizing health care services.
   C. control health claims expenses.
   D. All of the above

C. Cost containment measures have been instituted to control claims expenses.

---

2. What are four cost management approaches insurers have taken to control claims expenses?

   1. ______
   2. ______
   3. ______
   4. ______

1. Mandatory second opinions
2. Precertification review
3. Case management
4. Ambulatory surgery
(May be in any order.)

---

3. What three aspects of policy structure or design can be used to help control claims costs?

   1. ______
   2. ______
   3. ______

1. High deductibles
2. Coinsurance
3. Shorter benefit periods
(May be in any order.)

---

4. Which cost containment approach involves a specialist reviewing a claim as it develops?

   ______

Case management

5. Examples of managed care organizations (MCOs) include __________ and __________.

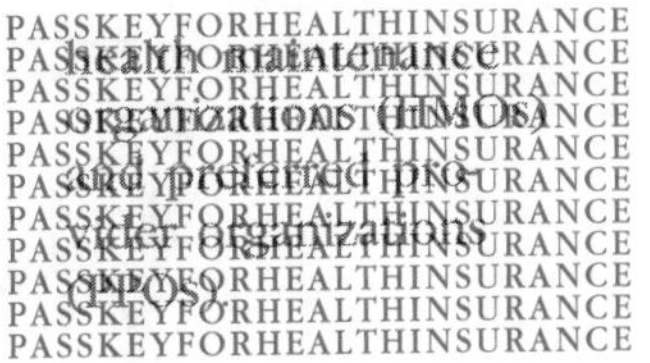

11

Group Health Insurance

Most of our discussion of health and accident insurance so far has focused on individual policies. However, the majority of Americans obtain their health insurance coverage through a group plan. Every year employers contribute billions of dollars for health insurance benefits for their employees. Students of health insurance should be familiar with the unique characteristics of this type of insurance protection.

NATURE OF GROUP HEALTH INSURANCE

Group health is a plan of insurance that an employer (or other eligible group sponsor) provides for its employees. The basic principle of group insurance is that insurance coverage for a number of people is provided under a single policy. The contract for coverage is between the insurance company and the employer, and a *master policy* is issued to the employer. The individual insureds covered by the policy are not given separate policies; instead, they receive *certificates of insurance* and an outline or booklet that describes their benefits. Generally speaking, the benefits provided under a group health plan are more extensive than those provided under an individual health plan, and the cost to the individual insured is lower. Group health plans typically also have higher benefit maximums and lower deductibles.

Characteristics of Group Health Insurance

The characteristics of group health insurance include eligibility standards for groups and for individuals within the groups, method of premium payments (contributory vs. noncontributory), lower cost, predetermined benefits, underwriting practices, conversion privileges, portability and preexisting conditions provisions. Let's briefly review each.

Eligible Groups

To qualify for group health coverage, a group must be a "natural group." This means it must have been formed for some reason other than to obtain insurance. Qualifying groups include employers, labor unions, trade associations,* creditor-debtor groups, lodges and the like.

State laws specify the minimum number of persons to be covered under a group policy. One state may stipulate 15 persons as a minimum number, while another state may require a minimum of ten. (Ten lives is the most typical minimum requirement.)

Some small businesses do not have enough employees to form a group large enough to qualify for group insurance. Insurance companies often permit small organizations of a similar nature to join together for group health coverage thereby forming a group of acceptable size. These groups are called *multiple employer trusts* (METs). (METs are discussed in greater detail in Chapter 13.)

Individual Eligibility

Most group health plans commonly impose a set of eligibility requirements that must be met before an individual member is eligible to participate in the group plan. It is common to find the following requirements:

- minimum of one to three months' employment service; and
- full-time employment status.

However, HIPAA prohibits a group health plan from establishing eligibility rules based solely on the following factors:

- health status;
- medical condition (physical or mental);
- claims experience;
- receipt of health care;
- medical history;
- genetic information;
- evidence of insurability; or
- disability.

With certain exceptions and limits, group health plans that are subject to HIPAA but do not comply with its provisions are subject to a penalty of $100 for each affected individual for every day they are not in compliance.

An insured group may consist of all employees working for an employer. But the group need not include all of the employees; a specific class or

---

* An association group must have been in existence for a minimum period of time, usually two years.

classes of employees within a company may be covered in a group plan, as long as employees are not excluded due to age, sex or race. Classes of employees to be insured may be defined in various ways, such as by:

- location—plant, office or city;
- pay—hourly, weekly or monthly;
- duties—executives, clerical or factory workers;
- department—sales, accounting or manufacturing; or
- length of service—one to four years, six to nine years or over ten years.

To illustrate, imagine a company in which the office supervisors and employees constitute a group covered by one group health plan and the plant workers who are excluded from *that* group, have their own group health insurance with somewhat different benefits. In very large companies, there may be several different groups, each having its own distinctive health plan.

Contributory vs. Noncontributory

Group health plans may be *contributory* or *noncontributory*. If the employer pays the entire premium, the plan is noncontributory; if the employees share a portion of the premium, it is contributory. Almost universally, noncontributory group health plans require 100 percent participation by eligible members, whereas contributory group health plans require participation by 75 percent of eligible members. The reason for these minimum participation requirements is to protect the insurer against adverse selection and to keep administrative expenses in line with coverage units.

---

1. Any size group can qualify for group health insurance.

   (True/False)

False

State laws specify a minimum number of persons to be covered, typically ten people.

2. Tucker Fabric Company, which has 1,200 employees, is considering a group health insurance plan. Must all the company's employees be declared eligible for coverage under the plan?

   (Yes/No)

No

The employer can specify specific classes of employees to be insured.

3. Rules used to determine whether an individual is eligible to participate in a group health insurance plan may be based on the individual's

   A. full-time employment status.
   B. medical history.

---

4. Cape Cod Fish Company establishes a group health insurance plan for its employees. Participating employees would each receive a

   A. master policy.
   B. certificate of insurance.

---

5. Each participating Cape Cod employee pays $50 per month toward the group health insurance premium and the company pays the balance of the premium.

   A. With that arrangement, the plan is called ______ .
   B. If Cape Cod paid the entire premium, the group health insurance plan would be termed ______ and ______ percent of eligible employees would be required to participate.

Lower Cost

Benefit for benefit, the cost of insuring an individual under a group health plan is less than the cost of insurance under an individual plan. This is because the administrative and selling expenses involved with group plans are far less.

Predetermined Benefits

Another characteristic of group health plans is that the benefits provided to individual insureds are *predetermined* by the employer in conjunction with the insurer's benefit schedules and coverage limits. For example, group disability benefits are tied to a position or earnings schedule, as are accidental death and dismemberment benefits.

Underwriting Practices

Generally speaking, the approach insurers take in underwriting group health plans is to *evaluate the group as a whole,* rather than evaluating individuals within the group. Based on the group's risk profile, which is measured against the insurer's selection standards, the group is either accepted or rejected in its entirety.

However, there are some changes taking place with regard to underwriting group medical expense plans, especially for small groups. Whereas for large group medical plans it is common to accept all currently eligible members and new members coming into the group, this is not necessarily true any longer for smaller groups. In smaller groups the presence of even one "bad risk" can have a significant impact on the claims experience of the group. Consequently, most insurers today reserve the right to engage in *individual underwriting* to some degree with groups they insure.

As the term implies, individual underwriting is the process of reviewing a group member's individual risk profile. Most commonly this is done on two occasions: when a group is first taken on by an insurer and when a group member (e.g., an employee) tries to enter the plan after initially electing not to participate. In the latter case, the underwriter's objective is to reduce the risk of adverse selection. In the former case, individual underwriting is only done on members for whom the initial application indicates a potential risk problem (such as a preexisting condition). If the member is found to represent too great a risk, the insurer often retains the right to exclude the member from participation in the plan, charge an increased premium or exclude coverage for the specified condition. It is important to note that if an insurer does reserve this right of individual underwriting, most states require the insurer to explain, in the policy, how it will exercise this right.

Rarely is an entire group rejected on the basis of one bad risk, unless the group is very small.

---

1. Group health plans typically provide less extensive benefits than individual health plans.

   (True/False)

2. Stockdone Chemical Company wishes to establish a group disability plan that ties benefits to an employee's earnings. Is this permissible?

   (Yes/No)

3. Which of the following statements is true regarding group health underwriting?

   A. Insurers typically look at individuals in a group when underwriting group health insurance.
   B. Insurers typically look at the group as a whole when underwriting group health insurance.

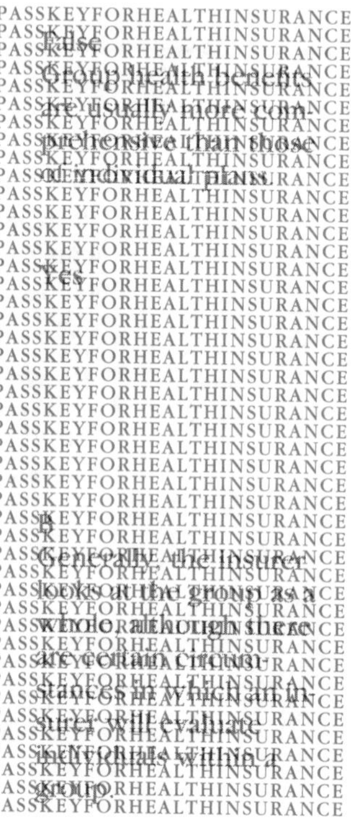

4. Under what two circumstances might an insurer engage in individual underwriting with a health insurance group?

1. ____

____

2. ____

____

1. When a new group is being insured and a member's application indicates potential risk.
2. When a member tries to enter the plan after initially electing not to participate.
(May be in any order.)

Conversion Privileges

Group health plans that provide medical expense coverage universally contain a *conversion privilege* for individual insureds, which allows them to convert their group coverage to an individual medical expense policy with the same insurer, if and when they leave their employment. Insurers are permitted to evaluate the individual and charge the appropriate premium, be it a standard rate or substandard rate; however, an individual cannot be denied coverage, even if he or she has become uninsurable.

The conversion privilege must be exercised within a given period of time, usually 30 or 31 days, depending on the state. During this time, the individual remains insured under the group plan, whether or not a conversion ultimately takes place. Conversion privileges generally are reserved for those who were active in the group plan during the preceding three months.

Portability

HIPAA provides that all employees are entitled to keep their health coverage when they switch or lose their jobs. This measure is effective for group health insurance plan years beginning July 1, 1997.

Under this *portability* provision, employees who change their jobs cannot be denied coverage under their new employers' group policy even if they have preexisting medical conditions. Such employees may be excluded from employer-sponsored group coverage for a waiting period of up to 12 months (18 months for late enrollees). However, this exclusion period must be reduced by one month for each month that the employee was covered at a previous job.

These portability rules do not apply to:

- government health plans;
- health plans covering fewer than two employees;
- accident insurance, disability income insurance, liability insurance and workers' compensation;
- long-term care insurance;

- Medicare supplement insurance; or
- coverage for a specified disease or illness.

Preexisting Conditions

Like individual health policies, group health insurance plans usually contain a provision that excludes preexisting conditions from coverage. However, whereas individual plans typically define "preexisting conditions" as those that first appeared before the policy was issued and were not cited on the application, a group plan typically defines a "preexisting condition" as one for which a participant received treatment during the three months prior to the effective date of the group coverage.

Group health plans that exclude preexisting conditions also usually specify when a condition will no longer be considered preexisting. For example, a plan may cover a preexisting condition once the group participant has gone without treatment for that condition for three months.

Under recent federal legislation, pregnancy may not be treated as a preexisting condition.

---

1. Walter quit his job two months ago. Upon his resignation his coverage under his employer's group medical expense plan immediately stopped.

   (True/False)

2. Martha quits her job due to poor health and would like to convert her group health certificate to an individual medical expense policy. Which of the following is true?

   A. Martha must exercise her option to convert immediately.
   B. The insurer must charge Martha the same premium that she paid under the group policy.
   C. The insurer may not deny Martha coverage, even if she is evaluated as an uninsurable risk due to poor health.

3. In group health policies, a preexisting condition typically is defined as one

   A. that appeared before the policy was issued and was not mentioned on the application.
   B. for which an insured received treatment during the three months before the policy's effective date.

4. Usually, if a group health policy excludes a preexisting condition, it is excluded for the life of the policy.

(True/False)

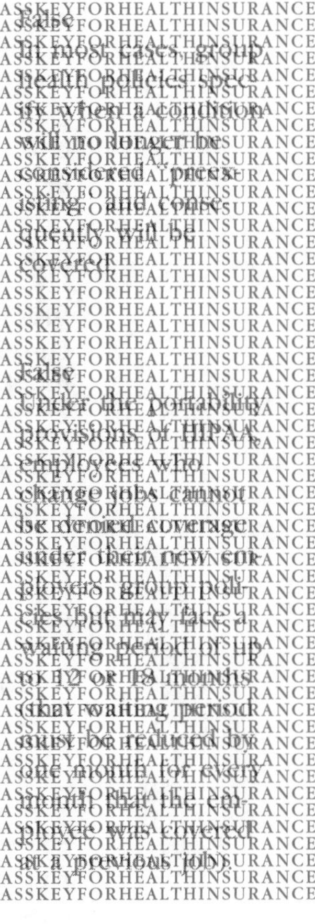

---

5. Under new rules regarding health insurance portability, every employee who leaves his or her old job is entitled to immediate health coverage with his or her new employer.

(True/False)

GROUP HEALTH INSURANCE COVERAGES

All of the types of health insurance coverages discussed in this text—medical expense, disability income and accidental death and dismemberment—are available for group plans. Rather than repeat the discussion of these policies—their purpose and functions are the same whether a group product or an individual product—let's focus on the unique features of these coverages when they are part of a group plan.

Group Basic Medical Expense

The three standard forms of basic medical expense insurance—hospital, surgical and physicians' expenses—are available for group insurance. In addition, a number of newer coverages have been developed in recent years, including dental and vision care.

Dental Care Coverage

Dental care coverage is designed to cover the costs associated with normal dental maintenance as well as oral surgery, root canal therapy and orthodontia. The coverage may be on a "reasonable and customary charge" basis or on a dollar-per-service schedule approach. Under the "dollar-per-service schedule" approach, covered dental services are categorized and each category is assigned a maximum dollar amount. The plan then reimburses the insureds for covered services up to the maximum amount.

Deductible and coinsurance features are typical (though some policies will cover routine cleaning and exams at 100 percent), as are maximum yearly benefit amounts, such as $1,000 or $2,000.

Vision Care Coverage

Vision care coverage usually pays for reasonable and customary charges incurred during eye exams by ophthalmologists and optometrists. Expenses for the fitting or cost of contact lenses or eyeglasses are often excluded.

Other Coverages

Other newer coverages include coverage for prescription drugs, home health care, extended care facilities, diagnostic X rays and laboratory services. In fact, some of these specified coverages, such as vision and dental care, are available only on a group basis.

A group basic medical expense plan can combine two or more of these coverages or it may consist of only one type of coverage, such as hospital expense only.

Group Major Medical Plans

Like individual major medical plans, group major medical plans may be offered as a single, extensive plan (comprehensive major medical) or superimposed over a group basic plan (supplemental major medical). Participants are usually required to satisfy an initial deductible with comprehensive plans and either a corridor or an integrated deductible with supplemental plans.

As we've stated, benefits provided by group major medical plans are usually more extensive than those of individual plans. For example, it is not uncommon to find group plans that offer individual benefit maximums of $1 million; still others do not set any maximum benefit limits. Too, deductibles are usually lower for group plans, typically ranging from $100 to $250, whereas deductibles for individual policies can be $500 or more.

Three other characteristics of group medical expense plans distinguish them from individual plans. These are the coordination of benefits provision, the treatment of maternity benefits and COBRA continuation of benefits.

Coordination of Benefits

The purpose of the *coordination of benefits* (COB) provision, found only in group health plans, is to avoid duplication of benefit payments and overinsurance when an individual is covered under more than one group health plan. The provision limits the total amount of claims paid by *all* insurers covering the patient to no more than the total allowable medical expenses. For example, an individual who incurs $700 in allowable medical expenses would not be able to collect any more than $700, no matter how many group plans he or she is covered by.

The COB provision establishes which plan is the primary plan, or the plan that is responsible for providing the full benefit amounts specified in its policy. Once the primary plan has paid its full promised benefit, the insured may submit the claim to the secondary provider for any additional benefits payable. In no case, however, will the total amount the insured receives exceed the costs he or she incurred.

Coordinating benefits is appropriate for married couples, when each is covered by an employer group plan. For example, John and Cindy, a young married couple, each are participants in their own employer's health plan and are also covered as dependents under their spouse's plan. John's plan would specify that it is the primary plan for John; Cindy's plan would be his secondary plan. Likewise, Cindy's plan would specify that it is the primary plan for Cindy; John's plan would be her secondary plan.

Maternity and Newborn Benefits

Whereas it is common for individual health plans to exclude routine maternity care from coverage, group medical expense plans *must* provide *maternity benefits*. This is the result of a 1979 amendment to the Civil Rights Act, which requires plans covering 15 or more people to treat pregnancy-related claims no differently than any other allowable medical expense.

As a result of recent federal legislation, group health plans are subject to certain additional requirements relating to benefits for mothers and newborns. A group health plan may not restrict hospital stay benefits in connection with childbirth for either a mother or newborn to less than 48 hours (or 96 hours, in the case of a cesarean delivery).

Furthermore, a group health plan cannot impose a preexisting condition exclusion on a newborn child provided the child was covered by a group health plan within 30 days of the child's birth (or within 30 days of adoption in the case of adoptees).

---

1. Edgar is covered by two group health insurance policies, one through his employer and the other through his wife's employer. What provision normally would prevent a duplication of benefits being paid to Edgar when he files a claim?

____

2. In question 1, which policy would normally be Edgar's primary plan?

   A. Edgar's group plan
   B. His wife's group plan

3. All of the following coverages are optional in a group health plan, EXCEPT:

   A. dental care coverage.
   B. home health care coverage.
   C. maternity coverage.
   D. vision care coverage.

C

Group health plans covering more than 15 people must provide maternity coverage.

---

4. Group basic medical expense plans that cover dental care must cover vision care as well.

   (True/False)

False

Dental and vision care are separate optional coverages.

---

5. Gerald's group health plan provides basic hospital expense coverage and supplemental major medical coverage. What type of deductible would Gerald have, if any?

   A. Flat
   B. Dual
   C. Corridor
   D. No deductible

C

Participants covered by a comprehensive major medical plan are usually required to satisfy a corridor or integrated deductible.

COBRA Continuation of Benefits

Participants in group medical expense plans are protected by federal law that guarantees a continuation of their group coverage if their employment is terminated for reasons other than gross misconduct. Practically speaking, the law protects employees who are laid-off, but not those who are fired "for cause."

This law, known as the *Consolidated Omnibus Budget Reconciliation Act of 1985* (or COBRA), requires employers with 20 or more employees to continue group medical expense coverage for terminated workers (as well as their spouses, divorced spouses and dependent children) for up to 18 months (or 36 months, in some situations) following termination.

Some important points about this law should be noted. It is *not* the same as the policy conversion privilege by which an employee may convert a group certificate to an individual policy. COBRA permits the terminated employee to continue his or her group coverage.

Also, the law does *not* require the employer to pay the cost of the continued group coverage; the terminated employee can be required to pay the premium, which may be up to 102 percent of the premium that would otherwise be charged. (The additional 2 percent is allowed to cover the employer's additional administrative expenses.) The schedule of benefits will be the same during the continuation period as under the group plan.

1. The purpose of the COBRA requirements concerns

   A. conversion of group health policies to individual policies.
   B. continuation of group health coverage.

B

COBRA allows terminated employees to continue their group coverage.

---

2. Which of the following is true regarding a terminated employee's continued coverage as compared to coverage before termination?

   A. The benefits can be less extensive but the premium must be the same.
   B. The benefits must be the same and the premium must be the same.
   C. The benefits must be the same but the premium can be higher.
   D. The benefits can be less extensive and the premium can be higher.

C

When a terminated employee decides to continue his or her group coverage, the benefits must be the same; however, the premium can be up to 102 percent of the premium that would otherwise be charged.

Group Disability Income Plans

Group disability income plans differ from individual plans in a number of ways. Individual plans usually specify a flat income amount, based on the person's earnings, determined at the time the policy is purchased. In contrast, group plans usually specify benefits in terms of a percentage of the individual's earnings.

Like individual plans, group disability can include short-term plans or long-term plans. The definitions of "short-term" and "long-term," however, are different for group and individual plans.

Group *short-term* disability plans are characterized by maximum benefit periods of rather short duration, such as 13 or 26 weeks. Benefits are typically paid weekly and range from 50 percent to 100 percent of the individual's income.

Group *long-term* disability plans provide for maximum benefit periods of more than two years, occasionally extending to the insured's retirement age. Benefit amounts are usually limited to about 60 percent of the participant's income.

If an employer provides both a short-term plan and long-term plan, the long-term plan typically begins paying benefits only after the short-term benefits cease. Often, long-term plans use an "own occupation" definition of total disability for the first year or two of disability and then switch to an "any occupation" definition.

Most group disability plans require the employee to have a minimum period of service, such as 30 to 90 days, before he or she is eligible for coverage. In addition, most group plans include provisions making their benefits supplemental to workers' compensation benefits, so that total benefits received do not exceed a specified percentage of regular earnings. In some cases, group disability plans actually limit coverage to nonoccupational disabilities, since occupational disabilities normally qualify for workers' compensation benefits.

1. All of the following statements regarding group disability plans are true, EXCEPT:
   - A. Benefits are specified in terms of a percentage of the participant's earnings.
   - B. Benefits paid under the group plan are supplemental to workers' compensation benefits.
   - C. Employees covered under both a short-term and long-term plan collect benefits from each simultaneously.

2. Employees are usually eligible for coverage under a group disability plan on their first day of work.

   (True/False)

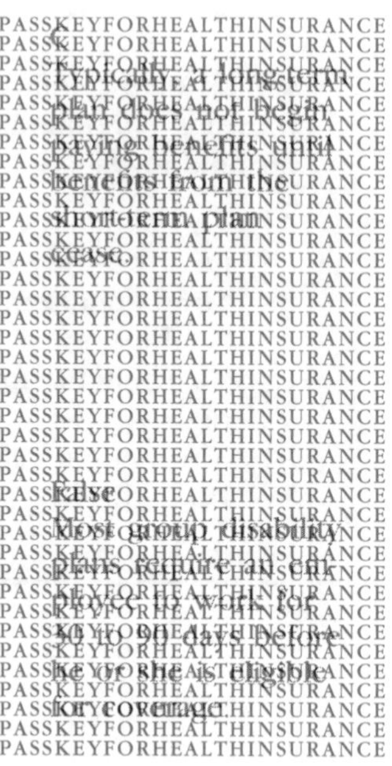

Group AD&D

Accidental death and dismemberment insurance is a very popular type of group coverage, frequently offered in conjunction with group life insurance plans. It may also be provided as a separate policy, in which case it is normally paid for entirely by the employee. Such employee-pay-all plans are called *voluntary group AD&D,* since plan participation is voluntary. Benefits may be provided for both occupational and nonoccupational losses, or for nonoccupational losses only. Voluntary group AD&D typically provides benefits for both types of losses.

Similar to individual AD&D, group AD&D pays a principal sum upon the insured's accidental death (or loss of any two body members). A capital sum is payable upon the accidental loss of one body member. Some group AD&D plans specify a higher death benefit if the insured dies while on company business.

Group AD&D, unlike group medical, normally does not include a conversion privilege.

Other Types of Group Health Plans

In addition to the typical group health insurance plan—as would be utilized by an employer, for example—additional types of plans are worth noting:

- blanket health insurance,
- franchise health insurance,
- credit accident and health insurance and
- medical savings accounts.

Blanket Health Plans

Blanket health insurance is issued to cover a group whose members are constantly changing but who, while they are part of the group, may be exposed to the same risks. A blanket health plan may be issued to an airline or a bus company to cover its passengers or to a school to cover its students.

Franchise Health Plans

Franchise health plans, sometimes called "wholesale plans," provide health insurance coverage to members of an association or professional society. Individual policies are issued to individual members; the association or society simply serves as the "sponsor" for the plan. Premium rates are usually discounted for franchise plans.

Credit Accident and Health Plans

Credit accident and health plans are designed to help the insured pay off a loan in the event he or she is disabled due to an accident or sickness. If the insured becomes disabled, the policy provides for monthly benefit payments equal to the monthly loan payments due.

Typically, group credit accident and health coverages are provided through banks, savings and loan associations, finance companies and retailers. A master policy is issued to the institution sponsoring the plan and sales commissions are paid to the insurance agent who places the business. Each insured debtor receives a certificate of insurance that defines the coverage.

To qualify for group credit accident and health insurance in most states, creditors must have a minimum number of debtors each year (typically 100). Debtors are usually required to pay part or all of the premium, but they are allowed to choose the insurer; they cannot be forced to take coverage from any one particular insurance company. The amount of insurance cannot exceed the amount of the debt.

Medical Savings Accounts (MSAs)

As you may recall from our discussion in Chapter 2, medical savings accounts are tax-favored trusts that are being tested as a new means by which the self-employed and small businesses (those with 50 or fewer employees) may help defray medical expenses. MSAs must be used in conjunction with a high-deductible catastrophic coverage plan; certain other requirements must be met as well.

If all the requirements are met, an individual may make tax-free contributions to the MSA up to certain limits. In addition, the individual may take tax-free distributions from the MSA provided the distributions are used to pay certain unreimbursed medical expenses of the account holder, his or her spouse or dependents.

---

1. A vacation cruise line that wants group health coverage for its passengers would purchase

   A. franchise health insurance.
   B. blanket health insurance.
   C. credit health insurance.

B

---

2. With blanket health insurance, the insureds (are/are not) issued individual policies.

are not

---

3. Group accidental death and dismemberment policies usually (do/do not) contain a conversion privilege.

do not

---

4. What is the purpose of credit accident and health insurance?

To pay off a loan in the event the debtor (the insured) becomes disabled.

12

Tax Treatment of Health Insurance Premiums and Benefits

The taxation of health insurance premiums and benefits depends on the type of policy in question. It is difficult to make definitive statements about the tax treatment of health insurance that would apply in every situation, but we can discuss the basic rules. To simplify the discussion, we will examine the issue of taxation as it applies separately to group and individual disability income and medical expense policies.

TAXATION OF INDIVIDUAL HEALTH INSURANCE

Taxation of individual health insurance premiums and benefits depends on the type of coverage.

Disability Income

Premiums paid by individuals for personal disability income policies are not tax deductible. However, any benefits that are received from such policies are tax free to the insured.

Individuals under age 65 who are permanently and totally disabled and are retired on disability are entitled to a tax credit on their disability income. This credit is based on the individual's tax filing status (single, married filing jointly, etc.).

Medical Expense

Individual medical expense insurance is treated a little differently than individual disability income. Incurred medical expenses that are reimbursed by insurance may not be deducted from an individual's income tax. Furthermore, incurred medical expenses that are not reimbursed by insurance may only be deducted to the extent they exceed 7.5 percent of the taxpayer's adjusted gross income. For example, an individual who has an adjusted gross income of $35,000 would be able to deduct only the amount of unreimbursed medical expenses that exceed $2,625.

For purposes of determining deductible medical expenses, the following can be included:

- prescription drugs,
- insulin,
- hospital expenses,
- physician and surgeon fees,
- rehabilitative treatments and
- medical expense insurance premiums (including qualified long-term care insurance premiums, within limits).

Benefits received by an insured from a personal medical expense policy are not included in his or her gross income, since they are paid to offset losses he or she incurred. However, medical expense insurance benefits must be included in gross income to the extent that reimbursement is received for medical expenses deducted in a prior year.

The rules for self-employed individuals are slightly different. Amounts paid for medical care insurance for self-employed individuals, their spouses and dependents are deductible within certain percentage limits. In 1998, the limit was 45 percent; however, this limit is being increased gradually until it reaches 100 percent, according to the following schedule:

Beginning Tax Year	**Deduction**
1998–1999	45%
2000–2001	50%
2002	60%
2003–2005	80%
2006	90%
2007 and beyond	100%

---

1. Hubert is the insured in a disability income policy for which he pays an annual premium of $408. Which of the following statements applies?

   A. Hubert's $408 premium is partially deductible for federal income tax.
   B. Hubert's $408 premium is not tax deductible.

B. Such premiums are not deductible.

2. Kathleen becomes totally and permanently disabled and is drawing $500 monthly benefits under her personal disability income policy. Which statement is correct?

   A. Kathleen must include the monthly disability benefits in her gross income for tax purposes.
   B. Kathleen is entitled to receive the $500 monthly disability benefits on a tax-free basis.

B

Disability benefits from an individual policy are not taxable.

---

3. In 1998, a self-employed individual may deduct all amounts paid for medical care insurance that covers the individual, his or her spouse and dependents.

   (True/False)

False

In 1998, self-employed individuals may deduct 45% of amounts paid for such medical care insurance.

---

4. Roscoe has an adjusted gross income of $28,000. He pays medical insurance premiums of $900 and has other itemized medical expenses of $800, which are not reimbursed. How much of his medical expenses can Roscoe deduct?

   $______

$0

Roscoe's medical expenses total $1,700. This does not exceed 7.5 percent of his adjusted gross income.

---

5. Rick, who has no health insurance, experienced $3,000 in medical expenses this year. Assuming his adjusted gross income was $29,000, how much of those medical expenses can he deduct from his income taxes, if any?

   A. $0
   B. $825
   C. $2,175
   D. $3,000

B

Unreimbursed medical expenses are deductible only to the extent that they exceed 7.5 percent of adjusted gross income. In Rick's case, 7.5 percent of adjusted gross income is $2,175. Rick's medical expenses totaled $3,000, which exceeds $2,175 by $825.

TAXATION OF GROUP HEALTH INSURANCE

As an incentive for employers to provide health insurance benefits to their employees, the federal government grants favorable tax treatment to group health insurance plans. These benefits are discussed below.

Medical Expense

Employers are entitled to take a tax deduction for premium contributions they make to a *group medical expense* plan, as long as the contributions represent an "ordinary and reasonable" business expense. By the same token, individuals who are covered by a group plan do not include employer contributions made on their behalf as part of their taxable income.

As we learned in the last chapter, many group plans are contributory, meaning that employees contribute a portion of the premium. As a general rule, these premium contributions are not tax deductible by the individual employees. Only when unreimbursed medical expenses—expenses that include any contributions to a group medical plan—exceed 7.5 percent of an individual's adjusted gross income can a tax deduction for group health premiums be taken by an individual. Any premiums the individual contributes for group disability or group AD&D coverage are not considered qualifying medical expenses when determining this excess.

Disability Income

When a *group disability* insurance plan is paid for entirely by the employer for employees and benefits are paid directly to individual employees who qualify, the premiums are deductible by the employer. The benefits, in turn, are taxable to the recipient. On the other hand, if an employee contributes to any portion of the premium, his or her benefit will be received tax free in proportion to the premium contributed.

For example, let's assume Michelle is a participant in a contributory group disability income plan in which her employer pays two-thirds of the premium and Michelle pays one-third. Her employer qualifies for a tax deduction for its share of the premium and, as is true with any group health plan, Michelle is not taxed on those contributions. The premium portion that Michelle pays does not qualify for a tax deduction by her.

Now assume Michelle becomes disabled and receives disability income benefits of $900 a month. One third of the monthly benefit—$300—would be tax free to Michelle, since it is attributed to the premium she paid; the remaining two-thirds of the payment—$600—would be taxable income, since it is attributed to the premium her employer paid.

---

1. Sally is covered by her employer's noncontributory group disability plan, the premium for which is $50 a month. If she were to become disabled and receive $1,000 a month, how much of each benefit payment would be taxable income to her?

   A. $1,000
   B. $950
   C. $50
   D. $0

A

Since Sally's employer paid 100 percent of the premium, 100 percent of the benefits would be taxable to Sally.

2. An employer's premium contributions to a group health plan (are/are not) considered part of an employee's taxable income.

---

3. Disability income benefit payments attributed to the (employer's/employee's) contributions are not taxable to the employee.

---

4. If the Teatray Corporation establishes and pays for a group disability income plan for its employees, can the company deduct the disability insurance premiums as a business expense?

   (Yes/No)

---

5. Susan is covered under her employer-sponsored disability group plan. The premium is $50 a month: Susan pays $10 and the employer pays $40. Assuming Susan were to become disabled and receive monthly disability benefits of $700 from the plan, how much, if any, of the monthly benefit would be taxable income to Susan?

   A. $560
   B. $140
   C. $70
   D. $0

Progressive Quiz No. 4

(Text reference numbers are shown under each correct response in the red column.)

1. All of the following factors are of primary importance in underwriting a health insurance policy, EXCEPT the applicant's

   A. physical condition.
   B. occupation.
   C. age.
   D. marital status.

D
(114, 117)

---

2. Jim, who is covered by an individual disability income policy, switched jobs from accountant to race car driver. Assuming his policy was continuously in force with the change of occupation provision attached, which of the following statements is true?

   A. Jim would receive reduced benefits on any claim submitted.
   B. Jim would receive the same benefits as before, but would have to pay higher premiums in the future.
   C. Jim would receive the same benefits, and his premiums would remain the same.
   D. Jim would receive reduced benefits but would pay lower premiums in the future.

A
(77)

---

3. Four policyowners, all the same age, purchase identical major medical policies at standard rates. Mary pays her premium monthly; Joyce, quarterly; Joan, semiannually; and Natalie, annually. Whose policy will cost the most?

   A. Natalie's
   B. Joyce's
   C. Joan's
   D. Mary's

D
(87)

4. In order to have an insurable interest in another person, one must meet which of the following requirements?

   A. Be a member of the other person's family
   B. Be expected to experience a financial loss if the person becomes ill or disabled
   C. Be married to the person
   D. Have a business relationship with the person

B
(114)

---

5. All of the following are techniques used to underwrite substandard risks, EXCEPT:

   A. charge an extra premium.
   B. limit the type of policy.
   C. reinsure the risk.
   D. specify an exclusion to avoid covering the extra risk.

C
(118)

---

6. Morbidity relates directly to all of the following, EXCEPT:

   A. birth statistics.
   B. sickness.
   C. disability figures.
   D. health insurance.

A
(6, 120)

---

7. All of the following statements regarding premiums are true, EXCEPT:

   A. The older the insured, the higher the applicable premium rate.
   B. Nonoccupational classifications carry higher premium rates than (occupational) classifications.
   C. Female premium rates frequently are higher than male premium rates for comparable coverage.
   D. A policyowner's premium may be affected by his or her occupation.

B
(26, 122)

---

8. Doris, who is covered under an individual disability policy, was involved in an auto accident. She was never totally disabled but is classified now as partially disabled and will

   A. receive the same benefits as a totally disabled individual.
   B. receive partial disability benefits indefinitely.
   C. receive partial disability benefits for up to one year.
   D. not receive partial disability benefits.

D
(25)

9. All of the following would indicate a high degree of moral hazard, EXCEPT:

   A. a poor credit rating.
   B. no church affiliation.
   C. dishonest business practices.
   D. excessive drinking.

---

10. Health insurance premium computations are complex because

   A. there are few morbidity tables.
   B. of competition among insurers.
   C. health insurance involves more than one type of benefit and claims are filed more frequently.
   D. the average claim is small.

---

11. Which is a true statement about the reserves of an insurer?

   A. Federal law mandates the minimum reserve requirements for health insurance.
   B. Premium reserves are for losses that have occurred but for which settlement is not complete.
   C. The reserves reflect an insurer's liability for future claims.
   D. Reserves are held for a specified period of time before being paid as dividends to stockholders.

---

12. A primary consideration as to occupational risk in the underwriting of health insurance is

   A. length of employment.
   B. experience on present job.
   C. probability of disability.
   D. past work experience.

---

13. Concerning the waiver of premium provision, all of the following are correct statements, EXCEPT:

   A. It exempts an insured from paying premiums during periods of permanent and total disability.
   B. The waiver may apply retroactively.
   C. The waiver generally drops off after the insured reaches age 60 or 65.
   D. It normally applies to accidental death and dismemberment policies.

14. Group dental care coverage usually includes the following provisions, EXCEPT:

A. elective indemnity.
B. coinsurance.
C. deductible.
D. maximum benefit.

---

15. Compared to benefits in individual policies, group health insurance benefits generally are

A. about the same.
B. more comprehensive.
C. more expensive.
D. less comprehensive.

---

16. What or who establishes the minimum number of persons to be insured under a group health insurance policy?

A. Federal law
B. Common practice
C. State law
D. The Insurance Commissioner

---

17. How are medical expense insurance premiums to be deducted by individuals for income tax purposes?

A. Any premium amount that exceeds 3 percent of adjusted gross income is deductible.
B. The premiums are fully deductible from gross income.
C. When premiums are lumped with other medical expenses, the total amount deductible is the amount that exceeds 7.5 percent of the taxpayer's adjusted gross income.
D. Ten percent of medical expense insurance premiums may be deducted from adjusted gross income.

---

18. Vance is totally and permanently disabled and draws an $800 monthly benefit from his personal disability income policy. Which statement concerning income taxes is correct?

A. Vance must include his disability benefits in his gross income for tax purposes.
B. He is entitled to receive the benefits on a tax-free basis.
C. Vance may deduct 50 percent of his disability benefits on his federal tax return.
D. He may deduct the premiums paid for the policy.

19. Which of the following statements concerning health insurance benefits is true?

    A. Each policy offers a single type of benefit.
    B. Claims and not benefits affect premium rates.
    C. Policyowners who have policies with identical benefits pay the same premiums.
    D. The greater the benefits, the higher the premium.

---

20. What is the total number of required uniform policy provisions?

    A. 11
    B. 12
    C. 15
    D. 23

---

21. All of the following are sources of insurability information, EXCEPT:

    A. inspection reports.
    B. the Medical Information Bureau.
    C. church records.
    D. applications.

---

22. Concerning the agent's report, all of the following statements are true, EXCEPT:

    A. It is part of the application.
    B. It is verified and signed by both the applicant and the agent.
    C. It contains statements by the agent about the applicant.
    D. It is a source of insurability information for home office underwriters.

---

23. Which type of group health coverage typically does NOT contain a conversion privilege?

    A. Basic medical expense
    B. Comprehensive medical expense
    C. Disability income
    D. Accidental death and dismemberment

24. Concerning the insuring clause, all of the following statements apply, EXCEPT:

A. It represents a company's promise to pay benefits for specific kinds of losses.
B. The clause identifies the insurer and the insured.
C. It usually specifies that benefits are subject to all provisions, terms and exclusions stated in the policy.
D. The clause usually appears on the last page of a policy.

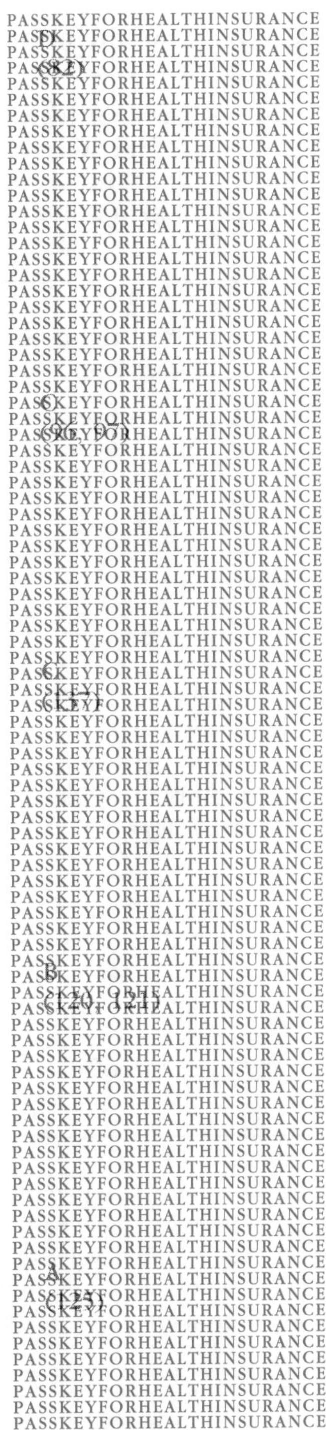

---

25. Inspection reports are prepared by

A. home office underwriters.
B. health insurance agents.
C. inspection services.
D. insurance agencies.

---

26. Which of the following MUST be included in a group health insurance policy?

A. Dental care
B. Vision care
C. Maternity care
D. Prescription drug coverage

---

27. Premium factors in health insurance include all of the following, EXCEPT:

A. benefits.
B. income.
C. interest.
D. expense.

---

28. Precertification review is one approach insurers use to

A. control costs.
B. underwrite risks.
C. adjust claims.
D. process claims.

29. A group health plan for which employees pay no part of the premium is referred to as a

A. participating plan.
B. contributory plan.
C. nonparticipating plan.
D. noncontributory plan.

---

30. Which of the following group health plans involves each participant being issued an individual policy?

A. Franchise health plan
B. Blanket health plan
C. Credit health plan
D. Long-term disability plan

---

31. Ed is a participant in his employer's group health plan. He quits his job and is notified that he has 31 days in which to choose to convert his health coverage to an individual policy. After a week passes, and before Ed has notified his former employer of his decision, he is involved in an automobile accident and is hospitalized with injuries. Which of the following statements is true?

A. The cost of Ed's hospitalization would not be covered.
B. The cost of Ed's hospitalization would be covered provided Ed is considered to be insurable.
C. Ed's hospitalization would be covered because his coverage continues under the group plan for the 31-day period.
D. None of the above

---

32. Julianne is covered by her employer's group disability plan. However, she pays $20 of the $200 monthly premium herself. If she were to start receiving monthly benefits of $2,000, what amount of those benefits would Julianne receive tax free?

A. $200
B. $400
C. $1,800
D. $1,980

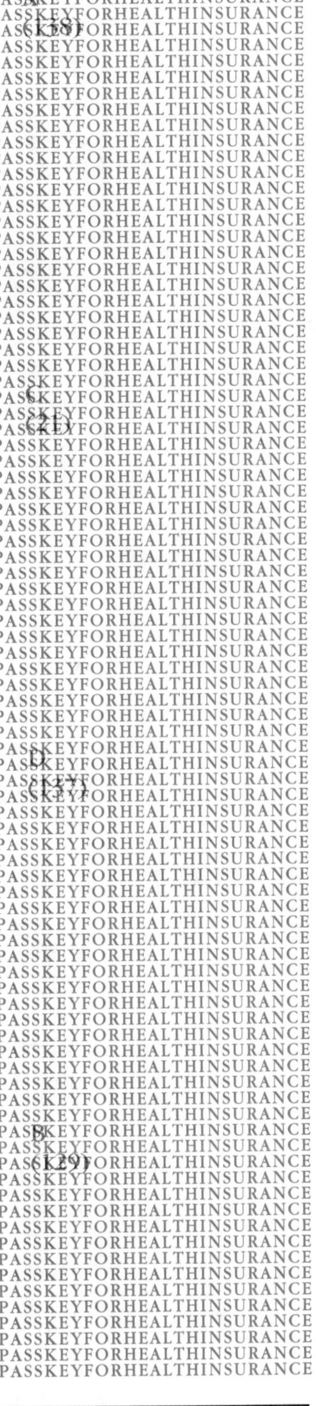

33. Which of the following statements regarding COBRA requirements is NOT true?

A. The employer must pay the cost of the continued coverage.
B. COBRA applies to employers with 20 or more employees.
C. The schedule of benefits remains the same.
D. Spouses, divorced spouses and dependent children can also continue coverage.

---

34. If funds contributed to an MSA are not spent, the funds

A. are distributed to the MSA account holder after a penalty tax is levied.
B. are applied automatically to the account holder's Medicare Part B premium.
C. accumulate to prefund future medical expenses.
D. become the property of the small employer who set up the MSA program.

---

35. Newborn children may not be excluded from coverage under an individual or group health plan during their first 12 months of life provided the newborn's parents

A. have no preexisting genetic conditions.
B. have the newborn undergo a physical exam within 7 days of birth.
C. have been with their current insurer for more than 24 months.
D. enroll the newborn in their group plan within 30 days of the child's birth.

---

36. Group health plans that are subject to HIPAA's requirements but do not comply with its provisions are subject to

A. an automatic flat penalty of $50,000.
B. a penalty of $100 for each affected individual for every day they are not in compliance.
C. misdemeanor criminal charges for the insurer's officers.
D. felony criminal charges for the insurer's officers.

13

Health Insurance Providers

When it comes to obtaining health insurance coverage, Americans have a variety of options from which to choose. Those providing health insurance can be divided into three general categories: private insurers, service providers and state and federal government. In all cases, though, the objective is the same: to provide protection against the costs associated with illness, injury or disability. How each provider approaches this task is unique. In this chapter, we will review the prominent types of health insurance providers.

PRIVATE INSURERS

Both group and individual health insurance policies may be written by a number of private insurers, including life insurance companies that specialize in one or more types of medical expense and disability insurance. Among life insurance companies, health insurance is offered by "ordinary" companies as well as "debit" (or home service companies). (Debit companies sell what are known as "industrial" policies.)

Private insurers function on the *reimbursement approach*. As you will recall from previous chapters, with this approach policyowners obtain medical treatment from whatever source they feel is most appropriate and, per the terms of their policy, submit their charges to their insurer for reimbursement. The *right of assignment* built into most commercial health policies lets policyowners assign benefit payments from the insurer directly to the health care provider, thus relieving the policyowner of first having to pay the medical care provider. The right to assign a policy's benefits, however, does not change the fact that the policy is reimbursing the insured for covered medical expenses.

Within this broad category of "private insurers" are specific types of insurance companies. Let's take a look at each.

Stock Insurers

A *stock insurance company* is a private organization, incorporated under state laws for the purpose of making a profit for its stockholders. It is structured the same as any corporation. Stockholders may or may not be policyholders. When declared, stock dividends are paid to stockholders. In a stock company, the directors and officers are responsible to the stockholders.

Mutual Insurers

Mutual insurance companies are also organized and incorporated under state laws but they have no stockholders. Instead, the owners are the policyholders. Anyone purchasing insurance from a mutual insurer is both a customer and an owner. He or she has the right to vote for the board of director members. By issuing participating policies that pay *policy dividends,* mutual insurers allow their policyowners to share in any company earnings. Essentially, policy dividends represent a "refund" of the portion of premiums that remains after the company has set aside the necessary reserves and has made deductions for claims and expenses. It can also include a share in the company's investment, mortality and operating profits.

Occasionally, a stock company may be converted into a mutual company through a process called "mutualization." Likewise, some mutuals are "demutualizing" by converting to stock companies. Stock and mutual companies are often referred to as *"commercial insurers."*

Risk Retention Group

A risk retention group is a mutual insurance company formed to insure people in the same business, occupation or profession (for example, dentists, pharmacists or engineers).

Reciprocal Insurers

Similar to mutuals, *reciprocal insurers* are organized on the basis of ownership by their policyholders. However, with reciprocals, it is the policyholders themselves who insure the risks of the other policyholders. Each policyholder assumes a share of the risk brought to the company by others. Reciprocals are managed by an attorney-in-fact, an individual to whom each policyholder gives authority to exchange insurance for him or her with other policyholders.

Fraternal Benefit Societies

Insurance is also issued by *fraternal benefit societies,* which have existed in the United States for more than a century. Fraternal societies, noted primarily for their social, charitable and benevolent activities, have memberships based on religious, national or ethnic lines.

To be considered a fraternal society, an organization must be nonprofit, have a lodge system that includes ritualistic work and maintain a representative form of government with elected officers. Most fraternals today issue insurance certificates with many of the same provisions found in policies issued by commercial private insurers.

Debit Insurers

Health insurance is also sold through a special branch of the industry known as *home service* or *"debit" insurers*. These companies specialize in a particular type of insurance called *industrial insurance*.

The major characteristics of *industrial health* insurance, when contrasted to "ordinary" insurance, are:

1. premiums are payable weekly or monthly and

2. premiums are usually collected regularly by agents in the field.

Industrial health insurance provides weekly benefits for disability due to sickness or injury and a designated sum per day for hospital confinement. Modest amounts for surgical operations according to a surgical schedule also may be included. Coverage likewise may include accidental death and dismemberment benefits.

Provisions in industrial health insurance normally include a grace period of four weeks. When a policy lapses, reinstatement is handled more liberally than with ordinary insurance; these policies typically can be reinstated with evidence of insurability and the payment of two weeks' premiums. A required provision is that insureds have a right to return the policies within a specified time and obtain a premium refund.

Premiums for industrial health insurance are somewhat higher than for similar ordinary policies for several reasons. Because premiums are collected more frequently, the company has less money to reinvest; and a higher premium makes up for the company's smaller interest earnings. Also, the disability rate is higher for industrial policyowners than for persons purchasing commercial health insurance. One reason is that coverage is available for persons who generally represent a higher risk because of more dangerous occupations.

---

1. Roland, a health insurance policyowner and not a stockholder of Secure Life, has a right to vote for new directors at the annual meeting of the company. Therefore, Secure Life is

   A. a mutual company.
   B. a stock company.

---

2. What is the process of converting a stock company to a mutual company called?

   ____

3. Which policyowner right does a policyowner exercise when he or she allows his or her insurer to make payments directly to a medical services provider?

The right of assignment

---

4. Which of the following is managed by an attorney-in-fact?

   A. A reciprocal insurer
   B. A fraternal benefit society

A Reciprocal insurers are managed by attorneys-in-fact.

---

5. List three characteristics of a fraternal benefit society.

   1. ______
   2. ______
   3. ______

1. Nonprofit
2. A lodge system that includes ritualistic work
3. A representative form of government

(May be in any order.)

---

6. What distinguishes the premiums for industrial health insurance from those of ordinary health insurance?

______

They are payable weekly or monthly and are collected regularly by agents in the field. They are also generally higher than ordinary health insurance premiums.

SERVICE PROVIDERS

Service providers are not insurers per se; rather, they operate on the principle that their subscribers (the term used in place of policyholders) receive medical care services as a result of their payment of premiums. Subscribers typically are not billed for services rendered by a medical care provider. Instead, the care provider—who has entered into an agreement with the service organization to provide medical care—is paid directly by the service organization. As you can see, this is the opposite of the reimbursement approach taken by private insurers. Under the service approach, the subscriber receives "benefits" in the form of medical services for which payment has already been made (via the premium).

This service approach is used primarily by three types of organizations:

1. Blue Cross and Blue Shield
2. Health maintenance organizations (HMOS)
3. Preferred provider organizations (PPOs)

Blue Cross and Blue Shield

Blue Cross and *Blue Shield* are health care service organizations. Blue Cross offers prepayment plans designed to cover hospital services; Blue Shield covers surgical expenses and other medical services performed by physicians.

Generally, Blue Cross and Blue Shield plans work in close cooperation with each other, within a given state or region within a state. In fact, in the past few years, most Blue Cross and Blue Shield plans have merged into single plans. Unlike private insurance companies, Blue Cross and Blue Shield organizations have contractual arrangements with hospitals and physicians. These contracts provide for payments for services rendered to subscribers with agreed-upon rate or fee schedules.

Consequently, in order to obtain full value from their service plans, subscribers are usually required to utilize the contracted hospitals and physicians for medical care. Payments for services are made directly by Blue Cross or Blue Shield to the hospitals and physicians; subscribers are responsible only for services not covered by their particular plans. (Blue Cross and Blue Shield plans offer a broad and comprehensive range of services from which the subscriber can choose.)

Blue Cross and Blue Shield plans are available on an individual, family or group basis.

---

1. Blue Cross plans cover (hospital services/physician expenses) while Blue Shield plans cover (hospital services/physician expenses).

hospital services
physician expenses

2. Emily, a Blue Cross and Blue Shield subscriber, is admitted to a contracted hospital for surgery. When she is discharged from the hospital, the charges for her covered expenses will be billed

   A. to Emily so she can submit a claim to Blue Cross and Blue Shield.
   B. directly to Blue Cross and Blue Shield.

B
Covered expenses are billed directly to Blue Cross and Blue Shield.

3. What is a major difference between private insurers and Blue Cross and Blue Shield?

____

Blue Cross and Blue Shield plans have contract agreements with hospitals and participating providers to provide payment for medical services per rate or fee schedules.

Health Maintenance Organizations

Although *health maintenance organizations,* or HMOs, have been in existence since the 1930s, The Health Maintenance Act of 1973, which provided some federal funding for these organizations, spurred the HMO movement forward. One of the Act's provisions requires employers with 25 or more employees to offer enrollment in an HMO if they provide health care benefits for their workers. This provision is often referred to as the "dual choice" provision.

Like Blue Cross and Blue Shield plans, HMOs offer health care services on a prepaid basis to subscribing members. Also like Blue Cross and Blue Shield plans, HMOs operate within a specific geographical region. This region is called the HMO's *service area*. HMOs are distinguished from other service providers, however, by the fact that they not only finance health care services for their subscribers, but they organize and deliver the services as well.

HMO subscribers pay a fixed periodic fee to the HMO and are provided with a broad range of health services, from routine doctor visits to emergency and hospital care. Care is rendered by physicians and hospitals who participate in the HMO. HMOs stress preventive care, the objective being to prevent disease from occurring or to treat diseases in their early stages and therefore reduce unnecessary hospital admissions and minimize the cost of treatment.

Unlike commercial insurers and Blue Cross and Blue Shield, HMOs rarely assess deductibles; when they do, the charges are nominal, such as $2 for prescription drugs or $5 for an office visit. Thus, the out-of-pocket expenses for members of an HMO are often lower than for individuals covered by medical expense plans. While the coverage provided by an HMO is often more comprehensive than that provided by medical expense plans, an HMO subscriber's choice of providers is limited. HMO members must choose a physician who is a *participating provider* in the HMO. That is, the physician must have a contract with the HMO to provide health care services to the HMO's members.

Often a physician is selected to serve as an HMO member's *primary care physician*. The primary care physician acts as a gatekeeper between the patient on one side and specialists, hospitals and other providers on the other side. It is the primary care physician who consults with other physicians in deciding whether to refer an HMO patient to a specialist or to recommend hospitalization.

Types of HMOs

There are two basic types of HMOs: *a group practice association model* and an *individual practice association model*.

1. *Group Practice Association Model.* A group practice association model (or "staff model") consists of physicians who are salaried employees of the HMO and work out of the HMO's facilities. Group practice models are also referred to as *closed panel plans* since subscribers must use physicians employed by the plan and these physi-

cians usually do not treat patients who are not members of the HMO.

2. *Individual Practice Association Model.* An HMO that operates on an individual practice association basis is characterized by a network of physicians who work out of their own private offices and participate in the HMO on a part-time basis. These plans are sometimes referred to as *open panel plans* since the physicians usually accept non-HMO patients as well as HMO subscribers.

Health maintenance organizations may be self-contained and self-funded based on fees from their subscribers, or they may contract for excess insurance or administrative services provided by insurance companies. In fact, some HMOs are sponsored by insurance companies.

Basic and Supplemental Health Care Services

In order to be federally qualified and thus eligible for federal funds, HMOs must provide what are called *basic health care services*. These include:

- physician's services,
- inpatient and outpatient hospital care,
- maternity care,
- well-baby care including immunizations,
- preventive health care including routine periodic examinations by a physician,
- mental health care (up to 20 outpatient visits) and
- emergency care (when medically necessary).

Services above and beyond these basic health care services are called *supplemental health care services* and are often subject to higher copayments than the basic services. HMOs may provide the following benefits as supplemental benefits or may exclude them from coverage altogether:

- long-term care services,
- vision care,
- dental care,
- mental health services exceeding those covered by the HMO,
- rehabilitative services,
- prescription drugs (when not given in a hospital) and
- out-of-area benefits (other than emergency care).

Complaint System and Quality Assurance

HMOs must have a system in place through which subscribing members can place complaints. Methods for resolving complaints within 180 days must also be in place. All HMOs must have an ongoing quality assurance program.

Evidence of Coverage

Within 60 days of enrolling a member, HMOs must provide the member with *evidence of coverage,* which describes the member's coverage and its limits. It must also identify the HMO, the providers and give other information regarding the terms and conditions of the coverage.

---

1. All of the following are features of HMOs, EXCEPT:

   A. health care services are prepaid.
   B. routine doctor's visits are covered.
   C. members pay a periodic fee that varies depending on which services the member uses.

C. The fixed periodic fee is the same regardless of which services a member uses.

2. An HMO whose physicians are salaried and work out of the HMO's facilities is called a ____________.

group practice association.

3. Why do HMOs stress preventive care?

____

____

____

Through preventive care, diseases are prevented or caught in their early stages, thereby reducing the cost of treatment.

Preferred Provider Organizations

Another type of health insurance provider is the *preferred provider organization* or PPO. A preferred provider organization is a collection of health care providers, such as physicians, hospitals, and clinics, who offer their services to certain groups at prearranged prices. In exchange, the group refers its members to the preferred providers for health care services.

Unlike HMOs, preferred provider organizations usually operate on a fee-for-service-rendered basis, not on a prepaid basis. Members of the PPO select from among the preferred providers for needed services. Also in contrast to HMOs, PPO health care providers are normally in private practice. They have agreed to offer their services to the group and its members at fees that are typically less than what they normally charge. In exchange, because the group refers its members to the PPO, the providers broaden their patient/service base. One of the features that attracts groups to PPOs is the discounted fees that are negotiated in advance.

Groups that contract with PPOs are very often employers, insurance companies or other health insurance benefits providers. While these groups do not mandate that individual members must use the PPO, a reduced benefit is typical if they do not. For instance, individuals may pay a $100 deductible if they use PPO services and a $500 deductible if they go outside the PPO for health care services.

---

1. Ben is covered by his employer's PPO. However, his physician is not a preferred provider. Which of the following is true?

   A. The PPO will not pay any benefits unless Ben switches to a preferred provider.

   B. Ben will be paid a reduced benefit unless he switches to a preferred provider.

---

2. HMOs usually operate on a (fee-for-service-rendered basis/prepaid basis) while PPOs usually operate on a (fee-for-service-rendered basis/prepaid basis).

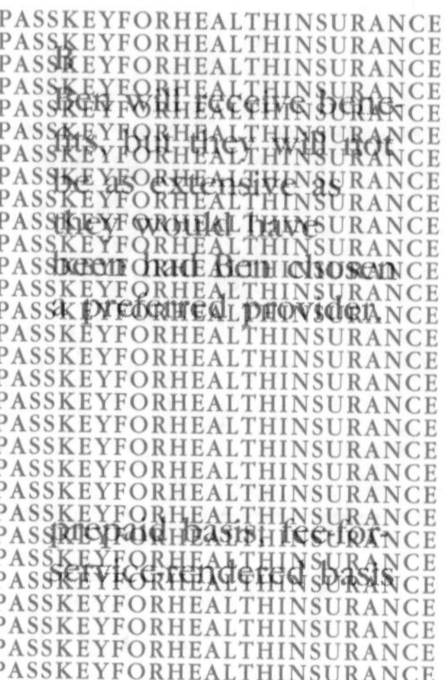

GOVERNMENT INSURANCE PROGRAMS

For many people, health care cost protection is made available through a state or federal government program. At the federal level, *Medicare* is the primary source of health insurance. It is a part of the Social Security program that also provides *disability income* to qualified workers under OASDI. Retired military personnel may be eligible for CHAMPUS (Civilian Health and Medicare Program of the Uniformed Services), which shares the cost of medical care in civilian facilities when care is not available at a military hospital. At the state level, *Medicaid* offers protection to financially needy individuals and state *workers' compensation* programs provide benefits for workers who suffer from occupational injuries or illnesses. The subject of Medicare was covered in Chapter 5; here we will look at Social Security disability, Medicaid, workers' compensation programs and CHAMPUS.

Social Security Disability Income

In addition to Medicare, the federal government also provides disability-related benefits through the Social Security "Old-Age and Survivors Disability Insurance" (OASDI) program.

Disability income benefits are available to covered workers who qualify under Social Security requirements. One of the requirements is that the individual must be so mentally or physically disabled that he or she cannot perform *any* substantial gainful work. In addition, the impairment must be expected to last at least 12 months or result in an earlier death. The determination of disability for Social Security purposes must be based on medical evidence; it is usually made by a government agency. In addition to meeting this very restrictive definition of disabled, the individual must have earned a minimum number of quarters of coverage under Social Security.

A five-month waiting period is required before an individual will qualify for benefits. During this waiting period time the individual must remain disabled. For example, if Jerry became disabled in January, he must wait five full months—February through June—before he will qualify for disability benefits. His first benefit payment would be for July, and it would be paid in August. No second five-month waiting period is required if the disabled worker recovers and then is disabled again within five years.

Social Security Taxes

The benefits provided by Social Security—retirement, survivor, disability and Medicare—are financed by a payroll tax on workers, their employers and the self-employed. Federal law specifies the rates of Social Security tax to be paid each year.

An employee pays Social Security tax on his or her annual earned income up to the amount of the year's designated wage base. In 1998, the employee and employer each paid 6.2 percent in taxes for Social Security and 1.45 percent for Medicare. The total of the current tax rate is applied each year to the earned incomes of employees and others who are self-employed on earnings up to the specified wage base. There is no maximum wage base for Medicare taxes.

The Social Security tax rates and wage base are subject to change, so agents should check regularly to keep up with the current rates and wage base.

---

1. Jerome, an employee of the Lextex Corporation, paid $2,250 in Social Security taxes based on his earnings for the year. Lextex then would have paid how much additional in Social Security taxes based solely on Jerome's earnings?

   A. $1,125
   B. $2,250

B. The employer pays the same amount as the employee.

2. In May, Ned became severely disabled and was unable to work for quite some time. In August, he returned to work in a position that required much less physical activity. Would Ned qualify for Social Security disability benefits?

   ____
   ____
   ____

No, because a five-month waiting period is required, during which the individual must remain disabled.

3. Horace, a 67-year-old worker "fully insured" under Social Security, becomes totally blind as the result of a chemical explosion. Would Horace be eligible for Social Security disability benefits? Why or why not?

No, because disability recipients must be under age 65. He would qualify, of course, for retirement benefits.

Medicaid

Medicaid is Title XIX of the Social Security Act, added to the Social Security program in 1965. Its purpose is to provide matching federal funds to states for their medical public assistance plans to help needy persons, regardless of age. If family income is below a specified level, Medicaid benefits generally are available. Although each state has some leeway in establishing eligibility requirements, Medicaid benefits are generally payable to low income individuals who are blind, disabled or under 21 years of age. The benefits may be applied toward Medicare deductibles and copayment requirements.

State Workers' Compensation Programs

All states have *workers' compensation laws,* which were enacted to provide mandatory benefits to employees for work-related injuries, illness or death. Employers are responsible for providing workers' compensation benefits to their employees and do so by purchasing coverage through state programs, private insurers or by self-insuring.

Although each state's laws differ with regard to procedures, requirements and minimum benefits, there is uniformity to the following extent:

- If a worker is killed in an industrial accident, the law provides for payment of burial expenses, subject to a maximum amount, and compensation for the surviving spouse or other dependents of the worker at the time of death.

- Regardless of whether the employer was negligent, he or she is liable for work-related disabilities that employees suffer.

- Under the law, a disabled employee is entitled to benefits as a matter of right, without having to sue the employer for benefits. However, in return for the benefits provided under the law, the employee gives up the right to sue the employer.

- Under most laws, a disabled employee is paid benefits on a weekly or monthly basis, rather than in a lump sum.

- The employer must provide the required benefits; the employee does not contribute to the plan.

The law provides for a schedule of benefits, the size of which is based on such factors as the severity of the disability and the employee's wages.

CHAMPUS

The *Civilian Health and Medical Program of the Uniformed Services* (CHAMPUS) is designed for all active and retired personnel and dependants who are unable to use government medical facilities because of distance, overcrowding or unavailability of appropriate medical treatment. Retired military personnel and their dependents and dependents of deceased personnel are compensated by CHAMPUS if they are not eligible for Medicare.

CHAMPUS provides payment (after a deductible amount) for medical care. It helps pay for inpatient and outpatient care, hospitalization, medical supplies and covered care at health care centers other than hospitals, such as drug and alcohol rehabilitation centers.

---

1. Which of the following statements regarding workers' compensation plans is/are correct?

   A. Benefit amounts are mandated by the federal government.
   B. A worker will qualify for benefits only if his or her disability or illness was a result of employer negligence.
   C. Benefits may be financed by private insurers, state funds or self-insurance.
   D. All of the above

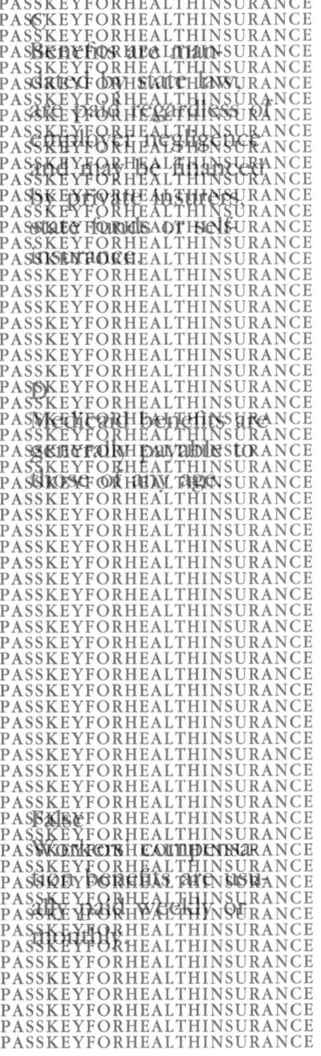

---

2. All of the following statements pertaining to Medicaid are correct, EXCEPT:

   A. It provides federal matching funds to states for medical public assistance plans.
   B. Its purpose is to help eligible needy persons with medical assistance.
   C. Medicaid benefits may be used to pay the deductible and coinsurance amounts of Medicare.
   D. It provides financial assistance only to persons age 65 or over who are in need of medical services they cannot afford.

---

3. Workers' compensation benefits are usually paid in a lump sum.

   (True/False)

4. CHAMPUS benefits are available to

____

____

ALTERNATIVE METHODS OF PROVIDING HEALTH INSURANCE

As the cost of health insurance has increased, businesses and individuals have turned to nontraditional methods of providing health insurance.

Self-Insurance

For businesses and individuals, an alternative to a private or service health insurance plan is *self-insurance*. Large corporations especially will self-insure their sick-leave plans for their employees. Labor unions, fraternal associations and other groups often self-insure their medical expense plans through dues or contributions from members. Others may self-insure part of a plan and use insurance to protect against large, unpredictable losses.

Many of these self-insured plans are administered by insurance companies or other organizations that are paid a fee for handling the paperwork and processing the claims. When an outside organization provides these functions, it is called an *administrative-services-only* (ASO) or *third-party administrator* (TPA) arrangement.

To protect a self-insured plan against a catastrophic loss, some groups adopt a *minimum premium plan* (MPP). These plans are designed to insure against a certain level of large, unpredictable losses, above and beyond the self-insured level. As the name implied, MPPs are available for a fraction of the insurer's normal premium.

Multiple Employer Trusts

As mentioned in an earlier chapter, a method of marketing group benefits to employers who have small number of employees is the *multiple employer trust (MET)*. METs may provide either a single type of insurance (such as health insurance) or a wide range of coverages (for example, life, medical expense and disability income insurance). In some cases alternative forms of the same coverage are available (such as comprehensive health insurance or basic health insurance).

An employer who wants to get coverage for employees from a MET must first become a member of the trust by subscribing to it. The employer is issued a joinder agreement, which spells out the relationship between the trust and the employer and specifies the coverages to which the employer has subscribed. It is not necessary for an employer to subscribe to all the coverages offered by a MET.

A MET may either provide benefits on a self-funded basis or fund benefits with a contract purchased from an insurance company. In the latter case the trust, rather than the subscribing employers, is the master insurance contractholder. In either case the employees of subscribing employers are provided with benefit descriptions (certificates of insurance) in a manner similar to the usual group insurance agreement.

In addition to alternative methods of funding benefits, METs can be categorized according to how they are administered, that is, whether by an insurance company or a third-party administrator.

Multiple Employer Welfare Arrangements

A *multiple employer welfare arrangement* (MEWA) is a type of MET for union employees that is self-funded and has tax-exempt status. Employees covered under a MEWA are required by law to have an "employment related common bond."

■ HOW HEALTH INSURANCE IS SOLD

As we've just discussed, health insurance is available to the public through a variety of means—private insurers, service providers and state and federal programs. With respect to private insurance, most coverage is purchased through licensed *producers* who present insurers' products and services to the public via active sales and marketing methods. Insurance producers may be either *agents* who represent one particular company or *brokers* who are not tied to any particular company and can represent many companies' products.

Agents

An insurance agent represents an insurance company in the following ways:

1. describing the company's insurance policies to prospects and explaining the conditions under which the policies may be obtained;

2. soliciting applications for insurance;

3. sometimes collecting payments (premiums) from policyowners or applicants; and

4. rendering service to both prospects and those who have already purchased policies from the company.

Agents have a contract with the insurer they represent. This contract, called a "contract of agency," clearly defines the scope of the agent's authority, as agreed upon by the company and the agent. Within the authority granted, the agent is seen as identical with the company under the law and the agent's acts are binding upon the company. The relationship between an agent and the company he or she represents is governed by *agency law*.

Principles of Agency Law

By legal definition, an agent is a person who acts for another person or entity (known as the "principal") with regard to contractual arrangements with third parties. Implicit in this definition is the concept of power—an authorized agent has the power to bind the principal to contracts (and to the rights and responsibilities of those contracts). From this concept of power come the main principles of agency law:

- The acts of the agent (within the scope of his or her authority) are the acts of the principal.
- A contract completed by an agent on behalf of the principal is a contract of the principal.
- Payments made to an agent on behalf of the principal are payments to the principal.
- Knowledge of the agent regarding business of the principal is presumed to be knowledge of the principal.

Agent Authority

Within agency law, agent authority is another key concept. Technically, only those actions for which an agent is actually authorized can bind a principal. In reality, however, an agent's authority can be quite broad. In essence, there are three types of agent authority: *express, implied* and *apparent.* Let's take a look at each.

Express authority is the authority a principal intends to—and actually does, in fact—give to its agent. Express authority is granted in writing by means of the agent's contract. For example, an agent has the express authority to solicit applications for insurance on behalf of the company.

Implied authority is authority that is not expressly granted, but which the agent is assumed to have in order to transact the business of the principal. For example, an agent's contract may not specifically state that he or she can print business cards that contain the company's name, but the authority to do so is implied.

Apparent authority is the appearance of, or the assumption of, authority based on the actions, words or deeds of the principal or because of circumstances the principal created. For example, by providing an individual with a rate book, application forms and sales literature, a company creates the impression that an agency relationship exists between itself and the individual. The company will not later be allowed to deny that such a relationship existed.

The public cannot be expected to know exactly what authority the contract of agency grants the agent. As a result, the agent and the company may be held legally responsible for any acts, even beyond the agent's authority, if the public could have reasonably assumed that the agent had authority to take the action he or she took.

Agent as a Fiduciary

Another legal concept that governs the activity of an agent is that of *fiduciary*. A fiduciary is a person who holds a position of special trust and confidence. Agents act in a fiduciary capacity when they accept premiums on behalf of the insurer or offer advice that affects people's financial security. Agents have fiduciary responsibilities to both their clients and the insurance companies they represent. Acting as a fiduciary requires that an agent:

- be fit and proper;
- be honest and trustworthy;
- have a good business reputation;
- be qualified to perform insurance functions;
- have knowledge of, and abide by, state laws and regulations; and
- act in good faith.

Brokers

While agents represent the insurer, brokers represent the buyer in an insurance sales transaction. The broker determines what kind and amount of insurance the client needs and makes a recommendation accordingly. The broker also selects the company with which to place the business.

A broker may place business with more than one company, while an agent normally places business only with the company with which he or she is under contract. An agent has an agent's contract; a broker must have a broker's contract. A broker may have broker's contracts with several companies, or may secure a one-time broker's contract for placing a single case.

In practice, the legal distinction between brokers and agents may not be that significant since both brokers and agents are licensed as insurance *producers* and both are subject to insurance laws and regulations.

Special Agents

In addition to agents and brokers, there are also *special agents,* who do not actually solicit insurance business, but who work as field representatives, helping a company's central office and the agency force in their territory.

Solicitors

Solicitors act for agents by seeking prospects, receiving applications or collecting premiums. However, solicitors generally do not have the power to bind coverage.

Consultants

Consultants are independent advisors who specialize in the design, implementation and administration of insurance sharing plans. Consultants are usually licensed agents.

1. Pat is a licensed agent with Full Life. As such, Pat is authorized to represent the company in accordance with terms defined in a ____________ .

contract of agency

2. James, a licensed broker, sells a disability income policy to a client and has the policy issued by the Fanfun Company. Technically, whom does James represent?

   A. The client
   B. The Fanfun company

A

Brokers represent their clients.

3. An insurance broker may place business with (only one/ more than one) insurer.

more than one

4. Authority that the insurance company intends to give the agent and does specifically give the agent is called

   A. express authority.
   B. binding authority.
   C. apparent authority.
   D. implied authority.

A

Express authority is given explicitly in the contract of agency.

5. A (consultant/solicitor) is an independent advisor who specializes in the design, implementation and administration of insurance sharing plans.

consultant

A solicitor acts for an agent by seeking prospects, receiving applications or collecting premiums, but generally does not have the authority to bind coverage.

AGENCY SYSTEMS

Generally speaking, there are three systems that support the sale of insurance through agents and brokers. These are the *career agency system, the personal producing general agency system* and the *independent agency system*.

Career Agency System

Career agencies are branches of major stock and mutual insurance companies that are contracted to represent the particular insurer in a specific area. In career agencies, insurance agents are recruited, trained and supervised by either a manager-employee of the company or a general agent (GA) who has a vested right in any business written by his or her agents. General agents may operate strictly as managers or they may devote a portion of their time to sales. The career agency system focuses on building sales staffs.

Personal Producing General Agency System

The *personal producing general agency* (PPGA) system is similar to the career agency system. However, PPGAs do not recruit, train or supervise career agents. They primarily sell insurance although they may build a small sales force to assist them. PPGAs are generally responsible for maintaining their own offices and administrative staff. Agents hired by a PPGA are considered employees of the PPGA, not the insurance company, and are supervised by regional directors.

Independent Agency System

The *independent agency system,* a creation of the property/casualty industry, does not tie a sales staff or agency to any one particular insurance company; rather, independent brokers represent any number of insurance companies through contractual agreements. They are compensated on a commission or a fee basis for the business they produce. This system is also known as the "American agency system."

Other Methods of Selling Insurance

While most insurance is sold through agents or brokers under the systems described above, a large volume is also marketed through *direct selling* and *mass marketing* methods.

With the *direct selling* method, the insurer deals directly with consumers—no agent or broker is involved—selling its policies through vending machines, advertisements or salaried sales representatives. Insurers that operate using this method are known as "direct writers" or "direct response insurers."

A large volume of insurance also is sold through *mass marketing* techniques, such as direct mail or newspaper, magazine, radio and television ads. Mass marketing methods provide exposure to large groups of consumers, often using direct selling methods with occasional follow-up by agents.

---

1. Which of the following is likely to recruit and train an insurance agent?

   A. A general agent
   B. A personal producing general agent

2. What three systems support the sale of insurance through agents and brokers?

   1. ______________________________
   2. ______________________________
   3. ______________________________

1. Career agency system
2. Independent agency system (or American agency system)
3. Personal producing general agency system

(May be in any order.)

---

3. Which system is a creation of the property/casualty industry?

   ____

The independent agency system

14

How the Insurance Industry Is Regulated

In order to protect consumers and preserve the solvency of insurance companies, the insurance industry is strictly regulated. This chapter gives a brief overview of the how insurers and agents are regulated by a number of authorities, including some within the industry itself.

HISTORY OF REGULATION

The insurance industry, unlike the securities or banking industries, is primarily regulated at the state level rather than the federal level. Though the history of insurance regulation shows a seesaw between state and federal authority—each at different times being the primary regulatory body—the matter was resolved in 1945 when Congress enacted the *McCarran-Ferguson Act*. This Act recognized that state regulation of insurance was in the public's best interest, but also allowed the federal government to apply antitrust laws "to the extent that such business (insurance) is not regulated at the state level." To avoid federal intervention, each state has revised its insurance laws to conform with federal requirements.

STATE REGULATION OF INSURERS

The insurance industry is regulated at the state level by *state insurance departments, divisions* or *boards*. These in turn are headed by a *commissioner, director* or *superintendent*, depending on the state. Though specific duties will vary from state to state, the head of a state insurance department is generally responsible for:

- issuing rules and regulations;
- licensing and supervising insurance companies formed within the state;
- licensing and supervising insurance agents and brokers;

- controlling the kinds of insurance contracts and policies that may be sold in the state;

- regulating the investment activity of insurers;

- determining the amount of reserves an insurer must maintain; and

- overseeing insurance companies' marketing practices and investigating consumer complaints.

Licensing of Insurers

All insurance companies doing business within a given state must be *licensed* or *certified* by that state. Thus, insurance companies are referred to as "licensed" or "nonlicensed." (In some states, the terms used to designate whether or not a company is licensed are "authorized" and "nonauthorized" or "admitted" and "nonadmitted.") In addition, the following terms are frequently used to describe insurance companies and their site of incorporation:

- *Domestic insurers.* An insurance company is a domestic insurer in the state in which it is incorporated.

- *Foreign insurers.* A foreign insurer is one licensed to conduct business in states other than the one in which it is incorporated.

- *Alien insurers.* Alien insurers are companies incorporated in a country other than the United States, the District of Columbia or any territorial possession.

Whether companies are considered domestic, foreign, or alien, they must be licensed in each state where they conduct business. State laws prohibit insurance companies that are not licensed or not authorized from doing business within their borders.

---

1. The Apex Insurance Company plans to expand its operations into three additional states. What must the company do before it can solicit applications in those states?

____

____

The company must become licensed in each of the three states.

2. List some of the duties of the head of a state insurance department.

____

____

____

____

____

____

____

____

3. An insurance company that is incorporated in Canada is a(n) (foreign/alien) company in the United States.

STATE REGULATION OF INSURANCE PRODUCERS

Every state requires that those who sell insurance have a license from the state. However, before an insurance department will issue such a license—whether it's to a prospective agent or broker—the candidate must pass a producer licensing exam administered by the department. In most states, a specific number of hours of approved prelicensing study also are required of applicants before they sit for the licensing exam. An additional common requirement for agents is that the insurance company that the applicant wishes to represent must file with the insurance department a *notice of appointment* authorizing the applicant to represent that insurer.

In some states, the agent's or broker's license may be perpetual unless revoked; in many states, however, it must be renewed at stipulated intervals and producers must meet specific continuing education requirements in order to qualify for license renewal.

Suspension or Termination of Licenses

Insurance commissioners have the power to refuse a license or to revoke or suspend a license after proper notice and hearing. Such action may be taken on the grounds that a licensee willfully violated the law or participated in fraudulent or dishonest business practices. A license also may be canceled or suspended if an agent had proven to be untrustworthy or incompetent or has made a material misrepresentation in his or her application for a license.

A license is terminated by an agent's death or if the insurer cancels the agent's appointment. However, brokers are licensed in their own right and severance from any company does not terminate their licenses to sell. Some states will issue a temporary license or "estate certificate of convenience" to the heirs or next of kin of a deceased agent or broker if they wish to carry on the business while arranging for a new permanent license or attempting to find a buyer for the business.

---

1. If Judith, a teacher, wishes to become a licensed insurance agent, all she must do is file an application with her state insurance commissioner.

   (True/False)

2. Jerry, a licensed agent, participates in dishonest business practices. What serious action may the state commissioner take to halt such practices?

   ____

   ____

Prohibited Practices

Every state dictates acceptable marketing and sales practices for its licensed producers. While there are different standards as to what are ethical and unethical practices, certain practices have long been punishable in virtually all jurisdictions: *misrepresentation, twisting, misuse of premiums* and, in some states, *replacement* and *rebating*. These are known as "prohibited practices."

Misrepresentation

Misrepresentation is a false or misleading statement or representation made intentionally or unintentionally by a producer regarding:

1. the policy he or she is proposing,
2. the policy of a competing agent or
3. a competitor company.

A buyer of health insurance is frequently confused or unclear about the language of policy provisions; thus it is the agent's responsibility to explain the exact nature of the policy being presented. Agents are not allowed to misrepresent a policy's terms or benefits or the nature of the coverage it provides. If policy dividends are payable, they cannot be represented as guaranteed.

State regulations impose varying penalties for misrepresentation, from reprimands to fines and imprisonment, depending on the circumstances.

Twisting

Twisting is the act of persuading a policyowner to drop and replace an existing policy with a new policy by misrepresenting the terms or conditions of one or the other. Typically, the motivation for twisting is simply to increase one's commissions by inducing the sale of a policy without regard to the potential disadvantages to the policyowner. Not only is twisting illegal, it is highly unethical.

Misuse of Premiums

Misuse of premiums includes diverting premium funds for personal use. Some states require that an agent establish a separate premium account if he or she holds the money for any time prior to turning it over to the insurer. Commingling premium funds with personal funds is prohibited.

Replacement

Replacement of one policy for another means convincing a policyholder to lapse or terminate an existing policy and purchase another. While replacement is not necessarily illegal, it may not always be in the best interests of the policyowner.

Where allowed, the practice of replacement is strictly regulated and requires full and fair disclosure to the policyowner of all facts regarding both the new coverage and the existing policy. For example, policyowners should be informed if health conditions covered under the existing policy will be subject to waiting periods or classified as preexisting conditions by the new policy. "No loss-no gain" laws provide that a replacing policy continue to cover all continuing claims that began under the policy being replaced. This is true even if the replacement policy excludes preexisting conditions or establishes waiting periods before benefits are payable.

Replacement is an area in which misconduct on the part of an agent could easily expose him or her to errors and omissions liability. ("Errors and omissions" insurance is professional liability insurance for agents.) To avoid this, agents should take care to fully inform the policyowner and to follow the regulations established in their states. Replacement also requires notice to both the existing insurer and the replacing insurer regarding the replacement.

Rebating

Rebating occurs when a buyer of an insurance policy receives any part of the agent's commission or if the agent gives the buyer anything of significant value in exchange for purchasing a policy. Most states prohibit the practice of rebating, terming it an "illegal inducement." In some states, it is not just the agent who gave the rebate who is seen as breaking the law, but the policyowner who accepted the rebate as well.

Where rebating is allowed, strict guidelines have been imposed to control and monitor its practice. Some states have set a dollar maximum and gifts valued above that maximum would be considered rebating. This allows agents the leeway to give away promotional items of minimal value. For example, a $25 gift certificate given in exchange for the purchase of a policy would be rebating in some jurisdictions, while giving a client a calendar valued at $3, or a wallet worth $10 would not.

Professionalism and Ethics

It is the responsibility of insurance agents to be knowledgeable about the products they have to offer, state laws and regulations affecting their business and any new developments in the insurance industry.

To meet this responsibility, agents can attend insurance seminars, take additional study courses in insurance, read trade publications regularly and attend insurance association meetings. By expanding their knowledge on a continuing basis, agents will be in a position to serve prospects and clients more effectively. They can provide a genuine, continuing service to clients, and by helping their clients, help themselves and place their own careers on a higher professional plane.

The Code of Ethics of the National Association of Health Underwriters, printed at the back of this book, can guide agents toward their personal goals of professionalism.

---

1. If an agent implies to an applicant that a major medical policy will pay all hospital expenses when the policy has an 80/20 coinsurance provision, what is the agent guilty of?

   ____

Misrepresentation

---

2. What is "twisting"?

   ____

   ____

   ____

   ____

   ____

Twisting is persuading a prospect to drop an existing policy in order to buy a new policy by misrepresenting or distorting the facts.

3. In some states, policyowners who accept rebates from agents would be violating the law against rebating and could also be subject to penalties.

   (True/False)

True

In some states both the agent and the policyowner are considered to have broken the law when rebating occurs.

---

4. Which of the following practices is NOT necessarily illegal?

   A. Twisting
   B. Misrepresentation
   C. Replacement

C

Replacement is not necessarily illegal, but strict regulations must be followed.

---

5. Which of the following agent examples represent a misuse of premiums?

   Henry uses premiums he has collected to have his car repaired and plans to replace the money the following month.
   A. (Yes/No)

   Marsha places premium money in her personal checking account to pay a large personal telephone bill at home.
   B. (Yes/No)

   Bill deposits premium collections in a separate account at the bank for safekeeping before forwarding the money to his home office.
   C. (Yes/No)

A. Yes

B. Yes

C. No

---

6. George sends birthday cards with 25 cents enclosed to the children of his policyowners. Would George be guilty of rebating?

   (Yes/No)

No

In order to be a rebate, the item given away must be of significant value.

■ NATIONAL ASSOCIATION OF INSURANCE COMMISSIONERS

All state insurance commissioners or directors are members of the *National Association of Insurance Commissioners* (NAIC). This organization has standing committees that work regularly to examine various aspects of the insurance industry and to recommend appropriate insurance laws and regulations.

Basically, the NAIC has four broad objectives:

1. to encourage uniformity in state insurance laws and regulations;

2. to assist in the administration of those laws and regulations by promoting efficiency;

3. to help protect the interests of policyowners and consumers; and

4. to preserve state regulation of the insurance business.

The NAIC has been instrumental in developing guidelines and model legislation that help ensure that the insurance industry maintains a high level of public trust by conducting its business competently and fairly. This group also develops standards for policy provisions, helping ensure that policies are more uniform than disparate across the country. Examples of this work are the model Medicare supplement policies discussed in Chapter 5. Notable among the NAIC's accomplishments was the creation of the *Advertising Code* and the *Unfair Trade Practices Act*, which have been adopted by virtually every state.

Advertising Code

A principal problem of states in the past was regulating misleading advertising and direct mail solicitations. Many states now subscribe to the *Advertising Code* developed by the NAIC. The Code specifies certain words and phrases that are considered misleading and are not to be used in advertising of any kind. Also required under this code is full disclosure of policy renewal, cancellation and termination provisions. Other rules pertain to the use of testimonials, statistics, special offers, etc.

Unfair Trade Practices Act

Most jurisdictions have also adopted the NAIC's *Unfair Trade Practices Act*. This act, as amended in 1972, gives insurance commissioners the power to investigate insurance companies and producers, to issue cease and desist orders and to impose penalties on violators. The act also gives commissioners the authority to seek a court injunction to restrain insurers from using any methods believed to be unfair or deceptive. Included in the context of "unfair trade practices" are misrepresentation and false advertising, coercion and intimidation, inequitable administration or claims settlement and unfair discrimination.

■ STATE GUARANTY ASSOCIATIONS

All states have established *guaranty funds* or *guaranty associations* to support insurers and to protect consumers if an insurer becomes insolvent. Should an insurer be financially unable to pay its claims, the state guaranty association will step in and cover the consumers' unpaid claims. These state associations are funded by insurance companies through assessments.

■ RATING SERVICES

The financial strength and stability of an insurance company are two vitally important factors to potential insurance buyers and to insurance companies themselves. Various *rating services* such as A.M. Best, Inc., Standard &

Poor's, Duff & Phelps and Moody's publish guides to companies' financial integrity and claims-paying ability. For instance, in *Best's Insurance Reports,* companies are rated as A++ to A+ (superior), A to A– (excellent), B++ to B+ (very good), B to B– (good), C++ to C+ (fair), C to C– (marginal), D (below minimum standards), E (under state supervision) and F (in liquidation). Experts generally recommend that insurance buyers purchase policies from companies that have a rating of A– or better, since this indicates financial stability.

---

1. Which of the following is NOT a broad objective of the NAIC?

   A. Promoting uniformity in state insurance laws
   B. Promoting uniformity in state insurance regulations
   C. Promoting competition among insurers
   D. Protecting the interests of policyowners

---

2. What model law has been adopted by states to regulate the advertising and solicitation of insurance by mail or by other means?

   ____

   ____

---

3. Under the Unfair Trade Practices Act, who has the power to investigate and take action against violators in cases of insurance solicitation by mail?

   A. State insurance commissioner
   B. State and municipal courts

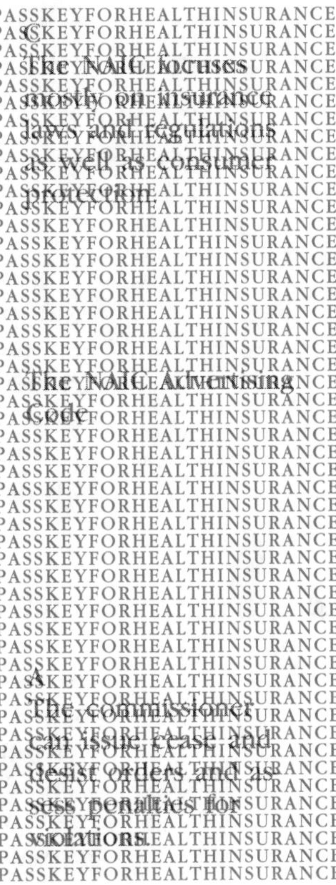

15

Uses of Health Insurance

It may at first seem that the uses of health insurance are self-explanatory: one purchases health insurance to protect against the cost of health care—or, more accurately, health insurance provides protection against the costs associated with the loss of one's health. However, the different types of health insurance plans can be used in various ways to meet an individual's or business's unique needs. This chapter looks at the question, "What are the uses of health insurance?"

INDIVIDUAL NEEDS FOR HEALTH INSURANCE

At one time it was acceptable to expect one's family to provide support when illness or disability struck. Those days are now long past; today, we all must prepare for and assume the responsibility of covering the cost of medical care. However, unless one is independently wealthy, the prospect of covering costs out-of-pocket is not an attractive one; indeed, it can be downright terrifying.

The loss of one's health can have wide-ranging consequences. Not only does the cost of medical care come with a high price tag, but the loss of income that often accompanies a disabling illness or injury can compound the devastating effects of the health loss. Current demographics, which show that most families have both parents working, emphasize the need to consider both parents' income needs when designing a complete health insurance program.

Medical Expense Insurance Needs

While it is difficult to measure the importance of one type of insurance over another, it is fair to presume that a health insurance program must begin with an adequate amount of medical expense insurance. Without proper protection devoted to these potential costs, even the most basic medical care can quickly exhaust an individual's savings; a catastrophic claim can spell financial disaster.

At one time, most medical policies were the basic medical expense type, those that offer "first-dollar" protection. However, today it is more common to find most Americans covered under some form of major medical policy or a service plan such as Blue Cross and Blue Shield or an HMO. If the policyowner can afford the cost, an ideal policy is a combination plan in which a basic plan is enhanced by a supplementary major medical plan. Under this approach, the insured obtains the "first-dollar" benefits of the basic plan and also has the expansive protection offered by the major medical plan.

Most policyowners, of course, are concerned with the cost of their health insurance and find that some financial sacrifice may be required. As we have seen, an individual major medical plan with a $100 individual deductible is going to cost more than a comparable plan with a $500 deductible. A plan with an 80/20 coinsurance provision will cost more than a comparable plan with a 75/25 coinsurance provision. The question the policyowner must answer is, "Am I willing to assume more of the cost risk of *possible* future claims in exchange for the *definite* cost savings offered by a plan with a higher deductible or coinsurance limit?"

Group vs. Individual Coverage

More Americans are protected under a group medical expense policies than individual policies. The benefit to the group member, even assuming the plan is contributory, is the significantly less out-of-pocket cost than a comparable individual plan. The group plan participant can also take comfort in knowing that even if he or she should terminate employment, continued coverage is guaranteed through the conversion privilege built into every group health policy.

---

1. A major medical plan with a $100 deductible is less expensive than one with a $500 deductible.

   (True/False)

2. More Americans are covered by individual medical expense policies than by group medical expense policies.

   (True/False)

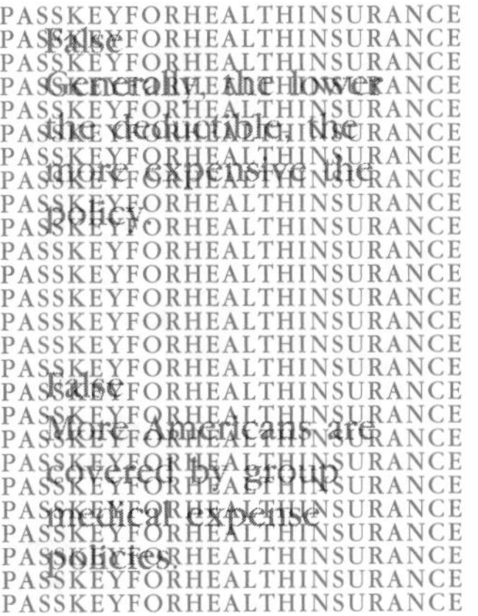

3. Nick is covered by his employer's group medical expense plan. Sheila has a comparable individual medical expense policy.

   A. Assuming their health care expenses are approximately equal, who is likely to pay more out-of-pocket, Nick or Sheila?

   ____

   B. What feature of Nick's group plan will guarantee Nick coverage should he quit his job?

   ____

A. Sheila
Group plans usually require participants to pay less out-of-pocket expenses than do individual plans.
B. the conversion privilege

Disability Income Insurance Needs

The importance of protecting one's earnings is sometimes overlooked in the insurance needs analysis process—a regrettable fact for the many people who become disabled every year. Americans too often assume that Social Security will provide the income necessary to survive if disability strikes. This is an unfortunate assumption; not only is the definition of "disabled" to qualify for Social Security benefits extremely narrow, but there is no assurance that the benefits will meet the disabled person's needs.

Social Security disability income should be viewed as a possible source of income to augment a personal plan. Whether the personal plan is based on a group policy or an individual policy, it should be regarded as the primary source of income if earnings are lost due to disability.

Policyowners can control the premium cost of a disability income plan by electing a longer elimination period than might otherwise be desired. The length of the benefit period also has a direct impact on the premium.

Because of the favorable tax treatment given to individually funded disability income policies, a plan that provides about 60 percent of predisability gross earnings can be considered sufficient. This is because disability income benefits are income tax free if the individual insured paid the premiums. An individual who earns $3,000 a month may only take home $2,000 after taxes. Consequently, a disability plan that provides a monthly tax-free benefit of $1,800 would likely be sufficient.

In the case of group disability income plans, the group member has little choice as to the level of benefits provided; the plan document must have a schedule of benefits that identifies what the participant will receive if disabled. On the other hand, the group member benefits to the extent the employer contributes to the disability income premiums.

If both parents in a family are actively employed, then disability income must be considered for each. If each parent's income is indispensable for the financial support of the family, then it is safe to assume that the loss of *either* income would present a financial problem.

1. A disability income policy with a six-month elimination period is (less/more) expensive than one with a 60-day elimination period, all other factors being equal.

2. The benefit payable under an individual disability income policy should equal the insured's gross monthly income.

   (True/False)

3. Methods of controlling the premium costs of a disability income policy include all of the following, EXCEPT:

   A. extending the elimination period.
   B. shortening the benefit period.
   C. increasing the deductible.

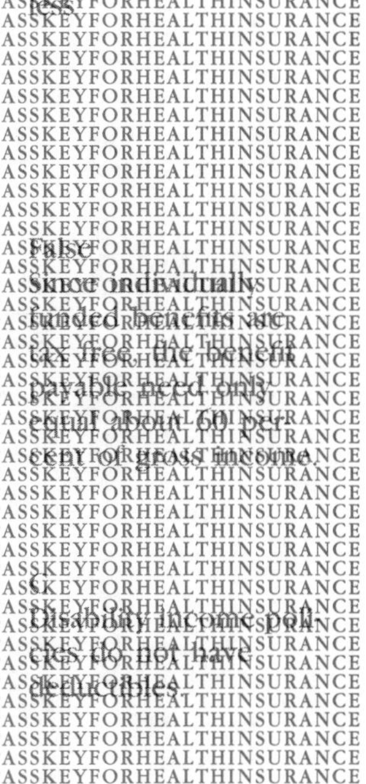

BUSINESS USES FOR HEALTH INSURANCE

Many health insurance producers have found a niche servicing the business market. There is a good, practical reason for this—the health insurance needs of the business market are as great as the needs of individuals.

Business uses of health insurance can be broadly divided into two categories: *employee benefit plans* and *business continuation plans*.

Employee Benefit Plans

While the term "employee benefit plan" can encompass a wide variety of benefit offerings—life insurance, a pension or profit-sharing plan, vacation pay, deferred compensation arrangements, funeral leave, sick time—it is rare when it does not include some kind of provision for health insurance or health benefits. The large and rapid increases in the cost of health care are likely the primary reasons for the popularity of employer-sponsored health plans, and many people rely on these plans as their sole source of health insurance.

Group Health Insurance

As we have learned, a group health plan can consist of medical insurance, disability income insurance or accidental death and dismemberment insurance—alone or in any combination. In fact, it is not uncommon to find all of these coverages included in a single group insurance plan.

By providing its employees with a plan for health insurance, an employer derives a number of benefits.

- The plan contributes to employee morale and productivity.
- The plan enables the employer to provide a needed benefit that employees would otherwise have to pay for with personal after-tax dollars (this helps hold down demands for wage increases).
- The plan places the employer in a competitive position for hiring and retaining employees.
- The employer can obtain a tax deduction for the cost of contributing to the plan.
- The plan enhances the employer's image in both public and employee relations.

Cafeteria Plans

Many times, employer-provided health insurance benefits are part of a *cafeteria plan*. As their name implies, cafeteria plans (also known as Section 125 plans) are benefit arrangements in which employees can pick and choose from a menu of benefits, thus tailoring their benefits package to their specific needs. Employees can select the benefits they value or need and forgo those of lesser importance to them. The employer allocates a certain amount of money to each employee to "buy" the benefits he or she desires; if the cost of the benefits exceeds the allocation, the employee may contribute the balance.

The types of flexible benefits usually available under a cafeteria plan include medical coverage, accidental death and dismemberment insurance, short-term and long-term disability, life insurance and dependent care. Some plans provide for "choices within the choices": an employee may have the option of selecting from various levels of medical plans or choosing from among a variety of HMOs, for example.

Business Continuation Plans

Just as life insurance provides a way to help a business continue in the event an owner or key employee dies, health insurance can help business continue in the event of a disabling sickness or injury. It does so through the following plans.

Business Overhead Expense Insurance

Business overhead expense insurance is designed to reimburse a business for overhead expenses in the event a business owner becomes disabled. It is sold on an individual basis to professionals in private practice, self-employed business owners, partners and occasionally close corporations.

Overhead expenses include such things as rent or mortgage payments, utilities, telephones, leased equipment, employees' salaries and the like—all the expenses that would continue and must be paid, regardless of the owner's disability. Business overhead expense policies do not include any compensation for the disabled owner; they are designed to help the day-to-day operation of his or her business continue during the period of disability.

The benefits payable under these kinds of policies are limited to the covered expenses incurred or the maximum that is stated in the policy. For example, assume Dr. Miller is the insured under a business overhead expense policy that pays maximum monthly benefits of $4,500. If Dr. Miller became disabled and actual monthly expenses were $3,950, the monthly benefits paid would be $3,950. If Dr. Miller's actual expenses were $4,700, the benefits payable would be $4,500.

The premium for business overhead insurance is a legitimate, tax-deductible business expense. The benefits when paid, however, are treated as taxable income.

Business Health Insurance

Business health insurance is available to indemnify a business for the loss of the services of a key employee, a partner or an owner should disability strike. Thus, these policies are often referred to as *key person disability insurance*. In the event of a disability, this insurance provides the business with funds to bridge the period necessary to secure and train a worthy successor.

The precise economic loss a business will face if a key individual becomes disabled is somewhat difficult to measure; the cost of securing an experienced, competent replacement or the income the employee or owner currently earns are two common approaches.

Disability Buy-Sell

A disability buy-sell agreement sets forth the terms for selling and buying a partner's or stock owner's share of a business in the event he or she becomes disabled and no longer able to participate in the business. It is a legal, binding arrangement, funded with a disability income policy.

Unlike typical disability income insurance plans that pay benefits in the form of periodic payments, the buy-sell plan usually contains a provision allowing for a lump-sum payment of the benefit, thereby facilitating the buy-out of the disabled's interest. However, if the owners desire, the plan often permits the buy-out to occur through the use of periodic income payments.

Disability buy-sell plans are characterized by lengthy elimination periods, often as long as two years. The reason for this is simple: since the plan involves the sale of a disabled partner's or owner's interest in the business, it is important to be quite sure that the disabled person will not be able to return to the business.

Considering the fact that a disabled partner can represent a double liability—the remaining partners must not only make up the slack left by the disabled partner's absence but usually must pay him or her an income as well—it is understandable why the disability buy-sell plan is popular with business owners.

---

1. Fred owns a small hardware store and is covered under a business overhead expense policy. If he becomes disabled, he can expect all the following expenses to be covered, EXCEPT:

   A. his employees' salaries.
   B. his salary.
   C. utility bills.
   D. property and liability insurance premiums.

B

Business overhead expense policies do not cover the disabled person's salary.

---

2. Which of the following characteristics is associated with disability buy-sell plans?

   A. A short elimination period
   B. The option to elect a lump-sum payment
   C. Provisions to cover the business's overhead expenses
   D. All of the above

B

Disability buy-sell plans have relatively long elimination periods and do not cover overhead expenses; however, they do provide the option of electing a lump-sum payment.

---

3. Which type of insurance indemnifies a business for the loss of a key employee's services in the case of disability?

   ____

Business health insurance or key person disability insurance

---

4. An employee benefit plan in which employees choose from a menu of benefits is called a ____________ .

cafeteria plan

Progressive Quiz No. 5

(Text page reference numbers are shown under each correct response in the red column.)

1. An insurance company has its home office in Illinois but is also licensed to do business in Indiana and Ohio. In the latter two states the insurer would be classified as what type of company?

   A. Alien
   B. Foreign
   C. Mutual
   D. Domestic

B
(176)

---

2. A mutual company is owned by its

   A. policyowners.
   B. directors.
   C. stockholders.
   D. underwriters.

A
(157)

---

3. Industrial health insurance is characterized by premiums paid

   A. quarterly.
   B. annually.
   C. semiannually.
   D. weekly.

D
(158)

---

4. Under the MedicarePlus Choice program

   A. Medicare will assign an individual to a health plan (such as an HMO) and Medicare will pay all costs associated with the plan.
   B. Medicare will assign an individual to a health plan and Medicare will pay the plan a certain amount per enrollee, with the individual paying certain out-of-pocket expenses.
   C. the individual will select a health plan and Medicare will pay the plan a certain amount per enrollee, with the individual paying certain out-of-pocket expenses.
   D. the individual will select a health plan and the individual will pay all costs associated with the plan.

C
(51)

5. An employer's contributions to an LTC insurance plan on behalf of an employee are

   A. included in the employee's gross income in all cases.
   B. excluded from the employee's gross income in all cases.
   C. included in the employee's gross income unless made as part of a cafeteria plan.
   D. excluded from the employee's gross income unless made as part of a cafeteria plan.

D
(62)

---

6. Nonoccupational policies exclude coverage for

   A. injuries received away from the place of employment.
   B. work-related injuries or illnesses.
   C. sickness but not for accidental injuries.
   D. persons in nonhazardous jobs.

B
(27, 140)

---

7. In general, statements made in an application for health insurance are considered to be

   A. warranties.
   B. statements under oath.
   C. factual.
   D. representations.

D
(85)

---

8. Health maintenance organizations (HMOs) are known for stressing

   A. preventive medicine and early treatment.
   B. state-sponsored health-care plans.
   C. in-hospital care and services.
   D. health care services mostly for government employees.

A
(161)

---

9. Who pays Social Security taxes?

   A. Employers
   B. Employees
   C. Self-employed individuals
   D. All of the above

D
(165)

10. All of the following may be classified as service organizations, EXCEPT:

A. health maintenance organizations.
B. Blue Cross and Blue Shield.
C. health insurance companies.
D. preferred provider organizations.

---

11. Technically, in a health insurance transaction involving a broker, whom does the broker represent?

A. A client
B. An agency
C. A state's insurance commissioner
D. An insurance company

---

12. Which of the following statements is true concerning Medicare or Medicare supplement policies?

A. Medicare Part B provides basic hospital insurance.
B. Medicare supplement policies generally pay all or part of the Medicare deductible and coinsurance amounts.
C. Most major commercial companies offer unique Medicare supplement policies.
D. A general enrollment period for Medicare is scheduled every two years.

---

13. All of the following statements about Blue Cross and Blue Shield are correct, EXCEPT:

A. Both are service type organizations.
B. Both have contractual arrangements with hospitals and physicians.
C. They are available on an individual, family or group basis.
D. Subscribers are billed directly by hospitals and physicians.

---

14. The waiting period before qualifying for Social Security disability benefits is

A. 6 months.
B. 12 months.
C. 5 months.
D. 3 months.

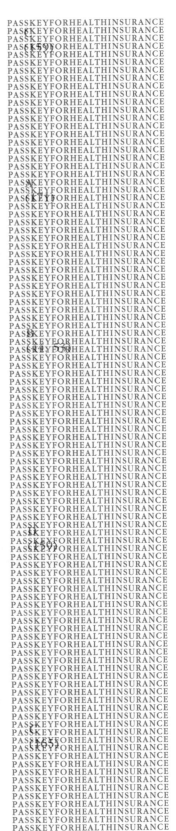

15. Which policy provision may help an insurance company avoid paying medical expense benefits for a claim attributable to a preexisting condition?

A. Coinsurance
B. Probationary period
C. Deductible
D. Elimination period

B
(28)

---

16. From a technical standpoint, whom does the agent represent?

A. A client
B. Himself or herself
C. An insurance company
D. A prospect

C
(169)

---

17. What is rebating?

A. Persuading a policyowner to lapse an existing policy in order to buy a new policy
B. Making disparaging remarks about a competing policy, agent or company
C. Giving a prospect the impression that an illustration of dividends is a guarantee of future dividends
D. Giving a policyowner part of a commission or anything of significant value as an inducement to buy insurance

D
(179, 180)

---

18. Which of the following is true regarding HMOs that operate on the individual practice association model?

A. The physicians only treat HMO patients.
B. The physicians are salaried HMO employees.
C. The physicians participate on a part-time basis.
D. The physicians work out of HMO facilities.

C
(162)

---

19. HMOs must provide new members with evidence of coverage within _____ days of enrollment.

A. 15
B. 21
C. 31
D. 60

D
(161)

20. All of the following are true regarding PPOs, EXCEPT:

A. Preferred providers are usually salaried PPO employees.
B. Provider fees are negotiated in advance.
C. PPOs operate on a fee-for-service-rendered basis.
D. If PPO members do not select a preferred provider, their benefits may be reduced.

A
(163, 164)

---

21. Which of the following is true regarding METs?

A. METs may be self-funded.
B. METs may be managed by a third-party administrator.
C. A MET may be funded through an insurance company.
D. All of the above

D
(168)

---

22. What is the name of the document that defines the authority of an agent?

A. Terms of agreement
B. Contract of agency
C. Agent's credentials
D. Rules of authority

B
(169)

---

23. Lionel has a major medical policy with a $500 deductible and an 80/20 coinsurance provision. He has a hospital bill for $4,200 of covered expenses. How much of that hospital bill will Lionel have to pay?

A. $1,240
B. $820
C. $1,150
D. $940

A
(16, 17, 18)

---

24. Which provision enables an insured to authorize that benefits be paid directly to a hospital or physician for services rendered?

A. Assignment
B. Coinsurance
C. Elective indemnity
D. Deductible

A
(87, 88)

25. Which of the following relates directly to the consideration clause of a health insurance policy?

A. Premium payment
B. Free look provision
C. Owners' rights
D. Exclusions

---

26. Your company will issue a maximum disability income monthly benefit of $4,000, as long as the applicant's total such benefits payable under all policies does not exceed 60 percent of regular monthly income. Your prospect, Marion, earns $5,000 monthly and has an existing policy that will pay $500 per month in disability benefits. What is the maximum monthly disability income benefit your company would issue to Marion?

A. $3,000
B. $2,500
C. $4,000
D. $2,400

---

27. All of the following would be rebating violations on the part of an agent, EXCEPT:

A. buying a hunting rifle for a policyowner, as promised when the application was signed.
B. paying weekend vacation expenses for a new policyowner.
C. mailing calendars with New Year's greetings to clients.
D. sharing part of a commission with a policyowner.

---

28. Insurance companies generally are classified according to the following classifications, EXCEPT:

A. domestic.
B. foreign.
C. home.
D. alien.

29. Under a qualified long-term care policy, which of the following events will trigger benefits for the insured under the policy?

    A. The insured is diagnosed as "chronically ill."
    B. The insured is hospitalized for three days.
    C. The insured is not expected to return to any substantial gainful activity in the next 12 months.
    D. The insured is diagnosed as "morbid."

---

30. All of the following statements apply to industrial health insurance, EXCEPT:

    A. Premiums are usually collected weekly or monthly by agents in the field.
    B. It can provide weekly benefits for disability due to injury or sickness.
    C. Lapsed policies may be reinstated without evidence of insurability.
    D. Premiums normally are higher than for similar commercial policies.

---

31. Which of the following terms relates to disability income insurance?

    A. Service basis
    B. First dollar
    C. Residual basis
    D. Coinsurance

---

32. A personal producing general agent is likely to

    A. recruit his or her own agents.
    B. train his or her own agents.
    C. maintain his or her own office.
    D. represent a number of insurance companies

---

33. There is a total of how many optional Uniform Policy Provisions?

    A. 12
    B. 11
    C. 10
    D. 8

34. Workers' compensation coverage is the responsibility of

A. the state.
B. employee unions.
C. employers.
D. employees.

C (166)

---

35. All of the following are typical duties of an insurance commissioner, EXCEPT:

A. issuing rules and regulations.
B. licensing insurance agents.
C. licensing insurance companies.
D. writing insurance laws.

D (175)

---

36. The miscellaneous hospital benefit in a basic hospital expense policy normally will cover

A. physicians' bedside visits.
B. medications administered in the hospital.
C. room and board.
D. All of the above

B (11, 12)

---

37. The period immediately following the onset of a disability when benefits are not payable is the

A. probationary period.
B. delayed disability period.
C. elimination period.
D. residual period.

C (28, 29)

---

38. Misrepresenting the facts in order to persuade a prospect to drop an existing policy and buy a new policy is known as

A. replacement.
B. rebating.
C. twisting.
D. None of the above

C (178, 179)

39. Which of the following is true regarding agent and broker licenses?

A. In many states agents and brokers are required to sit for the licensing exam each year in order to renew their licenses.
B. In many states agents and brokers are required to fulfill a continuing education requirement in order to renew their licenses.
C. Generally, agent and broker licenses are perpetual unless revoked.
D. If an insurer cancels a broker's appointment, the broker's license is terminated.

---

40. Group disability income benefits are tax free to the recipient to the extent that

A. the premiums are paid for by the recipient.
B. the premiums are paid for by the employer.
C. the benefits exceed the premium amount.
D. the benefits do not exceed 60 percent of the recipient's income.

---

41. When a policy is reinstated, any claims resulting from sickness will be paid only if the sickness occurs at least how many days after the reinstatement date?

A. 3
B. 7
C. 10
D. 14

---

42. All of the following statements concerning the probationary period in a disability income policy are true, EXCEPT:

A. The provision does not apply to accidental injuries.
B. Most states limit the probationary period to 45 days.
C. It precludes benefits being paid under certain conditions during an initial period of time commencing when the policy becomes effective.
D. The provision applies to sickness that is contracted or treated before the policy is in force.

43. Concerning the free look provision, all of the following statements are true, EXCEPT:

A. Most states have passed such a provision.
B. The provision generally must be printed on the first page of the policy.
C. The insured has free insurance protection for the number of days specified in the provision.
D. Policyowners may return their policies within the prescribed time limit (usually 10 or 20 days) and receive a full refund of any premium paid.

---

44. Concerning elimination periods in disability income policies, all of the following statements are correct, EXCEPT:

A. Elimination periods vary in the number of days specified.
B. A longer elimination period means a higher premium.
C. Benefits are not payable during an elimination period.
D. An elimination period follows the start of a disability.

---

45. When Lester is unable to work at his own occupation due to total and permanent disability, his disability income insurance policy pays him a monthly benefit of $1,200. A flat partial monthly disability benefit provided by the policy normally would pay Lester how much per month?

A. $900
B. $600
C. $400
D. $720

---

46. In health insurance, the guaranteed insurability option (or rider) is often available with which type of policy?

A. Family policy
B. Major medical insurance
C. Disability income insurance
D. Accident insurance

---

47. What term is NOT associated with an accidental death and dismemberment policy?

A. Coinsurance
B. Accidental results
C. Limited risk
D. Capital sum

48. All of the following are characteristics of a disability buy-sell plan, EXCEPT:

A. a relatively long elimination period.
B. the option to select a lump-sum payment.
C. provisions to cover business overhead expenses.
D. the option to select periodic payments.

---

49. Premiums for a key person disability insurance policy are paid by ______. If disability occurs, benefits are paid to ______.

A. the business; the key employee
B. the key employee; the business
C. the business; the business
D. the key employee; the key employee

---

50. Premiums for business overhead expense insurance are ______ while benefit payments are ______.

A. tax deductible; taxable
B. not tax deductible; taxable
C. tax deductible; not taxable
D. not tax deductible; not taxable

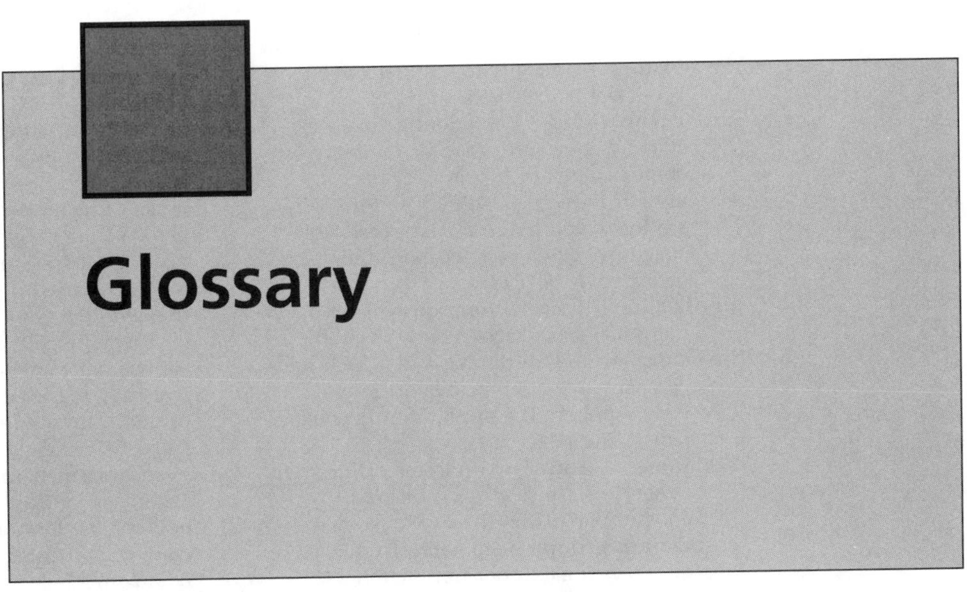

Glossary

This glossary of health insurance words and phrases will serve as a handy reference. Because the explanations are concise and the statements general, they should not be regarded or used as technically complete statements.

A

accident An unintended, unforeseen and unexpected event that causes injury. (26, 41)

accidental bodily injury Bodily injury resulting from an accident. Also called accidental results. (26, 41)

accidental death benefit A payment for loss of life due to an accident that was the direct cause of death. (40)

accidental dismemberment Often defined as "the severance of limbs at or above the wrists or ankle joints, or the entire irrevocable loss of sight." Loss of use, in itself, usually is not considered to be dismemberment. (40)

accidental means An unforeseen, unexpected and unintended cause of an accident. That means that cause the mishap must be accidental for any claim to be payable. (41)

accident and health insurance Insurance under which benefits are payable in case of disease, accidental injury or accidental death. Also called "health insurance," "personal health insurance" and "sickness and accident insurance." (4)

adhesion A health insurance contract is a "contract of adhesion" because buyers must "adhere" to the terms of the contract already in existence. They have no opportunity to negotiate for terms, rates, values, etc. (7)

administrative services only (ASO) plan— An arrangement under which an insurance carrier or an independent organization will, for a fee, handle the administration of claims, benefits and other administrative functions for a self-insured group. (168)

admitted company See **authorized company.**

adverse selection The tendency of persons with poorer-than-average health expectations to apply for insurance more so than do persons with average or better-than-average health expectations. (19, 61)

Advertising Code Rules established by the National Association of Insurance Commissioners (NAIC) to regulate insurance advertising. (182)

age limits Minimum or maximum age limits for the insuring of new applicants or for the renewal of policies. (61)

agent An insurance company representative who solicits insurance and services policyowners for the company. (169)

agent's report The section of an insurance application where the agent reports his or her personal observations about the applicant. (93)

alien company A company incorporated outside the United States. (176)

allocated benefits Payments (in some policies) for specified hospital services (X rays, drugs, etc.) that are limited to maximum specified amounts. (11, 12)

ambulatory surgery Surgery performed on an outpatient basis. (125)

any occupation A definition of total disability that requires that for disability income benefits to be payable, the insured must be unable to perform *any* job for which he or she is "reasonably suited by reason of education, training or experience." (24)

application A signed form on which an individual states facts requested by the company and on the basis of which the company decides whether or not to issue a policy. The application becomes part of the policy. (91)

assignment The signed transfer of the benefits of a policy by an insured to another party. (87)

association group A number of trade or professional association members insured jointly under one master health insurance contract. (129)

authority The actions and deeds an agent is authorized to conduct on behalf of an insurance company, as specified in the agent's contract. (170)

authorized company A company duly authorized by the insurance department to operate in the state. (176)

B

beneficiary Person to whom the proceeds of an accident policy are payable when the insured dies. The various types of beneficiaries are: primary beneficiaries (those first entitled to proceeds); secondary beneficiaries (those entitled to proceeds if no primary beneficiary is living when the insured dies); and tertiary beneficiaries (those entitled to proceeds if no primary or secondary beneficiaries are alive when the insured dies). (2, 76)

benefit A benefit may be either money or a right given to the policyowner upon the happening of the conditions set out in the policy. Not synonymous with "indemnity." (2) (See **indemnity**)

benefit period The maximum length of time that benefits will be paid for any one accident, illness or hospital stay. (11, 15, 29)

blanket policy Covers a number of individuals who are exposed to the same hazards, such as members of an athletic team, company officials who are passengers in the same company plane, etc. (141)

Blue Cross An independent membership organization providing protection against the costs of hospital care in a limited geographical area. Benefit payments are made directly to the hospital. Benefits vary among Blue Cross organizations. (159, 160)

Blue Shield An independent membership organization providing protection against the costs of surgery and other items of medical care in a limited geographical area. Benefit payments are made directly to the doctor. (159, 160)

broker A licensed insurance representative who does not represent a specific company but places business among various companies. Legally, the broker is usually regarded as a representative of the insured rather than the company. (171)

business health insurance Health coverage issued primarily to indemnify a business for the loss of services of a key employee, partner or active close corporation stockholder; or to buy out the interest of a partner or stockholder in a close corporation who becomes permanently disabled. (189)

business overhead health insurance (See **overhead insurance**)

C

cafeteria plan Employee benefit arrangements in which employees can select from a range of benefits. (188)

cancelable contract A contract of health insurance that may be terminated by the company or that is renewable at its option. (85)

cancellation The termination of an insurance contract by either party: the insured or the insurer. The company may not cancel unless the policy contains an optional cancellation clause. (85)

capital sum The amount provided for accidental dismemberment or the loss of eyesight. Indemnities for loss of one member or the sight of one eye are usually percentages of the principal sum. (41)

career agency system A method of marketing, selling and distributing insurance, it is represented by agencies or branch offices committed to the ongoing recruitment and development of career agents. (172)

case management The professional arrangement and coordination of health services through assessment, service plan development and monitoring. (126)

catastrophe insurance (See **comprehensive major medical and major medical expense insurance**)

certificate of insurance A document issued to persons insured under a group master policy that outlines the coverage provided. (128)

claim A request or demand on the insurer

for payment of benefits under the policy. (73)

classification The occupational category of a risk. (114)

closed-panel HMO A group of physicians who are salaried employees of an HMO and who work in facilities provided by the HMO. (161)

coinsurance (percentage participation) A principle under which the company insures only part of the potential loss, the policyowners themselves paying the other part. For instance, in a major medical policy, the company may agree to pay 75 percent of the insured's expenses, the insured to pay the other 25 percent. (17)

commissioner The head of a state insurance department. The public officer charged with the supervision of the insurance business in the state and the administration of insurance laws. Called "superintendent" in some states, "director" in others. (175)

comprehensive major medical insurance A policy designed to give the protection offered by both a basic and a major medical policy. It is characterized by a low deductible amount, coinsurance clause and high maximum benefits. (16)

concealment Failure of the insured to disclose to the company a fact material to the acceptance of the risk at the time application is made. (93)

conditional contract Characteristic of an insurance contract in that the payment of benefits is dependent on or a condition of the risk insured against. (6)

conditional receipt Receipts given to policyowners when they pay a premium at the time they make application. Such receipts bind the insurance company if the risk is approved as applied for, subject to any other conditions stated on the receipt. (99)

conditionally renewable contract A contract of health insurance that provides that the insured may renew the contract from period to period, or continue the contract to a stated date or an advanced age, subject to the right of the insurer to decline renewal only under conditions defined in the contract. (85)

confinement A clause in some policies that specifies that sickness income benefits are payable as long as the insured is confined at home, in a hospital or in a skilled nursing facility.

Consideration One of the elements of a binding contract. Consideration is acceptance by the company of the payment of the premium and the statements made by the prospective insured in the application. (82)

consideration clause That part of an insurance contract that sets forth the amount of initial and renewal premiums and the frequency of future payments. (82)

consultant An independent advisor specializing in the design, implementation and administration of insurance sharing plans. Consultants are usually licensed agents. (171)

contestable period Period during which the company may contest a claim on a policy because of misleading or incomplete information furnished in the application. (71) (See **Incontestable clause**)

Contingent beneficiary Person or persons named to receive proceeds in case the original beneficiary is not alive. Also referred to as "secondary" or "tertiary beneficiary." (76)

continuous disability Most contracts require that the insured's disability be continuous. However, a trial effort to return to work or work done as medical therapy, usually is not construed as breaking the continuity of disability. (29)

contract of agency A legal document containing the terms of the contract between the agent and company, signed by both parties. Also called "agency agreement." (169)

contributory plan A group insurance plan issued to an employer under which both the employer and employees contribute to the cost of the plan. Seventy-five percent of the eligible employees must be insured. (130) (See **noncontributory**)

conversion privilege The right granted insureds to change their coverage from group policies to individual policies within a specified period regardless of whether they are in good health at that time. (133)

coordination of benefits (COB) provision This is the provision designed to prevent duplication of group health insurance benefits. It limits benefits from multiple group health insurance policies in a particular case to 100 percent of the expenses actually incurred and designates the order in which the multiple carriers are to pay benefits. (136)

corridor deductible In supplemental major medical plans, a deductible amount between the benefits paid by the basic plan and the beginning of the major medical benefits. (17)

cost of living rider provides for indexing the benefit payable under a health policy to changes in the Consumer Price Index. (32)

creditors Third parties to whom the insured is indebted. (141)

credit report A summary of an insurance applicant's credit history, made by an independent organization that has investigated the applicant's credit standing. (97)

D

deductible An amount of expense or loss to be paid by the insured before the policy starts paying benefits. (16)

delayed disability A disability that manifests some time following an accident. (29)

dental insurance Covers dental expense, including treatment and care of dental disease and injury to the insured's teeth, within the framework of policy provisions. (135)

disability A physical or mental impairment that makes a person incapable of performing one or more duties of his or her occupation. (23)

disability buy-sell agreement An arrangement between business co-owners that provides that shares owned by any one of them who becomes disabled shall be sold to and purchased by the other co-owners or by the business using funds from disability income insurance. (189)

disability income insurance A form of health insurance that provides periodic payments when the insured is unable to work as a result of illness, disease or injury. (5, 23)

dismemberment See **accidental dismemberment, double dismemberment, and single dismemberment**.

dividend A policyowner's share in the divisible surplus of a company issuing insurance on the participating plan. (6)

domestic company A company is a domestic company in the state in which it is incorporated or chartered. (176)

double dismemberment Loss of any two members, sight of both eyes, or one member and sight of one eye. (40)

double indemnity A provision under which the principal sum in an accident policy (and sometimes the other indemnities) is doubled when accident is due to certain causes. (41)

dread disease policy See **limited risk policy**.

duplicate coverage A term usually applied to benefits other than loss of time where an insured is covered by several policies with one or more companies providing the same type of benefits, and often resulting in overinsurance. (136)

E

effective date The date a policy becomes effective. If the hour is not specified, the effective time is 12:01 A.M. on the appropriate date. (99)

elective indemnity Any insured who suffers an accidental injury resulting in a sprain, dislocation, fracture or amputation of fingers or toes, may elect to receive a lump sum, in accordance with the policy schedule, in place of any regular income payments provided. (87)

elimination period Duration of time between the beginning of an insured's disability and the commencement of the period for which benefits are payable. (28)

evidence of insurability Any statement or proof of a person's physical condition, occupation, etc., affecting acceptance of the applicant for insurance. (91, 132)

exclusions Specified hazards listed in the policy for which benefits will not be paid. (89)

experience rating A review of the previous year's claims experience for a group health insurance contract in order to establish premiums for the next period. (6, 132)

experience refund A provision in most group policies for the return of premium money to the policyowner because of lower-than-anticipated claims experience. (6)

F

Fair Credit Reporting Act Federal law requiring an individual to be informed if he or she is being investigated by an inspection company. (98)

family policy A health insurance policy covering eligible members of one family. (83)

fiduciary Person occupying a position of special trust and confidence, e.g., in handling or supervising affairs or funds of another, involving the exercise of confidence and trust. (170)

flat deductible An amount of covered expenses payable by the insured before major medical benefits are payable. (16)

foreign company A company is a foreign company in any state other than the one in which it is incorporated or chartered. (176)

franchise insurance Health insurance plan for covering groups of persons with individual policies uniform in provisions, although perhaps different in benefits. Solicitation usually takes place at an employer's business with the employer's consent. Generally written for groups too small to qualify for regular group coverage. May be called "wholesale insurance" when the policy is life insurance. (141)

fraternal benefit insurer Nonprofit benevolent organization that provides insurance to its members. (157)

fraud An act of deceit; misrepresentation of a material fact made knowingly, with the intention of having another person rely on that fact and consequently suffer a financial hardship. (93)

free look Provision required in most states whereby policyowners have either 10 or 20 days to examine their new policies at no obligation. (83)

fully insured A status of complete eligibility for the full range of Social Security benefits; death benefits, retirement benefits, disability benefits and Medicare benefits. (165)

G

grace period A period of time after the due date for a premium during which the policy will remain in force without penalty. (72)

group credit insurance A form of group insurance issued by insurance companies to creditors to cover the lives of debtors for the amounts of their loans. (141)

group insurance Insurance that provides coverage for a group of persons, usually employees of a company, under one master contract. (139)

group practice assocation model See **closed-panel HMO**.

guaranteed insurability (guaranteed issue) Arrangement, usually provided by rider, whereby additional insurance may be purchased at various times without evidence of insurability. (32)

guaranteed renewable contract Contracts that the insured has the right to continue in force by the timely payment of premiums for a substantial period of time during which period the insurer has no right to make unilaterally any change in any provision of the contract while the contract is in force, other than a change in premium rate for classes of insureds. (86)

guaranty association Established by each state to support insurers and protect consumers in the case of insurer insolvency, guaranty associations are funded by insurers through assessments. (182)

H

health insurance Insurance against loss through sickness or accidental bodily injury. Also called "accident and health," "accident and sickness," "sickness and accident" or "disability insurance." (4)

health maintenance organization (HMO) A health care center that stresses preventive health care, early diagnosis and treatment on an outpatient basis. Persons generally enroll voluntarily in an HMO by paying a fixed fee periodically. (161)

hospital benefits Benefits payable for charges incurred while the insured is confined to, or treated in, a hospital, as defined in the policy. (11)

hospital expense insurance Benefits subject to a specified daily maximum for a specified period of time while the insured is confined to a hospital, plus a limited allowance up to a specified amount for miscellaneous hospital expenses such as operating room, anesthesia, laboratory fees, etc. (11)

hospital indemnity A form of health insurance that provides a stipulated daily, weekly or monthly indemnity during hospital confinement. The indemnity is payable on an unallocated basis without regard to the actual hospital expense. (20)

hospitalization insurance The same as "hospital expense insurance." (11)

I

illegal holding of premiums State laws specify how premium monies collected by agents are to be handled. Unless these laws are followed, the agents may be accused of embezzlement or fraudulently converting funds to their own use. (179)

incontestable clause (time limit on certain defenses) A clause that makes the policy indisputable regarding the statements made by the insured in the application after a specified period of time has elapsed (usually one or two years). (71)

indemnity The payment of a benefit for loss insured under a policy. The insured is indemnified for a specified loss or part thereof.

independent agency system A system for marketing, selling and distributing insurance in which independent brokers are not affiliated with any one insurer but represent any number of insurers. (173)

individual insurance Policies that provide protection to the policyowner. (As distinct from group and blanket insurance.) Sometimes call "personal insurance." (8)

individual practice association model See **closed-panel HMO**.

industrial policy Provides modest benefits and relatively short benefit periods. Premiums are collected on a weekly or monthly basis by an agent who calls at the homes of insureds. (Also known as *debit policy*.) (158)

inpatient A person who is admitted to a hospital as a resident case (i.e., as a bed patient).

inspection report Report of an investigator providing facts required for a proper decision on applications for new insurance and reinstatements. (96)

insurability All conditions pertaining to individuals that affect their health, susceptibility to injury, as well as their expectancy of life, and go into the makeup of that insurance characteristics called insurability. (114)

insurability receipt A type of conditional receipt that provides coverage effective on the date the application was signed or the date of the medical exam (whichever is later), provided the applicant proves to be insurable. (99)

insurable interest Requirement of insurance contracts that loss must be sustained by the applicant upon the death or disability of another and it must be sufficient to warrant compensation. (114)

insurance Social device for minimizing risk of uncertainty of loss by spreading the risk over a large enough number of similar exposures to predict the individual chance of loss. (1, 2)

insured The individual covered by the contract of insurance. (2)

insuring clause A clause that defines and describes the scope of the coverage provided and the limits of indemnification. (82)

integrated deductible In supplemental major medical plans, a deductible amount between the benefits paid by the basic plan and those paid by major medical. All or part of the integrated deductible may be absorbed by the basic plan. (17)

intentional injury A injury resulting from an act, the doer of which intended to inflict injury. Self-inflicted injuries are not covered by an accident policy because they are not an accident. (89)

K

key-person insurance Protection of a business against financial loss caused by the disability of a vital member of the company, usually individuals possessing special managerial or technical skill or expertise. (Also called *business health insurance*.) (189)

L

lapse Termination of a policy upon the policyowner's failure to pay the premium within the grace period. (72)

law of large numbers Basic principle of insurance in that the larger number of individual risks combined into a group, the more certainty there is in predicting the degree or amount of loss that will be incurred in any given period. (2)

legal reserve The minimum reserve that a company must keep to meet future claims and obligations as they are calculated under the applicable state insurance code. (7)

level premium A premium that remains unchanged throughout the life of a policy.

license Certification issued by a state insurance department that an individual is qualified to solicit insurance applications for the period covered; usually issued for one year, renewable on application without need for repeating the original qualifying requirements. (177)

limited risk policies Those that restrict benefits to specified accidents or diseases, such as travel policies, dread disease policies, ticket policies, etc. (21, 43)

long-term care policy Health insurance policies that provide daily indemnity benefits for extended care confinement. Long-term care policies meeting certain standards qualify for tax-favored treatment and are known as "qualified" long-term care policies. (56)

lump sum Payment of entire proceeds of an insurance policy in one sum. (87)

M

major medical expense insurance Policies designed to help offset the heavy medical expenses resulting from catastrophic or prolonged illness or injuries. Generally, they provide benefit payments of 75 percent to 80 percent of all types of medical expenses above a certain amount first paid by the insured, and up to the maximum limit of liability and within the time period provided by the policy. (15)

malingering Feigning a disability in order to collect insurance benefits. (115)

managed care A system of delivering health care that involves agreements with selected providers, utilization review, quality standards and incentives for members to use selected providers. (124)

mandatory second opinion To control costs, many health policies provide that, in order to be eligible for benefits, insureds must get a second opinion before receiving non-life-threatening surgery. (125)

master policy Issued to the employer under a group plan; contains all the insuring clauses defining employee benefits. Individual employees participating in the group plan receive individual certificates that outline highlights of the coverage. Also called "master contract." (128)

Medicaid Provides medical care for the needy under joint federal-state participation (Kerr-Mills Act). (159)

medical cost management The process of controlling how policyowners utilize their policies. (125) (See **mandatory second opinion, precertification, ambulatory surgery** and **case management.**)

medical examination Usually conducted by a licensed physician; the medical report is part of the application, becomes part of the policy contract and is attached to the policy. A "nonmedical" is a short-form medical report filled out by the agent. Various company rules, such as amount of insurance applied for or already in force, applicant's age, sex, past physical history, and data revealed by inspection report, etc., determine whether the examination will be "medical" or "nonmedical." (96)

medical expense insurance Pays benefits for nonsurgical doctors' fees commonly rendered in a hospital. Sometimes pays for home and office calls as well. (4, 10)

Medical Information Bureau (MIB) A service organization that collects medical data on life and health insurance applicants for member insurance companies. (96)

medical report A document completed by a physician or other approved examiner and submitted to an insurer to supply medical evidence of insurability (or lack of insurability) or in relation to a claim. (95)

medically defined disability Definition of disability that requires the insured to be confined to a hospital or home in order to quality for disability benefits. (24)

medical savings account (MSA) A new method whereby the self-employed and small businesses can provide medical expense coverage by means of a tax-favored trust established to help defray medical expenses. Contributions to the MSA are not taxable; distributions from the account to pay the qualified medical expenses of the individual, his or her spouse and dependents are also not taxable. Requirements affecting the size of the employer, the amount of contributions and participation in a high-deductible catastrophic coverage plan must be met. (21)

Medicare A federally sponsored program of health insurance and medical care of persons 65 years of age and over. Administered under provisions of the Social Security Act. (44)

MedicarePlus Choice Program Scheduled for implementation after December 31, 1998, a program that will offer Medicare beneficiaries a variety of health coverage alternatives such as HMOs and PPOs, each of which must include currently covered Medicare services. Medicare will contribute a certain amount to the health coverage plan on behalf of the beneficiary; the beneficiary will pay out-of-pocket expenses that will vary according to the health plan selected. (51)

Medicare supplement policy Private insurance designed to fill in coverage gaps not met by Medicare. (52)

miscellaneous expenses Hospital charges other than for room and board, e.g., X rays, drugs, laboratory fees, etc., in connection with hospital insurance. (11)

misrepresentation The act of making, issuing, circulating or causing to be issued or circulated, an estimate, illustration, circular or statement of any kind that does not represent the correct policy terms, dividends or share of surplus, or the name or title for any policy or class of policies, which does not in fact reflect the true nature thereof. (178)

misstatement of age provision If the insured's age or sex is misstated in an application for insurance, the benefit payable usually is adjusted to what the premiums paid should have purchased. (78)

misuse of premium Improper use of premiums collected by an insurance producer. (179)

moral hazard Hazard arising from indifference to loss because of the existence of insurance. (115)

morbidity The relative incidence of disability due to sickness or accident within a given group. (3, 120)

morbidity table Shows the incidence and extent of disability that may be expected from a given large group of persons; used in computing health insurance premiums. (3, 120)

multiple employer trust Several small groups of individuals that need life and health insurance but do not have enough members to qualify for group insurance, may band together in a trust to purchase insurance. (129, 168)

mutual insurer One that is owned and controlled by the policyowners and is directly managed by a board of trustees or directors chosen by the policyowners. (157)

N

National Association of Insurance Commissioners (NAIC) An association of state insurance commissioners active in the discussion of insurance regulatory problems and in the formation and recommendation of model legislation and requirements. (181)

natural group A group formed for a reason other than to obtain insurance. (128)

noncancelable and guaranteed renewable contract A contract that the insured has the right to continue in force by the timely payment of premiums set forth in the contract for a substantial period of time, during which period the insurer has no right to make unilaterally any change in any provision of the contract. (86)

noncontributory A term applied to employee benefit plans under which the employer bears the full cost of the benefits for the employees. One hundred percent of the eligible employees must be insured. (130)

nondisabling injury One that requires medical care but does not result in a loss of time from work. (30)

nonduplication provision Stipulates that insureds shall be ineligible to collect for charges under a group plan if the charges are reimbursed under their or their spouse's group plan. (136)

nonoccupational policy A plan of insurance that insures a person against off-the-job accidents or sickness. (27)

nonparticipating A plan of insurance under which the insured is not entitled to share in the divisible surplus of the company. (6)

notice of claims provision Policy provision that describes the policyowner's obligation to provide notification of loss to the insurer within a reasonable period of time. (73)

O

occupational hazard A danger inherent in the insured's line of work. (115)

occupational injury An injury or sickness arising out of, or in the course of, employment. (27, 164)

occupational policy A plan of insurance that insures a person against both off-the-job and on-the-job accidents or sicknesses. (27)

Old-Age, Survivors, Disability and Hospital Insurance (OASDHI) Retirement, death, disability income and hospital insurance benefits provided under the Social Security system. (164)

open panel HMO A network of physicians who work out of their own offices and participate in the HMO on a part-time basis. (162)

optional benefit An additional benefit offered by the company that may be included in a policy at the applicant's request, usually for an additional premium. (87)

optionally renewable contract A contract of health insurance in which the insurer reserves the right to terminate the coverage at any anniversary, or, in some cases, at any premium due date, but does not have the right to terminate coverage between such dates. (85)

outpatient One who receives care at a clinic or hospital without being confined to that institution as a resident.

overhead insurance A type of short-term disability insurance that reimburses the insured person for specified, fixed, monthly expenses, normal and customary in the operation of his or her business or office. (188)

overinsurance An excessive amount of insurance carried by an insured. This might encourage the insured to prolong each period of disability, remain in a hospital longer than necessary, etc. (24, 78)

own occupation A definition of total disability that requires that in order to receive disability income benefits the insured must be unable to work at his or her *own* occupation. (24)

P

partial disability An illness or injury that prevents insureds from performing one or more, but not all, of their occupational duties. (25)

participating A plan of insurance under which the policyowner receives shares of the divisible surplus of the company. Such shares are commonly called "dividends." (6)

participating physician A physician who accepts Medicare's recognized charges and will not charge more. (49)

permanent disability A disability that

will last forever, or for an indefinite and undetermined period of time. (24, 26)

personal insurance The same as "individual insurance." (8)

personal producing general agency system (PPGA) A method of marketing, selling and distributing insurance in which personal producing general agents (PPGAs) are compensated for business they personally sell and business sold by agents with whom they subcontract. Subcontracted agents are considered employees of the PPGA, not the insurer. (173)

physical hazard The type of hazard that arises from the physical characteristics of an individual (e.g., impediments of hearing or sight). It may exist because of a current condition, past medical history, or physical condition present at birth. (115)

physical impairment A physical defect that makes an applicant a below-average risk. (115)

policy That document, including all endorsements and attached papers, that constitutes the entire contract of insurance. (2)

policy term The term of policy, usually the period for which the premium is paid. (83)

precertification The insurer's approval of an insured's entering a hospital. Many health policies require precertification as part of an effort to control costs. (125)

preexisting condition An injury, sickness or physical condition that existed prior to the issuance of a health policy. (66, 134)

preferred provider organization (PPO) A group of doctors or hospitals in a designated area who contract with insurers to provide health care services at a prearranged cost to the insured. For a small monthly fee, PPO participants may choose from among these health care providers. (163)

preferred risk A risk whose physical condition, occupation, mode of living and other characteristics indicate a prospect of longevity superior to that of the average longevity of unimpaired lives of the same age. (118) (See **standard risk.**)

premium The periodic payment required to keep a policy in force. (2)

presumptive disability Certain disabilities that are considered so serious that total and permanent disability is presumed. (26)

principal sum The lump sum payable for accidental loss of life, dismemberment or loss of sight. (40)

probationary period A specified number of days after the date of the issuance of a disability policy during which coverage is not afforded for sickness. Sickness protection does not become effective until after the end of such probationary period. (28)

producer A general term applied to an agent, broker, personal producing general agent, solicitor or other person who sells insurance. (169)

pure risk A risk that involves only the chance of loss; there is no opportunity for gain. (3)

R

reasonable and customary charge A charge for a health care service that is consistent with the going rate or charge in a given geographical area for an identical or similar service. (13)

rebating Returning part of the commission or giving anything of value to the insured as an inducement to buy the policy. Rebating is cause for license revocation in most states and illegal in others. In some states, rebating is an offense by both the agent and the person receiving the rebate. (179)

reciprocal insurer Insurance company characterized by the fact its policyholders insure the risks of other policyholders. (157)

recurring disability clause A provision that specifies a period of time during which the recurrence of a condition is considered a continuation of a prior period of disability or hospital confinement. (29)

reduction of benefits Automatic reduction in coverage under certain specified conditions, e.g., the monthly benefits may be reduced after the insured has reached age 60, 65, etc. (85)

reimbursement approach Payment of health policy benefits to insureds based on actual medical expenses incurred. (10, 156)

reinstatement Putting a lapsed policy back in force by producing satisfactory evidence of insurability and paying any past-due premiums required. (72)

reinsurance The acceptance by one or more insurers, called "reinsurers," of a portion of the risk underwritten by another insurer who has contracted for the entire coverage.

relation of earnings to insurance If at the time disability commences the total benefits payable under all coverages owned by the insured exceed the average earnings of the insured over the preceding two years, the benefits will be reduced pro rata to such amount. (79)

renewal Continuance of coverage under a policy beyond its original term. (85)

replacement The act of replacing one policy with another. May be done legally under only certain conditions. (179)

representation A statement made by an applicant that the applicant believes to be true. Under the laws of most states, statements made by an applicant in an insurance application are deemed to be representations and not warranties. (93) (See **warranty**)

reserve A fund held by the company to help fulfill future claims. (7)

residual disability benefits Benefits provided under a residual provision are payable in proportion to a partial loss of earnings as a result of disability as opposed to a full loss of benefits due to the inability to work full time. (25)

rider Strictly speaking, a rider adds something to the policy. However, the term is loosely used to refer to any supplemental agreement attached to and made a part of the policy, whether the conditions of the policy are expanded, additional coverages added or a coverage of condition waived. (31)

risk Technically, the degree or percentage of chance that a given contingency will occur—"the odds." The term is loosely used (a) to designate an insured; (b) to designate a peril insured again. (2)

risk pooling The spreading of risk (and cost) over a large group of individuals so that any one loss is shared by all. (2)

risk selection See **underwriting**.

S

schedule A list of specified amounts payable, usually for surgical operations, dismemberment, fractures, etc. (12, 13)

secondary beneficiary An alternate beneficiary designated to receive payment, usually in the event the original beneficiary predeceases the insured. (76)

self-insurance A program for providing group health-care benefits financed entirely through the internal means of the policyowner, in place of purchasing coverage from commercial carriers. (168)

service insurer A type of insurance provider that pays benefits in medical or hospital services rather than in dollars. Best-known examples of such coverage are the Blue Cross and Blue Shield plans. (159)

single dismemberment Loss of one hand or one foot, or the sight of one eye. (40)

Social Security Programs first created by Congress in 1935 and now composed of Old-Age, Survivors and Disability Insurance (OASDI), Medicare, Medicaid and various grants-in-aid, which provide economic security to nearly all employed people. (8, 44, 164)

Social Security rider Disability insurance rider that provides for additional benefits if social insurance payments are less than expected. (32)

solicitor A solicitor acts for an agent by seeking prospects, receiving applications or collecting premiums. However, solicitors generally do not have the power to bind coverage. (171)

special risk policies Those that cover unusual hazards normally not covered under ordinary health policies (43)

speculative risk a risk that involves the possibility of both loss and gain; a speculative risk is not insurable. (3)

standard risk—A person who, according to a company's underwriting standards, is entitled to insurance protection without extra rating or special restrictions. (118)

stock insurer An insurance company owned and controlled by a group of stockholders whose investment in the company provides the safety margin necessary in issuance of guaranteed, fixed premium, nonparticipating policies. (156)

stop loss provision Designed to stop the company's loss at a given point, as an aggregate payable under a policy, a maximum payable for any one disability or the like; also applies to individuals, placing a limit on the maximum out-of-pocket an insured must pay for health care expenses, after which the health policy covers all expenses. (18)

substandard risk Person who is considered an under-average or impaired insurance risk because of physical condition, family or personal history of disease, occupation, residence in unhealthy climate or dangerous habits. (118)

supplementary major medical insurance Medical expense policy designed to supplement the benefits of a basic policy. (15)

surgical expense insurance A policy that provides benefits to pay for the cost of surgical operations. (12)

surgical schedule A list of cash allowances that are payable for various types of surgery with the respective maximum amounts payable based upon the severity of the operations. The stipulated maximum usually covers all professional fees involved (e.g., surgeon, anesthesiologist). (12)

T

temporary license Some states permit agents to operate under temporary licenses, usually for six months. After that time, they must comply with the state's licensing requirements. (178)

term of policy The period for which the policy runs, which is usually the period for which a premium has been paid in advance. In some instances, it may be for a year, even though the premium is paid on a semiannual or other basis. (85)

third-party administrator (TPA) An organization outside the members of a self-insurance group which, for a fee, processes claims, completes benefits paperwork and often analyzes claims information. (168)

ticket insurance Accident-only protection that is issued in conjunction with a ticket for transportation on a common carrier. (43) (See also **limited risk policies)**

total disability Disability that prevents insureds from performing any duty of their usual occupations or from performing any occupation for remuneration. The actual definition in any case depends upon the wording in the policy. (24)

travel-accident policies Policies limited to idemnities for accidents while traveling, usually by common carrier. (43) (See also **limited risk policies)**

twisting Inducing a policyowner to drop an existing policy (especially one in another company) in order to take a similar policy from the agent doing the twisting. The act is usually defined in law as inducement "by misrepresentation." Twisting is cause for license revocation in most states and a legal offense in many. (179)

U

unallocated benefit Reimbursement provision, usually for miscellaneous hospital and medical expenses, that does not specify how much will be paid for each type of treatment, examination, dressing, etc., but only sets a maximum that will be paid for all such treatments. (11)

underwriter Company receiving premiums and accepting responsibility for fulfilling the policy contract. Also, company employee who decides whether or not the company should assume a particular risk. The agent who sells the policy. (113)

underwriting Process through which an insurer determines whether, and on what basis, an insurance application will be accepted. (113)

Unfair Trade Practices Act A model act written by the National Association of Insurance Commissioners (NAIC) and adopted by most jurisdictions empowering insurance commissioners to investigate and issue cease and desist orders and penalties to insurers for engaging in unfair or deceptive practices. (182)

Uniform Individual Accident and Sickness Policy Provisions Law NAIC model law that established uniform terms, provisions and standards for health insurance policies covering loss "resulting from sickness or from bodily injury or death by accident or both." (70)

unilateral Distinguishing characteristic of an insurance contract in that it is only the insurance company that pledges anything. (6)

uninsurable risk One that is not acceptable for insurance due to excessive risk. (118)

utilization review See **case management.**

V

voluntary group AD&D A group accidental death and dismemberment policy paid for entirely by employees, rather than an employer. (140)

W

waiting period The duration of time between the beginning of an insured's disability and the commencement of the period for which benefits are payable. Also called "elimination period." (28)

waiver An agreement that waives the liability of the company for a certain type (or types) of disabilities or injuries ordinarily covered in the policy. (89)

waiver of premium A provision included in some policies that exempts those insured from the payment of premiums after they have been disabled for a period of time (e.g., 90 days). (31)

warranty A statement made by an applicant that the applicant guarantees to be true. (93) (See **representation)**

wholesale insurance (See **franchise insurance**)

workers' compensation Benefits paid workers for injury, disability or disease contracted in the course of their employment. Benefits and conditions are set by law, although in most states the insurance to provide the benefits may be purchased from regular insurance companies. A few states have monopolistic state compensation funds. (166)